Managing Identity

Managing Identity

By Alison Pullen

First published 2006 by
PALGRAVE MACMILLAN
Houndmills, Basingstoke, Hampshire RG21 6XS and
175 Fifth Avenue, New York, N. Y. 10010
Companies and representatives throughout the world

PALGRAVE MACMILLAN is the global academic imprint of the Palgrave Macmillan division of St. Martin's Press, LLC and of Palgrave Macmillan Ltd. Macmillan® is a registered trademark in the United States, United Kingdom and other countries. Palgrave is a registered trademark in the European Union and other countries.

ISBN-13: 978–1–4039–4770–3   hardback
ISBN-10: 1–4039–4770–8   hardback

This book is printed on paper suitable for recycling and made from fully managed and sustained forest sources.

A catalogue record for this book is available from the British Library.

Library of Congress Cataloging-in-Publication Data
Pullen, Alison, 1971–
  Managing identity / by Alison Pullen.
    p. cm.
  Includes bibliographical references and index.
  ISBN 1–4039–4770–8 (cloth)
  1. Management. 2. Identity (Psychology)–Social aspects. 3. Organizational change. I. Title.

HD31.L477 2005
658.4'06–dc22   2005047534

10 9 8 7 6 5 4 3 2 1
15 14 13 12 11 10 09 08 07 06

Printed and bound in Great Britain by
Antony Rowe Ltd, Chippenham and Eastbourne

For Mam 1909–1998 and Cissie 1911–1989

Contents

List of Tables

List of Figures

Acknowledgements

My thanks to all the participants in the research for this book and in particular to the managers who spent many hours with me. A big thank you to Ursula Gavin for her original encouragement, and to Jacky Kippenberger and Rebecca Pash for their constant support. My gratitude goes to Peter Jackson, Dean of the Faculty of Social Sciences and former Director of the Management Centre at the University of Leicester who allowed me time and resources to complete the fieldwork; and to Steve Toms, Head of the Department of Management Studies at the University of York, for allowing me the time to complete this book. Heather Höpfl, Sue Clegg, John McAuley gave much appreciated feedback. To Steve Linstead for his dialogue and support throughout this project. My sincere thanks to Simon Pullen for completing the indexing; and fondest love to Lisa, Shona, Godfrey and Sonia Pullen for their support and encouragement always.

1
*Man*aging Identity

> ...the chaos of identities, and of strategies, in the world today
> is the effect of real, and highly structured, forces that are con-
> stantly felt in the lives of those trying to get from one day to
> the next (Friedman 1992: 363).

Background

Modern managers might well ask 'who are we and what are we becoming'? Two decades of downsizing, delayering, corporate liposuction,
lean manufacturing, empowerment, knowledge management and networked organization have shaken traditional assumptions about
management to their foundations. Postmodern conditions and post-
modernizing processes have fragmented established identity resources
and created a crisis of self-confidence, especially in middle managers.
In this book I draw on my own empirical studies in manufacturing
companies and recent theory on gender and power to explore the
impact of these changes on managers' sense of self and their responses
in constructing new and multiple identities. I start by viewing identity
as project – a process constantly changing, in flux, ambiguous and
fragile – and develop models for explaining and assessing largely
incomplete shifts from modern to postmodern management and the
associated processes of constructing managerial subjectivities.

Ironically, my research began as a study of the effects of the changing
conditions of organizational restructuring *on* middle managers, but
during the course of its development both the available reported empirical research on managerial work and critical research on managerial
identities grew enormously. It became clear that identity rather than
environment was the absorbing issue both for the managers in my

study and for the most recent theoretical studies, so my research was refocused accordingly. Long-established modes of studying managers have tended to concentrate on managerial work – *what do managers do and how is it changing?* – or on the nature of management – *what is management? how can it be defined or characterized?* Where identity issues have surfaced in this literature, they have been raised in the context of social role theory, or occasionally managerial psychology (Mead 1934; Merton 1957; Goffman 1959). The literature on managerial identity overlaps empirically with studies of managerial work but takes a very different theoretical line. It has developed interestingly in the past decade through studies influenced by the work of Michel Foucault that concentrate on how subjects are formed within discourse, a discourse being a patterned complex of everyday expression, rhetoric, institutional formations and practice (Knights 1990, 1992; Collinson 1994; Grey 1994; Kerfoot and Knights 1998; Gabriel 1999; Sotirin and Gottfried 1999). Managerial subjectivity therefore is not simply a property of the individual but is inherently *organized*. Alongside but not necessarily complementary to this we have a growing number of studies of organizational identity which differentiate identity from culture and distinguish it from the aggregate of individual identities in an organization, though influenced more by social psychological literature than poststructuralist sociology (Brown and Starkey 2000; Brown 2001; Hatch and Schultz 2002).

The importance of identity for organizations and for managers in the twenty first century parallels the attention that identity has received across the social sciences. Identity has become one of the fastest growing areas of interest in management and organization studies, much of which has been influenced by early developments in sociology and social psychology. For example both Hatch and Schultz (2004a) and Pullen and Linstead (2005a) acknowledge the importance of George Herbert Mead's symbolic interactionist social identity theory and the distinction between the "I" and the "me" in identity construction and Goffman's dramaturgical analysis of self-presentation. Hatch and Schultz also explore Cooley's analysis of the self and the social; and Tajfel and Turner's social identity theory in psychology. Moreover, Pullen and Linstead give credit to the part played by the functionalism approach of Talcott Parsons, influencing as it did the development of role theory by Robert Merton and Harold Garfinkel's ethnomethodological studies of how social membership is achieved through talk (and to which I will return shortly). They also highlight how the corporate culturism of the 1980s gave rise to the exploration of identity even though the importance of power and subjectivity in identity formation was acknowledged by few (Knights and Willmott 1985). They further comment that "Organizational Identity" effectively replaced corporate culture as focal topic and incorporated an externally facing consideration of identity as brand, whilst consideration of issues of power and subjectivity became synonymous with a Foucauldian approach to such management issues as strategy and HRM (Hatch and Schultz 2002/4b; Townley 1992; Pullen and Linstead 2005a: 1). Where more recent sociological and critical social psychological approaches to identity have explored self and subjectivity they have done it without a specifically organizational focus (Henriques et al 1984; Parker 1989; Elliot 1996; Craib 1998).

Hatch and Schultz (2004a) in tracing the early developments of organizational identity draw on the contributions of Albert and Whetten's statement of organizational identity; Schwartz's psychoanalytic framework for studying organizational identity; Ashforth and Mael's approach to organizational identification which has also been employed by Beech and Huxham (2003); Alvesson's application of the concept of organizational image to organizational identity; Dutton and Dukerich's (1991) work on reflexivity and organizational identity and image and Ginzel et al's employment of Goffman's approach to impression management for organizational image and identity. More recent developments are also presented in the book such as Pratt and Rafaeli's analysis of organizational dress as a symbol of multi-layered social identities; Golden-Biddle and Rao's introduction of the concepts of hybrid identity and identity conflicts in their analysis of organizational identity and corporate governance; Gioia et al's (2000) challenge to both Alvesson and Whetten's definition of identity and Dutton and Dukerich's definition of image, introducing the concept of adaptive instability; and Hatch and Schultz's own model of organizational identity formation which links organizational identity to culture and stakeholder images of the organization. To close this volume, Hatch and Schultz draw on Czarniawska's narrative approach to organizational identity and Alvesson and Willmott's labour-process theoretic model of identity regulation as a form of organizational control to reflect the growth in narrative and discourse in the field of identity. Yet although Hatch and Schultz's reader introduces identity as narrative and discourse whose work moves towards understanding subjectivity as constructed through language, it does not explore the relational view of power that embeds reading identity as project. However in other areas, power has been at the heart of many contributions to identity: the effects of societal changes and organizational restructurings on the identities of *managers* have been examined (e.g. Linstead and Thomas 2002; Thomas and Linstead 2002); the influence on professional identities has been debated (Parker 2000); the changing nature of the idea of "career" (see Grey 1994; McKinlay 2002) and the shift in significance from production to consumption have also been brought into a focus which addresses identity incidentally as a by-product of social fragmentation and simulation (du Gay 1996, 2001; Ritzer 1999, 2004); literature on diversity has shown an interest in the formation of ideas of *otherness* including gender, the effects of globalization and multiculturalism and the emergence of postcolonial critiques (Banerjee and Linstead 2001; Calás and Smircich 1996); and most importantly for viewing identity as project, literature on the fractal self has been drawn into the field of management and organization studies (Cohen 1994; Friedman 1992; Kellner 1992; Hassard 1993; Linstead and Grafton-Small 1992; Hancock 1999; Grafton-Small 2005). Building on this work on the fragmented and fractured self, Pullen and Linstead's edited collection (2005) develops existing work on identity in organizations by incorporating philosophical contributions to the area to *confront* established notions and assumptions about identity to look more closely and critically at the *performance* of identity in different organizational and societal contexts.

Middle managers and identity

This book is an attempt to contribute to the growing field of identity studies by offering a multidisciplinary study of middle managers' identity work, and to critically explore the creation and recreation of middle managers' subjectivities. Over the past two decades, restructuring discourses have fundamentally challenged, questioned and changed the legitimacy of middle managers in contemporary organizations initiating the construction and reconstruction of their identities and as such offered a particularly interesting research sample when this research was initiated. However, much of this research arises from positivistic epistemologies which reflect unitary, essentialist and homogenous representations of what is happening to middle management where difference is suppressed. To challenge existing functionalist theories this book re-genders middle managers' identity work to reveal how masculinist discourses dominate management practices whilst downplaying the feminine and rendering it abject.[1] Although there has been some gendered analysis of management, much of this research focuses on the behaviour and skills differences between men and women managers that create, reify, construct and legitimize masculinist organizational practices. This book focuses on the processes of subjective identity formation of middle managers in restructuring organizations and takes a gendered reading of these processes. The overall approach of *Managing Identity* is not to look at levels of identity as such (e.g. individual, role, group, professional, organizational, community, regional, national) although some of these considerations will surface, but to consider identity as project – a process rather than a product – a process which involves societal factors, psychological factors, interaction, reflection, practice and performance. This book developed alongside the growth in attention on identity in management and organization and emerged from more extensive work on changes in managerial subjectivities: the micro-processes of how middle managers come to identify as middle managers, or *become*. Recognizing the relative neglect of gender in the identity literature, which Hatch and Schultz's otherwise to be welcomed reader notably omits, the gender masks of managers – the ways in which managers present themselves as men or women – are explored. But the book is also about reading identity as project in a way that enables us to move beyond the presentation of identities as changing but relatively stable, as found in existing studies on managerial identities, towards the recognition of identity construction as a form of first order accounting characterized by paradox, fluidity, inconsistency and emergence. In chapters 5, 6 and 7 middle managers reveal in their persuasive accounts (Silverman 1975) the paradoxical nature of their identity construction in making sense of their work experiences. Identities are constructed in terms of the conjunction of past and future, as an explanation of previous events in a way that positions the constructor of the account advantageously for future episodes. Managers therefore move between reflecting on past experiences of

---

[1] Abjection is the act of casting away, casting out, but not completely. The abject cannot be ejected, nor fully rejected, nor can it be subjected – it is neither in nor out of the frame. The abject remains attached and represents something which is part of us, a dark side, which we want to suppress but which remains present and has, therefore, to be defended against. Its viscosity, or stickiness, always has a structuring effect on the subject. Thus even the most masculine and positive of discourses are shaped by the constant need to defend themselves against the suppressed but persistent abject feminine.

restructuring that were relatively stable and the legitimizing and securing of their future roles by drawing on discourses of performance (commitment and the need to be flexible and fluid) to accommodate the needs of their organizations. Identities are therefore masks that are created as resources in a project of becoming for participation in an ongoing masquerade. Foucault would argue that social analysis is a matter of revealing masks, although this is a process which reveals yet other masks behind the façade. Masks are necessary tools for individuals to achieve social and managerial success. Masks are simultaneously false representations of "identity", and yet are essential to the creation of "selves". They conceal, exaggerate, accelerate, displace and separate. They enform and inform, and occasionally deform. They mark the boundary between things and define those things themselves – and often they form what is held to lie beyond or behind the masking. The masks used by managers in their performance of the self may actually enable the managers to be and say what they would fear to otherwise. The paradoxical nature of masks suggests that masks may function to both conceal and perform the natural. This masking initiates the re-creation of managers' identities. The gendered masks, masks of masculinities, not only conceal but reveal individual subjectivities and serve to reinforce the masculine signifiers of organization.

I am interested in this book in providing greater awareness of the fragmentary nature of middle managers' narratives grounded in specific accounting practices within a flow of accountability, including their emergent qualities. The book sets out to aid the understandings of these middle managers' fractal "truths" with the objective of accommodating and appreciating difference, diversity and voice without trivialisation, and in doing so moves away from the deployment of fixed classifications of gender. As such, this book investigates how middle managers *do* identity work. To generate data on middle managers' subjectivities the research appropriated both an inductive (the exploratory study highlighted in Chapter 2) and deductive (the main part of this book) qualitative methodologies to develop theory (see appendices 1 and 2 for a full methodological justification). Prior knowledge from the inductive exploration informed the development of the 'Management in Three Movements' framework outlined in Chapter 3 and subsequent research design. The organizations at the time of selection were based on a sample that had undergone major restructuring and ranged from small to large sized companies. The respondents and participants (middle managers and other individuals such as team leaders, senior managers and shopfloor personnel) were selected and comprised a range of age, gender, race and occupational, professional and hierarchical groups. The organizations were private sector firms with diverse geographical locations and included manufacturing, engineering, logistics, and privatized utilities. The three organizations drawn from this larger sample that are presented in this book are all manufacturing organizations.

This book looks at and theorizes the processes of individual identity construction and the organizational conditions that shape them and the ways in which these accounts display effects which might be attributed to wider economic and social changes. Therefore reading across the accounts attempted to track common constructs throughout these accounts which might be attributed to meta organizational influences (see Jackall 1988 for comparable approach). In each of the three data chapters one significant dimension of identity construction (the dualities of hierarchy/networking; accountability/seduction; achievement/commitment) are investigated respectively within each organization. This approach has been taken because although it would have been possible to fully present data from each organization on each of these dualities there is a need to present data which are symbolically and discursively rich but within a chapter structure that is manageable. After the three chapters (chapters 5–7) in which the data are presented and initially analyzed against the modified Gowler and Legge model of content analysis, the processual features of identity construction across the whole data set are analyzed through the Modes of Subjectivities framework developed in this book in Chapter 8.

This book has six aims: first it advances the shift in attention in management studies from the general conditions affecting middle *management*, such as restructuring, Total Quality Management or Business Process Reengineering, to the processes of formation of the subjectivities of middle *managers* (Casey 1995; Kumar 1995; du Gay 1996), a question of identity production. Second, it identifies a useful model of the criteria underpinning modern managerial identity (see Chapter 3) and through a thorough literature review deduces how shifts in the conditions surrounding the practice of contemporary management might be expected to have affected the criteria for identity formation. Third, it develops new frameworks, for connecting "modern" and "postmodern" identity (Friedman 1992) criteria and for identifying specific modes of subject formation and resistance (Collinson 1994; Knights and Willmott 1999; Weedon 1999; Fleming and Sewell 2002; Knights 2002). Fourth, as a result of examining qualitative case data, it discovers that the shift from modern to postmodern is incomplete for these managers. Fifth, it identifies how modern and postmodern criteria are both linked vertically across the three movements hierarchy (developed in this book in Chapter 3) and how the criteria overlap, making some, in each paradigm, more dominant than others. Sixth, it identifies some issues which cut across the movement of hierarchy to networking, accountability to seduction, and achievement to commitment, interfering with the predicted horizontal trajectory to the postmodern – narcissism, gender and resistance (Chapter 8). Overall, the conclusion is that whilst postmodern conditions may have arrived at a general societal level, modernity is still the dominant framework through which managers understand their situations and identities (Giddens 1991; Lash and Friedman 1992).

Identity from the modern to the postmodern?

From a modernist position, Castells (1997: 8) discusses the idea of *project identity* where "social actors draw on the cultural materials available to them", which Pullen and Linstead (2005a) refer to as identity capital, to create new identities and effects social change (which could also be organizational change where conditions are appropriate). Castells argues that where legitimizing identities produce civil society and resistance identities produce community, project identities produce subjects. Pullen and Linstead disagree with his terminology in the latter two cases, as his use of the term subject appears to be more Hegelian and set against sovereignty at the level of the state rather than as a form of autonomy. But Pullen and Linstead retain the notion of project identity as a form of purposeful collective identity performance which can achieve small and potentially large scale social change. Hatch and Schultz (2004a) suggest that early definitions of identity as essence can be fused with what they term "postmodernist definitions of identity as flux and multiplicity", however in keeping with Pullen and Linstead, I would have to disagree (see Letiche 2004 for a telling critique of this sort of assumption; Pullen and Linstead 2005b for a critique of multiplicity).

For Friedman (1992) narcissism or self-obsession is closely linked to the changing nature of identity formation in the shift from modernity to postmodernity. Kellner (1992) somewhat wryly observes that identity has always been experienced as a problem, and has not just recently been problematized by the postmodern, although the postmodern condition has accelerated and fragmented the processes of identity formation. For Kellner, what is left may be a disaster of instability, a totally "fragmented, disjointed life subject to the whims of [managerial] fashion" or it may be a new set of opportunities for reconstructing the self. Friedman sees that postmodern narcissism accordingly cannot be one where the self-obsessed narcissist seeks support for their existence in any coherent or unified way, but in which the whimsicalities of that existence, seen almost as a *game,* conscript others into supporting or subordinate roles which shift as the rules of the game themselves shift. In considering how subject formation may be said to occur, then, this book identifies five categories, or modes, grounded in power, knowledge and language through which the "game" may be said to pass. These are perhaps best conceived in terms of the five questions which they address:

1. *Mode of Incorporation* (the ways that individuals accommodate organizational goals in a climate of change and restructuring) – The question here is how individuals align themselves with new organizational goals and objectives and accommodate visions which may be at odds with what they previously held or currently hold. These may range from enthusiastic embrace to attempts at avoidance, examples being; vision/advocacy (seduction); acceptance; accommodation; consent; citizenship; legitimation; "knowledge management", where what is acknowledged to be known is selective, and the unpalatable denied an the "dual identity" system where contrasting and often opposing identities and values are simultaneously subscribed to.
2. *Mode of Disciplined Subjectivity* (how individuals fit themselves into gendered organizational social systems/discursive structures) – The question here is how individuals identify with new systems with different requirements of them and different means of controlling and evaluating them as organizational members. Where the mode of incorporation deals with values and beliefs this mode is more grounded in the praxis of membership and what sort of a member the subject becomes. Examples are social subject/team player (surveillance); leading subject; political subject; professional subject; "acting subject" (performer of a role or roles).
3. *Mode of Subjective Identity* (the means by which individuals position, or see themselves positioned within/identify with wider social discourses) – The question here is how the individual weights organizational discourse to other wider discourses of which they may be a part. Here we are dealing with the subject in relation not just to the organization, but to who they *see* themselves being in the world,

and the tensions, strains or opportunities that may ensue. Alvesson and Willmott (2002) discuss self-identity in a relevant but slightly more restricted way than reading identity as multiplicity and fluidity. This is more about the "I" I Mead's terms than the "me". Examples may be personal; familial; professional/careerist; ethical; aesthetic etc.

4. *Mode of Resistance* (how individuals resist, transgress and change established discursive structures or create new ones) – Here the question is how individuals resist being colonized by discourses of which they do not approve or in which they do not believe, and how they resist having unacceptable identities inscribed upon them. Castells (1997: 8) argues that collective resistance identities may be formed from common modes of resistance permeating a group or society. Examples of both individual and collective can include political opposition; non-cooperation; subversion; symbolic/ discursive opposition; counter-seduction; transgressive reinscription; reflexive critique; dissent.

5. *Mode of Autonomy* (how individuals convert identity into agency and how praxis can thereby be enabled and realized) – The final question is how individuals are able to create identities which they can use to establish some sovereign epistemological space which can become a resource for change and development. Examples are political agency; emancipation; empowerment; networking and alliances; bricolage/ improvization; play; managing boundaries.

The modes may be thought of themselves as involved in deploying masks, at a tactical level, whilst simultaneously cohering to form different dimensions of a larger mask. Different masks may consequently be employed *within* different modes of subject formation to achieve a common objective or a specific combination of modes of subject formation may constitute one particular mask.

Gendering management

Researching gender in management and organization theory has largely involved establishing the idea of difference in terms of masculinity and femininity, predominantly in a dichotomous form. It is only more recently that degrees of difference in terms of multiple forms of masculinities or femininities has been recognized (see for example Connell 1995; Collinson and Hearn 1996; Kerfoot and Knights 1998) even though there is a great deal of research on men and women in management (see for example the works of Fagenson 1993; Vinnicombe and Colwill 1995; Marshall 1995; Ledwith and Colgan 1996). The notion of identity has been debated across the various feminisms, especially feminist standpoint research which has focused on the presence of an essential, fixed self – womanhood (see for example Oakley 1981). Poststructuralist feminists (Weedon 1987, 1999; Benhabib 1992) deny the presence of this unitary subject resting their analysis on how the socially constructed nature of the subject and how the subject is constituted within and through discourses of social relations, constantly in flux and always since subjectivity is "precarious, contradictory and in process, constantly being reconstituted in discourse each time we think or speak" (Weedon 1987: 33). Following a poststructuralist line to investigate gendered identities as project, this book is concerned with the move away from the search for "truth" to recognize that inconsistency, complexity and ambiguity is integral to knowledge production. The stability of knowledge is questioned and offers a means for overcoming charges of essentialism, located within the foundationalist claims of the Enlightenment, of much middle management research. The ontological and epistemological assumptions underlying management theorizing that presents management work as objective, neutral, observable activities have been criticized in a range of studies of management. Although these influences are acknowledged I wish to adopt the perspective that all knowledge is recognized as being partial, situated, localized and self-referential (Foucault 1980) in relation to middle management, where it is considered to be long overdue. Research on managerial identities requires therefore movement away from unitary, stable even if multiple categorizations of gendered identities representing the multiplicity, diversity, and processual nature of individual subjectivities towards identity as project in which the individual is the "site for competing and often contradictory modes of subjectivity which together constitute a person. Modes of subjectivity are constituted within discursive practices and lived by the individual as if she or he were a fully coherent intentional subject" (Weedon 1999: 104).

French feminist theorists Cixous, Irigaray and Kristeva, despite their many differences regarding their writings on psychoanalytic issues, sexuality and femininity, all reject the notion of individual subjectivity as unified and stable. However the usefulness of Lacanian and Freudian models of gendered subjectivities – which are still seen to retain significant masculinist features by many interpreters remains a contested area within feminism, as does their reinscription by feminist theorists such as Kristeva and Irigaray to Butler and Grosz (see for example Driscoll in Buchanan and Colebrook 2000). Grosz (1994), Butler (1999) and Weedon (1999) have challenged ideas of fixed meaning, unified subjectivity and centred theories of power. Meta-narratives of feminist theories are questioned, to open spaces for "alternative voices, new forms of subjectivity, previously marginalized narratives, and new interpretations, meanings and values" (Weedon 1999: 4). Subjectivities are therefore constantly in process and constructed and reconstructed in discourse within specific interactions with the "other" (Potter and Wetherell 1987; Chia 1996; Mumby and Clair 1997). Through this perspective the deconstruction of taken for granted assumptions inherent in organization and management is achieved, using theories of language, subjectivity, and social processes to reveal the underlying power relations (Calás and Smircich 1992a; 1992b).

The book develops in four phases. In the first phase I explore the context and background of contemporary middle managers to argue for a gendered analysis of middle managers' generic roles that explores the power relations involved in the construction and reconstruction of their identities. In Chapter 2 data generated from an exploratory study of middle managers' roles from a wider sample of organizations (see Appendix 2 for a full justification of the research design and methods employed) are used to highlight pertinent issues surrounding their experiences (however these data will not be considered in the rest of this book). Appreciating the treatment of power in the theoretical approach of Gowler and Legge (1996), their Meaning of Management/ Management of Meaning framework is critiqued from both a feminist and poststructuralist perspective in Chapter 4. This examination concludes that Gowler and Legge's approach needs development by giving greater attention to gender and power issues and by investigation of non-rhetorical factors. Gowler and Legge's model is then developed to provide an analytical framework that deductively explores the predicted shifts in middle managers' concerns over time. This framework identifies dimensions of subject positioning, through the shift from modernist modes of achievement, accountability and hierarchy (Gowler and Legge) to postmodern features of commitment, seduction and networking (see Chapter 3).

The second phase of this book – chapters 5–7 – presents the empirical data according to the above conceptual framework. The data were analyzed to explore the intersections of modern and postmodern features of managerial identity construction, namely the dualities between hierarchy and networking (Carlux in Chapter 5); accountability and seduction (Nylons in Chapter 6); and achievement and commitment (Larts in Chapter 7); in three case study organizations that had undergone, and were undergoing, organizational restructuring at the time of the inquiry. Qualitative interviews with approximately ten middle managers and other individuals in each company were conducted to explore individuals' experiences of their roles and how they construct their identities within their organizations (see Appendix 2 for the research methods adopted).

This book extends existing theory on middle managers' identities in its third stage by developing Gowler and Legge's Meaning of Management framework and offers a conceptual supplement – The Modes of Subjective Identity – developed during data analysis to consider the ways in which subjectivities, grounded in power, knowledge and language, are constructed (Chapter 8). The variety of ways in which the individual managers interviewed constructed their identities within these modes (discussed previously) are plotted from the data. This analysis illustrates the ways in which different masks may be employed *within* different modes of subject formation or how a specific combination of modes of subject formation may constitute one particular mask.

This book does not attempt to provide fixed conceptualizations of middle management subjects in contemporary situations. What it does attempt to develop are aids to an understanding of middle managers' ever changing subjectivities. These subjectivities are always in play, and as I have suggested, managers don and discard masks according to the ways in which they read the game they find themselves in. Over the next few chapters we will explore these games of self, gender and power, and the ways in which individual managers make sense of, and in some cases, transgress Jill Johnson's claim that "Identity is what you are according to what they say you can be" (cited in Shotter and Gergen 1989). After all, as Foucault contends:

> The main interest in life is to become someone else that you were not at the beginning... The game is worthwhile insofar as we don't know what will be the end.

2

Restructuring Middle Management

Stuck in the middle ... but of what?

Organizational restructuring over the past two decades has stimulated considerable empirical interest in the changing roles and careers of middle management as a consequence (Dopson and Stewart 1990; Floyd and Wooldridge 1997; Dopson and Neumann 1998; Thomas and Linstead 2002; Linstead and Thomas 2002; Littler et al 2003; Sims 2003; Balogun and Johnson 2004). As organizations face increasing global competition, turbulent markets and rapid change, it is suggested that there is a need for organizational structures to become more flexible, flat, responsive and lean (Peters 1987; Kanter 1989a). Accordingly, the middle management cohort are restructured and re-formed, since they, rightly or wrongly, come to be perceived as the root cause of many of the problems associated with the traditional hierarchical organizational form – and an obstacle to change. Scarbrough and Burrell (1996: 178) suggest that middle managers have been accused of being:

> costly, resistant to change, a block to communication both upwards and downwards. They consistently underperform; they spend their time openly politicking rather than in constructive problem solving. They are reactionary, undertrained and regularly fail to act as entrepreneurs.

Middle management have for some years been seen as being "stuck in the middle" of tall hierarchical structures but more recently they have also been "stuck in the middle" of academic debates between pessimistic and optimistic role experiences (Dopson and Stewart 1990). Research in this tradition has been trapped within the positive and negative modes of this dualism, drawn to investigate the impact of discourses of restructuring on the current "state" of middle management – work roles, functions, attitudes and behaviours, mindsets, and projected futures. Middle management research is also trapped between subject-object (what is happening to middle managers /what are they doing) and locked within epistemological treatments and methodological approaches that reinforce the generation of findings that may be easily generalized from a homogenized group of middle managers to construct middle manage*ment*. Before returning to critique existing research on "what is happening *to* middle management?" I briefly discuss the positive and negative experiences of middle managers to develop the critique made in this book.

What is happening *to* middle management?

Whether middle management has a role to play in new organizational forms has been an open question for some time. Some commentators, such as Kanter (1989a), the accessible academic; Peters, (1992) the revolutionary consultant; and Semler, (1993) the frame-breaking entrepreneur consider middle management to be a barrier to achieving a more cost competitive, customer focused, and flexible organization. What everyone seems to agree upon is that middle management has changed, although there is considerable diversity on what the most important influences have been on these changes. The most common suggestions are massive managerial redundancies and job insecurity (Cameron et al 1991; Heckscher 1995); the reconstitution of management roles (Floyd and Wooldridge 1997); careers (Noer 1993; Arthur et al 1995) and managers' self-identities (Watson 1994; Thomas and Linstead 2002; Linstead and Thomas 2002). The exact relationships between these influences are not linear or uni-directional – for example, redundancies may be for the reconstruction of roles, or it may be the other way round, depending on whether organizational change is a planned improvement or a forced response to the competitive environment. Pessimistic accounts report that these changes lead to a disillusionment and demoralization, and experiences of long working hours, work intensification, job insecurity, increased accountability and monitoring and psychological withdrawal from the organization (Scase and Goffee, 1989). Studies of "survivor syndrome" (Brockner et al 1992; Thornhill and Saunders 1997) amongst middle managers in both the UK and US (Guest and Peccei 1992; Doherty et al 1995; Dopson and Neumann 1998) have shown that prolonged periods of downsizing have resulted in work intensification, impoverished lifestyles and stress related illness, with commitment to the organization based on fear of job loss rather than any positive factors (Thornhill and Gibbons 1995; Newell and Dopson 1996; Benbow 1996; Charlesworth 1997; Thomas and Dunkerly 1999). Thompson and Warhurst (1998) sound a cautionary note against sounding the death-knell of the middle management prematurely due to the diverse macro influences of recession and restructuring on public and private organizations. That having been said, the initial exploratory inductive research phase of the study presented in this book on the experiences of middle managers in restructured organizations did reveal pessimistic moments in middle managers' texts. Fragments from middle managers' accounts are presented in the next section to highlight some of the issues that some of the middle managers face in the restructured and restructuring organizations researched. It is not my intention to attempt to generalize from this small sample either between middle managers or between organizations. Nevertheless, some of their more pessimistic accounts resonated with other studies in centring on greater intensification of work; presenteeism; broken psychological contracts; and job insecurity as underlying reasons for their instability, insecurity and ambiguity. To illustrate, the following accounts provide a flavour of middle managers' experiences.

With streamlining we have lost a about a third, there are fewer people who need to work harder. Before the change I used to read two or three books a week because there were so many of us. It's not like that now, now I can't get home, and when I'm there I get called back in (Kevin Larts).

You need to adapt yourself to different areas of the factory... I learnt the hard way... It was a case of figuring out what worked where, and changing yourself to get what you wanted done (Brian Carlux).

I get very, very stressed with some of the responsibilities I've got. I'm sitting at home, it can be ten o'clock at night and I've got to come in. I live ten miles away... I'm contracted 37 hours, but I'm expected to do the necessary hours to get my job done. We have 24-hour responsibility but that doesn't mean we have to be here 24 hours a day (laughter)... The job is bigger because there are fewer guys to get more done, and it's different work, not just the production stuff. It's the other stuff that takes the time... there's a feeling that you have to be in this place, not only to get the job done but to be seen to be doing extra (Wayne Larts).

It has changed the moral of people, at least with the old form there was some form of career path where you can see your career development... now it's a bit of a morass of who does what where... When you go from the shop floor to a team leader in the new structure there is a clear step, but after that they don't really know where to go (Dan Wire Products).

In this flat structure, where do you go? You either go across the company or go out of the company (Dave Dinky Products).

You've got all the pressures from above from the Directors and at the same time there are the operational pressures. All these pressures are pressed in at our level. This is a real balancing act; you have to be a juggler. I'm very much the piggy in the middle (Sue Parcel Co).

The accounts selected above reveal some of the greater pressures that these managers face within restructuring organizations. These demands centre on "doing more [work] with less [managers]" which means increased workloads, longer hours and more generic roles and responsibilities amongst all of the managers that experienced delayering. Not only were managers facing work intensification and working longer to "get the job done" there were escalating pressures to improve performance. Working longer hours was also a consequence of presenteeism as an intention to demonstrate individual commitment to their companies. This presenteeism surfaced in the data from increased feelings of insecurity as traditional forms of psychological contracts became redundant and heightened role ambiguity from the lack of career direction became evident. The loss of hierarchical progression was seen to be a fundamental attack on the status and identity of these managers. These preliminary findings confirm many of the frustrations experienced by middle management documented by earlier research (cf. Kanter 1983). The image of the middle managers presented here is reflective of the research data and portrays elements of the pessimistic book of middle management that influences the control they have over their working lives, increasingly having to sacrifice their personal life to meet the demands of the organization. That said existing research and the exploratory data reveal a more upbeat image of middle management.

More optimistic studies emphasize the growthful and positive aspects of the changes, seeing middle management as having a very different future, one which, transformed by restructuring, is now itself transforming, more flexible, autonomous and with more opportunities for development (Dopson and Stewart 1990). These managers are no more "stuck in the middle" of the organizational hierarchy (Dickson 1977; Stewart 1993) although downsized middle management cohorts are now found in many organizations. Optimistic advocates for "new" roles and opportunities for middle managers assume that they now have an increased strategic content to their roles, are more entrepreneurial, more personally involved, and with enriched roles have high intrinsic motivation (Dopson and Stewart 1990; Neumann et al 1995; Newell and Dopson 1996; Floyd and Wooldridge 1997). The concept of "commitment" is reconfigured into a more "mature" psychological attachment based on loyalty to task rather than to the organization, arguing for a "new managerial work" which constitutes the basis of a broader "new professionalism" (Heckscher 1995). From this perspective, greater autonomy leads to greater meaning and involvement, which delivers increased commitment and enthusiasm for the task, and rewards managers with the opportunity to gain skills and experiences which improve their employability and job mobility – which may, of course, seem a contradiction in terms, but commitment does not automatically entail loyalty as professionalism implies loyalty to performance standards rather than organizational culture. The texts from the exploratory research suggest that some middle managers were extremely positive about the *impact* of change on their roles:

Initially it was taking on responsibility... as a foreman, before I did anything you went to see the superintendent or manager, but when you went to making decisions with your team, well if it works it works and if it fails it fails. We get on with it now, and so do the teams and team leaders. We soon realised, as a company, that the skills and talents had been there all the time (Adam Larts).

We are more involved in the running of our sections, we have more responsibilities, so there's no more passing the buck. The buck stops with us. But we are now in control, we are in charge and we meet with our senior manager to discuss our targets but then we just get on with it. Of course this has a downside, we have to perform because we are more visible with performance and target settings (Nick Nylons).

Since I have taken on this role I have much more involvement with senior management issues, it's not just about doing your bit, it's about seeing the bigger picture. You feel more valued because of that, if you get on with your boss that is. We need to think about quality, reducing costs and things like improving production. It's also about improving our selves and our staff, some staff can be improved and some can't. But I'm much more responsible for my people now. I'm a manager and not another body but I suppose it's because there is fewer of us around these days (Joyce POC Ltd.).

I'm contracted 37 hours, but I'm expected to do the necessary hours to get my job done. We have 24-hour responsibility but that doesn't mean we have to be here 24 hours a day (laughter)... The job is bigger because there are less guys to get more done, and it's different work, not just the production stuff. It's the other stuff that takes the time... there's a feeling that you have to be in this place, not only to get the job done but to be seen to be doing extra...I'm also studying for my degree but I've studied all the time I've been with the company, it's the only way to get on and make sure you progress. I enjoy it but it's hard work (Wayne Larts).

There's no more passing the buck, the buck stops with us. We are in control now, we are in charge and we just meet with our manager to discuss targets. We just get on with things now, of course there is a downside 'cos we have to perform. We are more visible with the targets (Chris Nylons).

With restructuring they implemented the teams and much of our new roles is about managing these teams. Of course some managers have the skills that you need to manage people and others don't. Our jobs can be much better if you see it as working with a group and sharing the responsibility to get the work done and it's good. But, that's when it's working. If it's not, then, well, you have to manage hard and get control and that's the difficult bit because people have different expectations of the managers now (Brian Wire Products).

These more upbeat accounts from middle managers partially stem from greater control and discretion to make decisions and problem-solve within more "innovative roles" (Dopson and Stewart 1990; Dunford and Heiler 1994). However these flexible roles were associated with having more stress from doing more and having new and challenging responsibilities. Clear performance targets and increased visibility of individual performance alongside increased opportunities to engage in entrepreneurial activity resulted in pressures to work harder and longer. Heightened awareness of surveillance and pressures to manage their professional identities influenced managers' engagement with me, whereby they presented high levels of commitment and loyalty to their organizations. Managers commented on high levels of job satisfaction and fulfilment from their organizations, and were keen to present a committed, hard working and loyal image to their organizations in turbulent periods.

To summarize then, the literature on middle management presents a contradictory and inconclusive picture. On the one hand the majority of accounts paint a pessimistic future for middle management. In contrast, optimistic accounts suggest that new middle management has emerged from the ruins of the drastic reductions of downsized and delayered organizations and is now more strategically involved, more empowered, more innovative and entrepreneurial, with work perceived as more enriching and meaningful. Managers do not have the pervasive sense of loss of identity, demoralization and self-doubt that flavours the pessimistic accounts; optimistic accounts see managers as energized by possibility and embracing the opportunity to become autopoietic, creating their identities anew. Recent accounts have revealed that the picture is mixed and inconclusive and do not endorse the positive/negative, either/or approach of previous research, but although contradictory messages on the "state" of middle management have not gone unnoticed, critical research in the area remains very small (Watson 1994; Dopson and Neumann 1998; McGovern et al 1998; Thomas and Linstead 2002; Linstead and Thomas 2002). The middle managers' texts from the exploratory study reveal contrasting, contradictory and incomplete experiences both *of* individual managers as well as *between* managers (within organizations and across different organizations). So, the question remains whether existing research has failed to breakout of the positive and negative dualism, remaining stuck in the middle where Dopson and Stewart began.

Stuck in the middle – the subject-object dualism

Contemporary discourses of restructuring have questioned the economic and social function – indeed the very existence – of middle managers in periods of uncertainty, intensification of work and role ambiguity. Managers are seemingly constantly engaged in identity work to order and reorder, construct and reconstruct their subjectivities. The nature of the question of what is happening *to* middle management suggests that middle management have been the *object* of restructuring. Issues of identity are brushed aside with middle managers being seen as deterministically pushed, pulled and shaped this way or that, with no apparent agency, in this literature (Scarbrough 1998). Change impacts *on* middle management. Middle managers are also portrayed as univocal and homogeneous entities that are passive victims rather than active agents constructing, resisting and challenging the subjectivities offered them (Thomas and Linstead 2002). Furthermore middle managers have more often than not been researched as a univocal, homogenous entity: what is happening *to* middle management is the key consideration rather than exploring the experiences of middle managers and accounting for differences between them. In doing so, individual difference is denied, diversity of experience between vertical and horizontal groups (Mulholland 1998), and context is ignored.

To address this neglect of agency and the treatment of cause and effect this book, following earlier work with Thomas (Thomas and Linstead 2002), shifts the focus from what is happening to management, beyond what are managers doing about it, to how are managers *becoming*. We have seen the extensive literature on *what is happening to middle management*; have a little knowledge on *what it is doing to middle management* but have limited experience of *what middle managers are doing about it*. What it is doing to managers and what middle managers are doing about it are intertwined processes of becoming, deconstructing the subject-object dualism that has previously reinforced reductionist representations of middle managers in existing literature. The question therefore moves from *what* are middle managers becoming to *how* are middle managers becoming and with what outcomes – in other words, the means are the end, and as the means are constantly emergent, so must be the ends. Furthermore this book moves beyond this to explore the *multiplicity of becomings* that are simultaneously at play in managers' representation of "self".

Labour process theory has been guilty of neglecting managerial work (Hill 1991; du Gay 1996; Scarbrough and Burrell 1996). Managers, of course, are both, to a degree, beneficial subjects as agents of capitalist relations of production and targets of control processes as objects of those self-same relations. This equivocal position – arguably a class seduced to work against itself – for commentators such as Willmott (1997) is sufficiently significant as to require a "reconstruction" of labour process theory. Similarly informed by labour process theory, Scarbrough (1998) has argued that middle managers are facing a process of proletarianization as their knowledge (what distinguishes them from the Other, i.e., non-managers), is increasingly diffused amongst the workers by technologies of the self. Whilst such research may confirm the move towards proletarianization, it does not help to explain the contradictory images held between and by individual managers. However to focus on analyzing the individual is not to resort to the individualism and voluntarism (O'Doherty and Willmott 1999). Redressing this imbalance requires a method of analysis which focuses more specifically on the issue of difference, and the accounting and representational practices through which individual managers construct and deconstruct their difference and sameness in relation to the other – the non-manager.

In this book managerial identities are seen as changing but relatively stable, towards the recognition of identity construction as a form of first order accounting (Garfinkel 1967) characterized by paradox, fluidity, inconsistency and being constantly emergent which appreciates and accommodates diversity, difference, and voice of middle managers' "equivocal positions" (Willmott 1997: 1337). I suggest that identity construction is not a matter of resolving ambiguity and making clear cut choices, but is often characterized by confusion and conflict within the individual as well as in the context. Identities are not only embedded in the present, but are constructed in terms of the conjunction of past and future, as an explanation of previous events as episodes in an unfolding narrative in a way that positions the constructor of the account advantageously for future episodes. Identities can be seen as masks that are actively used, manipulated and created as resources for participation in an ongoing masquerade (Goffman 1959). That said, these masks are gendered – middle managers draw on gendered masks to negotiate their "self as manager" which I examine in chapters 5–7.

A critical, gendered reading of identity work in this book, enables a move away from generalizable accounts on the state of middle *management* which has denied difference, context, history, and agency to a reading of middle *managers'* actively constructed accounts (as Linstead and Thomas (2002) did by employing a poststructuralist feminist perspective). Analyzing identity as project in this way presents middle managers as a diverse and fragmented cohort and argues that, regardless of sex, both male and female managers' experiences of restructuring illustrate the further masculinization of management. The feminine here is suppressed as "other" (Cixous 1998) as individuals reinforce and legitimize their identities within what remain masculinist organizational frameworks of managerial work. Before returning to this argument the ontological and epistemological positions of existing research are discussed to explore the implications for methodology.

Stuck in the middle between ontology and epistemology

Knowledge claims in research on managerial work customarily ground their own validity in realist claims of greater empirical accuracy which produces a better representation of the "true picture" of the situation. Although some attention has been paid to the research methodologies adopted (Watson 1994) the epistemological underpinnings of this research had been virtually ignored. This book recognizes the neglect of ontology (as managers' lived experience) and epistemology (in both academic and manager constructions of "self"-knowledge) in a great deal of existing middle management research. Ontologically, much of the previous research has regarded the evidence on management work as objective, observable activities rather than socially and linguistically constructed processes. Middle managers are therefore not victims of restructuring, no longer passive subjects. Knights and Willmott (1999) assert that managers are active agents engaged in the construction of discourses as well as being subjected to them. Through the process of engagement with the "other", middle managers' identities "become", rather than operating as an autonomous base from which action "proceeds". Furthermore, as researchers we actively influence, and are influenced by, the research subjects. The nature of the research process could be argued as focusing on reducing the complex nature of this identity work to a manageable and meaningful "story". Paraphrasing Grint, managers when making sense of and representing their lives and experiences are influenced and "constrained by virulent external forces" that threaten them. However Grint reminds us of the possibility of agency and how managers are torn between different and contested "overlapping constructions" (1995: 66). Managers' *persuasive accounts* therefore represent involvement, manipulation, façade and storytelling to maintain their sense of organizational reality (see Weick 1979).

Research on middle management has to a great extent been locked within positivist epistemologies and realist ontologies which reflect the dominance of essentialist representations of what is happening to middle management in the field. Much of the work in this area is not grounded in substantial or extensive *and* detailed empirical work, being based instead on single case studies (Dopson and Stewart 1990; Newell and Dopson 1996; Redman et al 1997) or questionnaire surveys (Wheatley 1992; Inkson 1995). The limited generalizability of context specific single case studies is counter-balanced by rich, in-depth portraits of middle management in the midst of problem-solving and decision-making. Questionnaire-based surveys (Charlesworth 1997; Worrall and Cooper 1998) offer breadth and depict broad trends but have difficulty in explaining how direction changes and how trends may become significantly reversed, extrapolating what is to what will be without understanding the processes of becoming.

Methodologically then there are shortcomings in the existing literature. Where attempts have been made to address these shortcomings, responses have nevertheless been more of the same, although grounded in claims of empirical superiority – a larger sample of middle managers, a larger and/or more diverse sample of organizations, or greater depth and richness (Wheatley 1992; Redman et al 1997; Dopson and Neumann 1998). Different contexts have been addressed in some literature, but even here the complexity of the context is simplified, reduced or treated as irrelevant (see for example Dopson and Neumann 1998). The dichotomous nature of theorizing has been supported by the dichotomous nature of research.

Epistemologically, the extant research then can be criticized for adopting a power-blind, unitarist perspective where difference is effectively denied. Such unitarist analysis ignores, reinforces and promotes systems of oppression in the organization, in terms of class, gender and race (Thompson and McHugh 1995; Scarbrough 1998). Functionalist analysis of organization concentrates on debating the performatives of efficiency and effectiveness, and loses a sense of historical development or contextual dependence adjustment and choice, and as structure becomes privileged over agency the involvement of middle managers in their own reconstruction is occluded (Willmott 1997; Scarbrough 1998). In order to understand how management is not only affected by but also affects the social and political discourses which shape it, management can be seen as a "text". Watson's study (1994) of one organization attempts to illustrate the ways in which managers are reflexively constituted and constructed through the interactive operations of discourse. Taking a non-essentialist perspective on managerial identities, Watson argues that identity is in constant flux, ever-emerging and illustrates how managers draw on discourses to both manage others as well as to manage their selves. He identifies two conflicting dominant discourses, either of which may be accessed to work *for* the managers or work *upon* them. The discourse of *new management*, of empowerment, skill and growth is set against the discourse of *control*, of jobs, information and costs. This contradictory image underlines how researchers are caught between the problems of producing text accurately to capture the meaning of managers' lives and the challenges of moving towards more fluid understandings of identity. Furthermore, to research middle managers' identity work researchers need to explore what multiplicity of becomings are simultaneously at play in managers' representation of "self", highlighting the complexities and contradictions that surface discourses of power and inequality (Knights and Willmott 1999).

This book sees *identity as project* to investigate the gendered mask of middle managers' identity construction, which moves away from the search for "truth" to recognize that inconsistency, complexity and ambiguity are integral to knowledge production. The stability of knowledge is questioned and offers a means for overcoming charges of essentialism and foundationalism of much research into managerial identities and in particular middle managers' identities. The ontological and epistemological assumptions underlying management theorizing that presents management work as objective, neutral, observable activities have been criticized in a range of studies of management in which knowledge is recognized as being partial, situated, localized and self-referential (Foucault 1980). Being influenced by poststructuralism enables research on managerial identities to move even further away from unitary, stable even if multiple categorizations of gendered identities representing the multiplicity, diversity, and processual nature of individual subjectivities. The individual manager then is the "site for competing and often contradictory modes of subjectivity which together constitute a person. Modes of subjectivity are constituted within discursive practices and lived by the individual as if she or he were a fully coherent intentional subject" (Weedon 1999: 104). Researching difference in managers' identity work emphasizes fluid, unstable, contradictory and fractured managerial subjectivities. The gendered mask that individual managers employ to construct, perform and legitimize the "self as manager" is explored, uncovering how managers use this mask to position their "self" in work in order to articulate and legitimize themselves within the organization. Here one can see that managers draw on identity as a construct and resource in producing their own first order accounts (Garfinkel 1967) of their situations and its paradoxical nature emerges as we examine the stable yet fluid dimension to their constitution of their identity. This process is episodic in character as managers periodically restructure and reconstruct their identities – sometimes in response to outside pressure, crisis, or the punctuated equilibrium cycle characterized by short intensive periods of restructuring activity followed by relatively longer periods of stability. In doing so they not only make sense of past organizational performances to legitimize the gendered discourses that are revealed in their texts, such as the relationship of commitment to the neglect of family life, they also position their "self" in anticipation of future organizational episodes ensuring some consistency and certainty whilst maintaining "poise" – the ability to move rapidly and appropriately when the need arises. For these managers, the exit from one organizational stage is the entrance to another. This "identity work" is complex and unpredictable as Knights and Vurdubakis observe:

> ...the routine discourses and practices through which subjects are constituted (and constitute themselves) as, for instance, unitary autonomous individuals, are fraught with contradictions. Self-identity can therefore be realised only as a constant struggle against the experience of tension, fragmentation and discord. Subject positions are made available in a number of competing discourses... Identity is thus of necessity always a project rather than an achievement (Knights and Vurdubakis 1994: 185).

Rejecting essentialist notions of identity; subjectivities are therefore constantly in process and constructed and reconstructed in discourse within specific interactions with the "other" (Potter and Wetherell 1987; Chia 1996; Mumby and Clair 1997). Through this perspective the deconstruction of taken for granted assumptions inherent in organization and management is achieved, using theories of language, subjectivity, and social processes to reveal the underlying power relations (Calás and Smircich 1992a/b).

This book began by appreciating the opaque nature of management work (Hales 1993; Watson and Watson 1999) and the ambiguous boundaries around the "middle" (Livian and Burgoyne 1997). The aim of the book to deconstruct the boundaries between the dualisms that exist between pessimistic/optimistic futures for managers, subject/object, and ontology/epistemology have been discussed. This approach moves beyond functionalist debates about whether restructuring is good or bad for middle managers and asks the question "what do I want/what will I be allowed to be in the organization?" As Parker observes:

Organization is a contested process, a continually shifting set of claims and counter claims and there is surely no place or time from which it can be finally captured and presented as fact (1997: 134).

Gendering management: masks of masculinities

...masculine discourses and practices are so dominant in business that, regardless of sex, they have to be adopted or complied with if a person seeks to have any influence as a manager (Kerfoot and Knights 1998: 8).

Management theory has until relatively recently, and with notable exceptions such as Kanter (1977), neglected the issue of gender. From the classical studies of Fayol (1949) and Urwick (1952), behavioural and empirical studies of Mintzberg (1973), Stewart (1989), Hales (1993) and Willmott (1984), and even including the critical management analyses of Watson (1994), Linstead et al (1996) and Alvesson and Willmott (1998), the gendered nature of management has not been explored as part of the nature of management – even though some of these authors have written about gender in other works. More specifically, when considering different variations within managerial activity, research investigating middle management work has been dominated by functionalist perspectives and has therefore ignored the gendered nature of management and organization (Dopson and Stewart 1990; Newell and Dopson 1996; Floyd and Wooldridge 1997). However, contemporary critical and (pro) feminist writing on management and organization has argued and frequently demonstrated that gender should be an integral part of management analysis (Collinson et al 1990; Mills and Tancred 1992; Calás and Smircich 1996; Collinson and Hearn 1996; Kerfoot and Knights 1998; Knights and Willmott 1999). The area of study that has become known as the "women in management" field has largely explored the work experiences of women managers and has focused on the differences between, for example, feminine and masculine styles of leadership and image or sources of motivation (Sheppard 1989; Cockburn 1991; Davidson and Cooper 1992; Marshall 1995; Metcalfe and Linstead 2003).

In the broader management literature it has been widely documented that organizational restructuring has influenced the "state" of middle management and its quasi-professional status (Dopson and Stewart 1990; Floyd and Wooldridge 1997; Dopson and Neumann 1998). More recently there are now a small number of studies on middle management that explore the gendered implications of change and how it influences management roles, careers and identities (Collinson and Collinson 1997; Whitehead 1998; Prichard and Deem 1999; Thomas and Linstead 2002; Linstead and Thomas 2002). Nevertheless, much of the middle management and restructuring research is criticized for being ahistorical and decontextualized, serving to ignore, reinforce and promote systems of oppression in the organization of class, gender and race (Scarbrough 1998). Women, men and middle managers have been treated as homogeneous, unitary, and univocal resulting in the suppression of difference both of and between middle managers. Redressing this imbalance requires a method of analysis which focuses more specifically on the issue of difference, and the accounting and representational practices through which individual managers construct and deconstruct difference, sameness and identity to challenge the institutionalized practices of inequality that create, reify, construct and legitimize masculinist discourses of management and organization (Collinson and Hearn 1996; Kerfoot and Knights 1996, 1998; Messner 1997). It is argued, therefore, that middle management is imbued with particular notions of masculinity. The feminist voice has been slow to be heard in organization and management probably because management theory and practice has been dominated by men and discourses that privilege the trappings of masculinity (Hearn et al 1989; Weedon 1987, 1999; Collinson and Hearn 1996).

One consequence of such neglect is to reproduce the so-called gender neutrality of management and organizational theory in the middle management field (Wilson 1996). This produces analysis that supports rather than subverts the dominance of masculine discourses that exclude, downplay, and subordinate the feminine. Feminist researchers have however challenged this gender neutrality highlighting that both the researchers and researched in the research process, and the knowledge generated, are gendered (Hearn and Parkin 1983; Acker 1990; Jacobson and Jacques 1990; Calás and Smircich 1992a, 1992b, 1996; Linstead 2000a; Pullen forthcoming). Accordingly, and whilst not necessarily arguing that organizations as a whole are gendered, there has been some research that has examined the differential impact of restructuring on women managers (Edwards et al 1996, 1999; Woodhall et al 1997) and on male and female managers (Sinclair 1994; Wajcman 1998; Watson and Harris 1999). Research on women's identities at work has largely focused on the skills that women "naturally" possess (Fondas 1997) that more often than not promote images of weakness, passivity, and emotionality (Young 1990, cited in Kerfoot and Knights 1998: 9). Kerfoot and Knights (1998) suggest that this "passivity" is not absent in men and does not include *all* women, but for many women, "femaleness" becomes a phenomenon that they must manage, as it can be used to undermine or deny women's authority, silence their voices and restrict their involvement in decision-making. Wajcman's (1998) research for example suggests that many women find that they have to emulate masculine characteristics in order to manage successfully, a trait which ironically Wajcman is also criticized for reproducing in her writing (see Linstead 2000b). Leadership differences between men and women are therefore largely seen as a *negative* difference (see Sinclair 1994, 1998).

In studies of gender *per se*, there appears to be an emergent bipolarity. On the one hand the "feminization of management" book (Rosener 1990; Calás and Smircich 1993; Alimo-Metcalfe 1995) has been said to challenge masculinist management and working practices by offering new possibilities for women as their "special" skills and qualities are recognized and incorporated into the management canon (Newman 1995; Maile 1995). A critique of restructuring grounded in this perspective suggests that restructuring promotes new forms of ordering as another way of reinforcing the gender binary by disconnecting and subordinating the feminine, the "other", from and in relation to the hierarchically dominant masculine norms, albeit in new ways (see Spivak in Derrida 1976; Cixous 1998). Thus regardless of gender or sex managers become subjected to, and rendered incapable of resisting, increasingly masculinist career patterns and management practices.

On the other hand, research on managerial masculinities (such as Kerfoot 1999) has also served to challenge the so-called gender neutrality of management, drawing on poststructuralist approaches, to emphasize a more fluid interpretation of gendered identities in management and organizational theorizing. Masculinity is neither necessarily uniform nor easy to accomplish, even for males. Studies of masculinity have grown extensively in recent years, with a good body of studies now being in the public sector (Collinson and Hearn 1996; Prichard 1996; Goode and Bagilhole 1998; Kerfoot and Knights 1998, 1999; Leonard 1998; Whitehead 1998; Whitehead and Moodley 1999). Despite offering new insights in management and organization, there is a tendency in some of these studies to use masculinities, notably competitive masculinity, in too broad a way, losing the complexities of the empirical data.

To summarize, this book critically explores the creation and recreation of middle managers' subjectivities. This chapter has critiqued existing middle management, restructuring and gender literature to highlight the "state of middle management", a "state" that has been well overdue for a radical overhaul. In this chapter I have firstly critiqued those general accounts of the state of middle *management* which have denied difference, context, history, and agency and moved towards a reading of middle *managers'* actively constructed accounts. Secondly, to address this neglect of agency and the treatment of cause and effect this book shifts the focus from what is happening to managers, beyond what are managers doing about it, to how are managers becoming. The book further explores the multiplicity of becomings that are synchronously at play in managers' representation of "self". Thirdly, I argue that to theorize identity as *project* enables research on managerial identities to move away from unitary, stable even if multiple categorizations of gendered identities to accounts representing the multiplicity, diversity, and processual nature of individual subjectivities. This book has therefore already proceeded in this direction by introducing the deconstruction of the dichotomies of pessimistic/ optimistic, subject/object and ontology/epistemology that exist in existing middle management research – arguing that middle management are not so much "stuck in the middle" of organizational hierarchies anymore but rather stuck between the dualities that reinforce the "state of middle management" per se.

In this chapter by exploring studies of gender in management I have suggested that middle management is imbued with particular notions of masculinity. Although restructuring has provided the potential to feminize management it appears on the surface to support hierarchical dominance whereby the feminine is suppressed as other, marginalized by the dominant masculine. Thus the gender dichotomy in management theory is perpetually reinforced. This book progresses existing gender and management theory by moving towards a more fluid understanding of gender to retheorize managerial subjectivity. Having now taken a few moves forward, I move into chapters 3 and 4 by turning back in order both to underpin and to develop our critique of management theory further by retheorizing and developing Gowler and Legge's "Meaning of Management" (1996) thesis from perspectives of gender and power.

3
Management in Three Movements: Theorizing Middle Managers' Subjectivities

> Our ways of accounting for ourselves, our accounting practices, work both to create and maintain a certain pattern of social relations, a social order, and to constitute us as being able to reproduce that order in all our practical activities.
>
> Shotter (cited in Shotter and Gergen (1985))

Introduction

The exploratory inductive research conducted in this study, the themes of which have been highlighted in Chapter 2, demonstrated that further research into how middle managers construct and reconstruct their identities in contemporary restructured, and restructuring, organizations was required. Existing research in the management, and especially the middle management, field was critiqued for its epistemological and methodological orientations which take a largely functionalist, role and task-focused orientation to the subject. The exceptions to this fall into two categories:

a) Gowler and Legge's (1983) work on rhetoric in "The Meaning of Management and the Management of Meaning" (reprinted in Linstead et al 1996). Gowler and Legge's conceptual analysis is one of the earliest discussions of management – rather than managers – that investigates the socially constructed and hence *fluid* nature of management. Other work on rhetoric since then has not concentrated on the identity of management as such, but has examined the use of rhetoric in specific contexts (see for example Linstead 1995; Watson 1995a; Hamilton 1997; Alvesson 2001; Cunliffe 2001).

b) The growing body of work on discourse, both organizational and managerial, and its analysis (see Keenoy et al 1997; Grant et al 1998; Grant et al 2004; Hardy et al 2005). Some of this work has related the concept to the formation of subjectivities, but again this work has been empirically based and has considered subject formation in particular organizational contexts (Knights and Willmott 1992; Kerfoot and Knights 1993; Watson 1994).

Gowler and Legge's work is a landmark because, although it does not claim to address identity as such, it examines public claims which managers make about what management is, and conditions where that might seem to be contested or threatened. Managers' self-definitions then are part of their experienced identity, and intervene in a discourse to which they are held to be subject. However, Gowler and Legge's investigation was not into the conditions of subjectivity, or subject formation, as it did not focus on specific managers (as subjects) or specific contexts. Nevertheless, in their analysis of rhetoric they identify three important themes in the discursive construction of modern (or modernist) management at the beginning of the 1980s – management as hierarchy; management as accountability and management as achievement. I will discuss these further below.

As I have noted previously in Chapter 2, the conditions under which managers manage have changed in the past two decades and there is increasing empirical evidence to monitor these changes. It is important, however, to ask of these data three questions:

Firstly – if, as existing middle management research argues, the context has shifted, have Gowler and Legge's organizing themes changed or dissolved? Do managers still talk about the "meaning" of management as a major part of their understanding of their identity as a manager? If so, how do they do it?

Secondly – in addition to bringing out more strongly the theme of identity in Gowler and Legge's work are there other themes which have received greater prominence in the past two decades which they did not emphasize?

Thirdly – Gowler and Legge's work was one of the earliest pieces to mark the beginning of a transition from modern to postmodern analysis of management. What further developments need to be incorporated to take this move further?

In this chapter, the first question is examined by looking at some of the broader commentaries on postmodern social and organizational shifts, and I will propose that each of the three themes of Gowler and

Legge could be seen to have shifted along a continuum – hierarchy towards networking; accountability towards seduction; achievement towards commitment. I will suggest some of the characteristics of these shifts and the processes by which they are achieved in developing the model which I will call "Management in Three Movements". In subsequent chapters my own data are used to interrogate the model.

Having established this framework in this chapter, in Chapter 4 I will discuss Gowler and Legge's work and will note that two relatively neglected dimensions in their analysis – power and gender – have more recently become of critical importance to contemporary organizational analysis and I will suggest ways of bringing these back into more focused consideration through taking a critical feminist perspective. Next, I will consider developments in forms of poststructuralist analysis which have taken place in the last 20 years and will identify some theoretical issues which need to be incorporated into the analysis of the current situation of managerial identity formation. Finally, I will indicate a move forward, over the next few chapters, of the three moves from modernist to postmodernist forms of organization and managers' practices in making sense of their roles in the model developed – deductively investigating middle managers' subjectivities from a gender perspective. In brief, I will characterize the shift in analysis as being from *what management means to management* to what it *means for individual managers to be a manager*.

The meaning of management and the changing context of the management of meaning

Taking the first question first: if, as existing middle management research argues, the context has shifted, have Gowler and Legge's organizing themes changed or dissolved? If so, do managers still talk about the "meaning" of management as a major part of their understanding of their identity as a manager? If so, how do they do it? To address this, in this section I will explore Gowler & Legge's research; discuss how the literature suggests how organizational and societal contexts have shifted from modernist to postmodernist forms; develop Gowler and Legge's Meaning of Management framework to be more specifically applicable to the analysis of middle managers' subjectivities; and prepare to explore this framework through analyzing contemporary commentaries for the emergence of the shifting dualities of hierarchy to networking, accountability to seduction and achievement to commitment.

Looking back...

Gowler & Legge draw on empirical research on managerial roles and work (Mintzberg 1973; Stewart 1976) to illustrate the importance of communication as a function of management's activity. "The Meaning of Management and The Management of Meaning" analyzes management as an oral tradition, exploring rhetoric to establish the "meaning of management" and accomplish the "management of meaning". Gowler and Legge's analysis suggests that the identity of management is given meaning in a manager's attempts to persuade others what management is.

Rhetoric for Gowler and Legge is "the use of a form of word-delivery (Parkin 1975: 114) which is lavish in symbolism and, as such, involves several layers or textures of meaning" (Gowler and Legge (1981) cited in Gowler and Legge 1996: 34). Gowler and Legge explore management using four themes in "the rhetoric of bureaucratic control, that is, highly expressive language that constructs and legitimizes managerial prerogatives in terms of a rational, goal-directed image of organizational effectiveness" (ibid.: 35). Gowler and Legge's focus on the constitution of language and meaning, through an anthropological examination, conceives of management as:

> a subculture – a social collectivity whose members share a set of implicit and explicit meanings acquired through innumerable communicative exchanges. Furthermore, the possession of these shared meanings can only be demonstrated or utilised in communication, or in acts related to communication (ibid.: 35).

Gowler and Legge therefore offer a socially constructed perspective of the nature of meaning and highlight how managers actively shape and construct talk (and one could infer identities) through their interaction. Gowler and Legge highlight how practical rhetoricians, that is, managers, are "partly creations of their own talk and other social practices" (Harre (1980: 205) cited in Gowler and Legge (1996: 35)). Gowler and Legge's framework suggests that "the rhetoric of bureaucratic control conflates management as a moral order with management as a technical-scientific order, while submerging the former" (1996: 35). More importantly the authors demonstrate that:

> through the management of meaning, the rhetoric of bureaucratic control contributes to management as a political activity concerned with the creation, maintenance, and manipulation of power and exchange relations in formal organizations (1996: 35).

Therefore the "management of meaning is an expression of power, and the meanings so managed a crucial aspect of political relations" (Cohen and Comaroff (1976:102) cited in Gowler and Legge (1996: 35)). Gowler and Legge draw our attention to the significance of inherent *power relationships* in shaping the nature of management and meaning however, as will be seen in the next chapter, contemporary analyses of management need to address more fully the different issues of *relational power*.

Focusing on managers' language as the primary unit of analysis, Gowler and Legge investigate the rhetoric of management's texts in published letters highlighting how:

> When managers express views about their speech acts, they tend to emphasise the unambiguous articulation of aims, means, outcomes, and achievements... while managers often espouse the virtues of, and commitment to, plain speaking, they frequently adopt a type of speech that is highly ambiguous – rhetoric (Gowler and Legge 1996: 36).

Rhetoric for Gowler and Legge, as Linstead (2001a: 220) summarizes, is:

> the use of language to a) justify and legitimise actual or potential power and exchange relationships; b) eliminate actual or potential challenges to existing power and exchange relationships and, at a deeper level c) express those contradictions in power and exchange relationships that cannot be openly admitted, or, in many cases, resolved.

Gowler and Legge's analysis of the rhetoric of bureaucratic control demonstrates two distinct but interrelated areas of their analysis, namely the moral-aesthetic and the techno-social order, to identify the concerns of management and meaning. A great deal of management writings account and indeed privilege task – the functions, roles and technical requirements of management, foregrounding Gowler and Legge's specific, clear and intentional "techno-social" meanings (1996: 37) over the more metaphorical, ambiguous and suggestive "moral-aesthetic" arena that transmits the ideological agenda (for further discussion of aesthetics of organization see for example the contributors to Linstead et al 1996; Strati 1999; Linstead and Höpfl 2000). Put more simply, managers try to transmit the idea of the moral rectitude of management – that it is right and good to do these things – by talking about the technical demands of management – that it is necessary and efficient to do these things. However as Linstead (2001a) argues the rhetoric of bureaucratic control discussed by Gowler and Legge is only one possible variety of rhetorics of control. Additonally, rhetorics of resistance and emancipation also exist and I will discuss these in the next chapter. To develop Gowler & Legge's framework for exploring middle managers' subjectivities I am interested here in analyzing and extending the associated themes in the rhetoric of bureaucratic control:

- *Management-as-hierarchy* refers to the hierarchy of roles, systems of power and expertise to maintain control and efficiency. Relating this to middle management then hierarchy supports and legitimates the formal positions, work roles and status of middle management in traditional organizational forms as I discussed in Chapter 2. As has been seen in our discussion of middle management and organizational change, restructuring has influenced, and in many cases made redundant, the roles of many middle managers in traditional organizations. Indeed I could infer that the control and power achieved through middle management is now a resource retained for senior management as flexible working is implemented. But the hierarchy is also, as I have suggested, a moral one rather than simply a task – rights and duties go along with the job.
- *Management-as-accountability* refers to the accounting practices and accountability where roles and structural relationships are linked to and assist with constructing the "moral environment" which then becomes "the right to manage power and exchange relationships" (Gowler and Legge 1996: 42). This form of control provides middle managers with functional role clarity deriving from task and goal directed behaviours upon which performance is assessed. It renders management activity *visible* in particular ways. Restructuring middle managers' roles as has been seen in Chapter 1 has emphasized the loss of directive functional responsibilities and associated performance criteria, promoting increased participation and autonomous roles and increased performance measures upon which managers are assessed. Control shifts from structurally related accounting practices to cultural control that is often tied up with managerial and professional discourses. Ambiguity surrounding managers roles suggest that managers have more generic roles but experience more accountability in terms of their performance – greater visibility – which leads us into our discussion of achievement.

- *Management-as-achievement* refers to control that rests on the basic principles of "getting things done well" (Gowler and Legge 1996: 47) and is associated with "success", "competition", and "performance" (ibid.). The changing context of work where emphasis is placed on performance rather than productivity provides the possible foundation of achievement albeit inextricably linked to accounting practices. Middle managers, as a result of changing roles and performance accountability, therefore are on enhanced and different performance criteria as they account for their achievements. There is also emphasis on what is a "good" manager with the discourse of *performativity*.

So, Gowler and Legge's framework presents several unique contributions to the management field of its time and assists us to understand middle managers from a constructivist position. Firstly, Gowler and Legge's analysis implies a critique of management that has been dominated by the techno-social discourses of management that inform and construct the functional requirements of managers task related role behaviours such as planning, directing, decision-making, communicating and so forth (Mintzberg 1973; Stewart 1989; Hales 1993). These studies emphasize the importance of what *good* management should be and what being a good manager entails (see for example Stewart 1976). Gowler and Legge's analysis of plain speaking unpacks the taken for granted assumptions evident in much management writings and presents a more sophisticated, ambiguous picture by demonstrating the operation of rhetoric in secondary texts of management and consequently positions the moral-aesthetic order of management (and I could infer managers' identities). Gowler and Legge's work could be seen as supporting an early shift from modern to postmodern organization and management theory which will be discussed later.

Secondly, the authors' appreciation of the ambiguity, tensions and depths behind the managers' "talk" provides the multiplicity of meaning missing from a great deal of the research on management (particularly the writings up until the early 1980s). This ontological and epistemological advancement provides an early constructivist account of management that appreciates the fluidity of meaning. As Gowler and Legge in their discussion of rhetoric state:

Through language and social interaction, those involved participate in the creation and maintenance of shared meanings (1996: 38).

These constructivist undertones capture the fluidity of text that promote the "order of meaning" as "indeterminable"; "abstract"; lacking "concrete boundaries"; are "arbitrarily chosen from among the many others with which they are interwoven"; the "orders of meaning may exercise an influence upon one another"; "indistinct and "messy" processes"; "symbolic complexity" and the "flux of complex social interactions and contexts" (Gowler and Legge 1996: 38 *ff*). Therefore the fluidity of meaning derived from Gowler and Legge is imperative to developing contemporary critiques of management and managerial identities that are characterized by multiplicity, fluidity, contradiction, ambiguity and process. This fluidity of meaning knowingly addresses the "ability to stimulate flows of meaning from one order to another *(from techno-social to moral-aesthetic and vice versa)* that rhetoric derives its evocative and directive powers..." (Gowler and Legge 1996: 38). Gowler and Legge continue to say that "the exercise of these powers requires that the rhetorician and his audience be "on the same wavelength" (ibid.). It is at this stage of their argument that possible avenues for developing Gowler and Legge's early attempts to move towards the postmodern in management to examine relational power and reveals the potential to explore *difference* within and between managers, especially the gendered nature of management and organization can be seen.

Finally, Gowler and Legge's study provides a preliminary indication of possible routes for developing qualitative and "postmodern" research methodologies that focus on language in creating and maintaining meaning in our management. Although Gowler and Legge explored managers' talk, more recently researchers have investigated the role of language in management within specific contexts (Watson 1994; 1995a, 1995b; Alvesson and Karreman 2000; Westwood 2001; Sims 2003; Gabriel 2004a, b; Gabriel and Griffiths 2004; Hardy et al 2005).

Two fundamental conclusions can be generated from our analysis of Gowler and Legge's research. First it implies managers' *active* construction of their subjectivities as Linstead comments:

> ...many managers frequently communicate to themselves and each other as a collectivity in negotiating and establishing their subjectivity, their distinctiveness as a collective, and the nature of the managerial enterprise (1995: 236).

Although Gowler and Legge did not discuss managers' identities directly it can be inferred that managers' subjectivities are shaped and governed by the modes of control – hierarchy, accountability and achievement – that they develop. However I have suggested in our discussion of middle managers in Chapter 2 that these controls have changed. Gowler and Legge perhaps anticipate this by raising the importance of fluidity, complexity, ambiguity and uncertainty in the changing constitution of managers' identities. Their work can therefore be read as a move towards postmodern research in organization (see for example Linstead 1995, 2001a). The research conducted in this book taking a poststructuralist line will seek to expose the ambiguities, fractures, conflicts and contradictions that are not exposed in a great deal of existing research on managerial identities.

Second, Gowler and Legge explore the rhetorical themes of the management of meaning that bring about the closure between two discursive fields – the techno-social and moral-aesthetic (Linstead 1995: 239). In this research I am interested in the shifting rhetorical themes that emerge in postmodern situations rather rhetoric itself. Existing research on rhetoric has explored the use of rhetorical forms in management talk (see Watson 1995a, 1995b). Moreover Hamilton (1997) and Linstead (2001a) both argue that there has been a lack of exploration regarding the distinctions between rhetoric and discourse. In this research I am interested in the discursive formation of managers' subjectivities and therefore shift the focus from the juncture of discursive fields that form rhetoric, as Gowler and Legge successfully achieved, to widening our analysis of the discursive fields themselves.

So, to return to our first question of whether: if, as existing middle management research argues, the context has shifted, have Gowler and Legge's organizing themes changed or dissolved? If so, do managers still talk about the "meaning" of management as a major part of their understanding of their identity as a manager? If so, how do they do it? To address this, in the next section I first discuss the shifting trends in modernist to postmodernist organizational and societal contexts. Having accomplished this Gowler and Legge's "Meaning of Management" framework is extended to deductively investigate middle managers' subjectivities in chapters 5–7. Second, by analyzing contemporary commentaries, the dualities are developed that represent the ideological shifts between modernist and postmodernist *modes* of organizing – namely hierarchy to networking, accountability to seduction, and achievement to commitment – are elucidated.

Moving forward? The immanence of the postmodern

As seen in Chapter 2 the influence of societal and organizational changes on work identities are now well rehearsed (Casey 1995, 1996; Kumar 1995; du Gay 1996; Thompson and Warhurst 1998). Appreciating that change is neither stable, certain nor linear it can be said with a degree of confidence that organizational change is ongoing and influences the ways in which managers' subjectivities are constructed although these processes are characterized by multiplicity, ambiguity and fluidity. The managers in Gowler and Legge's study operationalized concepts in their rhetoric which suggest a highly "modern" vision of management. Hierarchy, accountability and achievement are aspects of three modernizing processes – differentiation, rationality and commodification. Each of these processes was the critical focus of the sociologies of Durkheim (and later Parsons), Weber and Marx respectively. Though each process may be found in each of Gowler and Legge's themes, hierarchy is clearly the dominant example of structural differentiation; rationality the underlying principle of accountability; and commodification the principle by which action can be turned into outputs which are associated with reward, the defining feature of achievement.

Modernist societies develop on the basis of increasing differentiation and specialization which necessitate the development of integrating mechanisms; the growth of systems based on objectified knowledge and impersonal abstract sources of authority; increasing technical control over persons and things, including relationships, and the externalization of action, or alienation of human subjects from the outputs of their efforts which take on a life of their own and an unwarranted significance.

Modernist societies are "organized" – they are complex in differentiation and systematic in organization (Crook et al 1992: 15). They are characterized by large production enterprises which are capital intensive but in which ownership is separate from control and which exert considerable power over supply and demand through advertising and promotion. Markets are predominantly "mass" markets (Lee and Munro 2001). State regulation tends to be central, and a large part of economic activity is devoted to services rather than goods. Mental and manual work are separated and technologies (including "scientific management") are used to render as much as possible calculable, deskilling the former and enskilling the latter. Management increases its power through manipulating knowledge and information.

Under late capitalism, however, several tendencies occur to pull apart society's homogeneity into more heterogeneous varieties. Indeed, the fact that Gowler and Legge's managers *need* to indulge in persuasive rhetoric over the nature of management would suggest that this is a reactive response to the problematization of "management". As the tendencies of differentiation (specialization, complexity) and organization (rationalization, commodification) accelerate, the divergent tendencies between them start to fragment. One driving force for this is technology which makes it possible to decouple organizational function from structure. Whilst some large industrial bureaucracies survive many were dismantled or downsized during the 1980s and 1990s as new forms – market niche producers, cooperatives, technocratic partnerships, segmented organizations, subcontractors, home and outworkers, networks of producers – continue to proliferate and hyperdifferentiate. This increasing *structural* differentiation is also facilitated by *de*-differentiation *within production processes* utilizing flexible technologies, flatter and more adaptable internal organizational structures, faster communication and better information systems which can interface unproblematically (Crook et al 1992: 33). Under conditions of hyperdifferentiation the consequences of any given piece of economic, bureaucratic or managerial manipulation cannot be predicted. Chaos and uncertainty proliferate and organizations teeter on the edge of being unmanageable. Hierarchies are collapsing, as power/knowledge bases shift from bureaucratic authority to "social capital" and the ability to shape discourse (Adler and Kwon 2002); lines of accountability are less obvious; paths to achievement and its sustainability are no longer clear. Where money and power tended to derive from specific and well understood sources in modernity, in postmodernity, where information in contexts that are often virtual is the key commodity, they may accrue or be dissipated quickly and unpredictably from a bewildering variety of sources. Traditional sources are no longer oligopolistic and they lose their ability to effect social control. Organizations thus face increasing problems in maintaining order, and managers are at the heart of this.

Performativity, Lyotard (1984) argues, increasingly attempts to deliver outputs at lower cost and the ability to do this replaces truth or merit as the measure of knowledge or worth. The ability of cultural forms on a larger scale to generate loyalty and commitment is correspondingly reduced and organizations need therefore to put more effort into dominating local narratives to create commitment on a smaller more intensive scale (Crook et al 1992: 31). Furthermore cultural dedifferentiation may mean that organizations become sources of values no longer available elsewhere, such as in religion or education, whilst simultaneously those sources may become sources of profit traditionally the province of economic organization, e.g. TV evangelism, consultancy.

For Baudrillard (1975; 1998), the unpredictability and chaos of postmodernity mean that it is not the relations of production but the conditions of consumption that have social force. The producing (and consuming) subject is decentred, so it is the signs and symbolic constructs that position and shape subjectivity that are important. As Bauman argues:

> Postmodernity... brings "re-enchantment" after the protracted and earnest, though in the end inconclusive, modern struggle to disenchant it (or, more exactly, the resistance to dis-enchantment, hardly ever put to sleep, was all along the "postmodern turn" in the body of modernity). The mistrust of human spontaneity, of drives, impulses and inclinations resistant to prediction and rational justification, has been all but replaced by the mistrust of unemotional, calculating reason. Dignity has been returned to emotions; legitimacy to the "inexplicable", nay irrational...We learn to live with acts that are not only not-yet-explained, but (for all we know about what we will ever know) inexplicable. We learn again to respect ambiguity, to feel regard for human emotions, to appreciate actions without purpose and calculable reward (Bauman 1993: 33 cited in Ritzer 1999: 74).

Baudrillard (1990) sees re-enchantment as happening through the process of seduction. As Ritzer notes, the "complete clarity and visibility associated with modernity" are replaced by the play and illusion which are offered by seduction. For Baudrillard (1981) subjects are fluidly positioned and repositioned in time and space by signs and symbols rather than fixed by social and economic "realities". Identity therefore will be fluid and multiple and constructed and reconstructed discursively through symbolic processes such as rhetoric and discourse.

Management in Three Movements

In this section I will introduce the Management in Three Movements framework (Table 3.1) developed to encapsulate the shifts in social and organizational conditions from social and management theory discussed above and their effects on the processes of managerial subjectivity, and will then go on to introduce the Management in Three Movements model (Figure 3.1) of the overall process. I will discuss the framework and the model further in the context of delineating the possible shifts in the dualities at each level common to both the framework and the model. The framework and the model incorporate dimensions of Gowler and Legge's rhetoric of bureaucratic control at the levels of hierarchy, accountability and achievement to explore ontological, epistemological

and behavioural assumptions respectively. The modernist, objective discourse of Gowler and Legge has been extended to introduce a postmodernist, subjective discourse of management which explores how the
discourses of management may have changed in the past 15 years or so.
The shifts I have observed in the literature discussed above between differentiation and dedifferentiation; rationality and enchantment and
commodification and consumption are incorporated to indicate what
the theoretical dimensions and empirical characteristics of such changes
may be. This framework (Table 3.1) does not portray a fixed empirical
shift between the objective and subjective or an irreversible epochal shift
between the modern and the postmodern, rather there is a *discursive*
shift between the modernist (objective) and postmodern (subjective).
These dualities are therefore relational and legitimize the configuration
and reconfiguration of managerial subjectivities. Furthermore subjectivities are discursively produced and subjects draw on multiple "technologies of the self" to shape and construct their subjectivities. Within
modernist discourses of management managers' identities are based on
unitary conceptions of the self. In contrast the postmodern discourse
shifts the focuses towards analyzing the decentred subject that offers
multiple, contradictory and fluid ways of exploring subjectivities
(Sampson 1989; Knights and Vurdubakis 1994; Grafton-Small 2005;
Pullen and Linstead 2005). The model resting on this framework
attempts to represent this fluidity by implying that fluidity is precisely
that, and may be horizontal, vertical, reversible, or in any direction,
although it is most likely to have particular characteristics which the
model foregrounds. Also, multiplicity implies that the modern and the
postmodern features may be coexistent to varying degrees. The levels of
the framework are adapted into the model to relate hierarchy to structure; accountability to representation and achievement to behaviour,
and at each level the appropriate shift – differentation/dedifferentiation,
rationality/enchantment, commodification/consumption is indicated.
However, at the behavioural level the framework is subverted on the
subjective side to highlight how change at this level influences the
ontological and epistemological subjective dimensions (reversals of cus-
tomary top-down approaches) to arrive at a fluid and relational framework of management that recognizes difference and opens up a way
forward for re-theorizing resistance in management and organization
(see Chapter 8).

In the next section of this chapter I discuss the Management in
Three Movements framework and model in terms of the dualities of
hierarchy and networking; accountability and seduction; achievement

Table 3.1   Management in Three Movements: from the Modern to the Postmodern?

Modern (Objectivist)	Postmodern (Subjectivist)
Hierarchy	**Networking**
Structural rigidity	Flexibility
Differentiation	Dedifferentiation
Functional role demarcations	Autonomy
Authority	2 way exchange
Externalization	Internalization
Vertical accountability	Horizontal accountability
Vertical career progression	Cross-functional projects
Bureaucracy	Cluster, fluidity of boundaries
Expert knowledge	Distributed knowledge
Managerial sovereignty	Social Capital
Accountability	**Seduction**
Rationality	Enchantment Competitive
Vertical,meritocracy, qualifications	Peer surveillance
Goal/task orientated	Performativity/self-interest
Moral dimension, ethics	Corporate Cultural control
Order of things	Symbolic order
Accounting	"Professionalism"
Reciprocal Power/Exchange	Insecurity /uncertainty
Relationship	Ambiguity
Clarity	Rhetorical
Concrete	Unquantifiable
Quantifiable	Portfolios
Specialization	
Achievement	**Commitment**
Performance in Job	Performance of Company
Outputs = Rewards	Rewards Complex ≠ Inputs +
Competence	Outputs
Competition	Surveillance, concertive
Recognition	control
Job enrichment	Impression management
Narrowly defined roles	Broader, changing, multiple
Dyadic Communication	accountability – wider roles
Persuasion	Control through HRM
Productivity	Simulation
Long-term	Credibility, presenteeism
Stable	Short-term
	Unstable

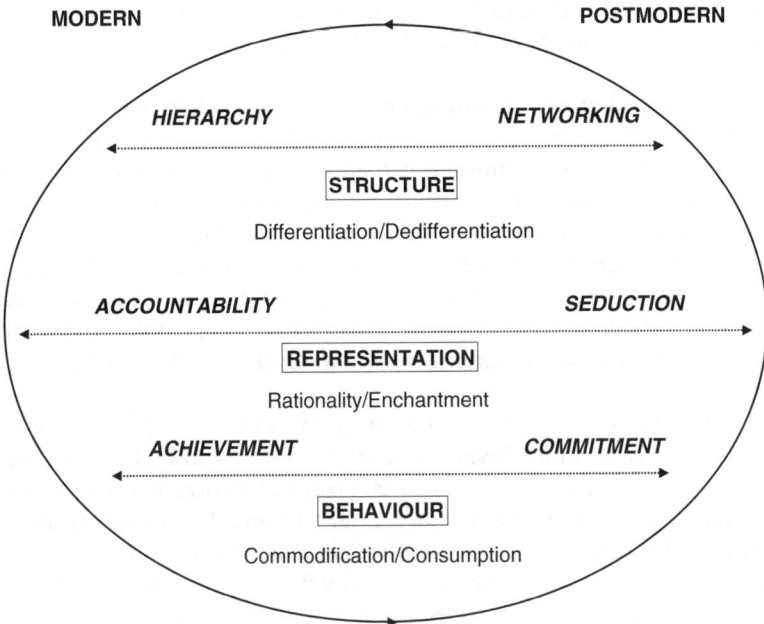

Figure 3.1   The Management in Three Movements Model

and commitment. The shift between the modern and postmodern dimensions, again I must emphasize, is not an oppositional break but rather the constructs of each duality represent a discursive shift between modernist and postmodernist discourses on managerial subjectivities.

From hierarchy to networking... towards fluidity

I have discussed earlier that hierarchy is a principle feature of modernism, having tendencies of differentiation (specialization, complexity) and organization (rationalization, commodification) which are pulled apart by technological advancements which make it possible to decouple organizational function from structure. The shift from structural order, rigidity and linearity to flexible specialization has dominated writings on Neo-Fordism, Post-Fordism, post-industrialism and the information society (see Piore and Sabel 1984; Kanter 1989a; Kumar 1995; Hancock and Tyler 2001). The importance and influence of technology and flexibility on organizations is summarized by Clegg:

> Where modernist organization was rigid, postmodern organization is flexible. Where modernist consumption was premised on mass forms, postmodernist consumption is premised upon niches. Where modernist organization is premised on technological determinism, postmodernist organization is premised on technological choices made possible through 'de-dedicated' microelectronic equipment. Where modernist organization and jobs are highly differentiated, demarcated and deskilled, postmodernist organization and jobs are highly de-differentiated, de-demarcated and multi-skilled (1990: 181).

Clegg's analysis also draws our attention to the role of power in new forms of organization. Discursive shifts in power/knowledge underpin the changing nature of organization. Postmodern organization deconstructs traditional, modernist structural and functional boundaries of work and organization through advancements in social and technological networking that are characterized by fluidity and which emphasize the virtual. Structures of control and co-ordination are broken down and replaced by new and more flexible alternatives (Thompson and Warhurst 1998); indeed the literature is overwhelmed by new terms constructed to represent structural changes such as "federalism" (Handy 1992), the "reengineered corporation" (Hammer and Champy 1993), the "networked organization" (Castells 1996), the "virtual organization" (Davidow and Malone 1992), the "knowledge-creating company" (Nonaka and Takeuchi 1995), the "high performance" or "high commitment work system" (Pfeffer 1998), the "boundaryless company" (Devanna and Tichy 1986) and the "transnational solution" (Bartlett and Ghoshal 1989). Jackson's (1999) classification of virtual working highlights the importance of the dimensions networking which is seen as: "*informating*" *or information processing* (see Zuboff 1998; Castells 1996) and is often associated with a growth in information workers and knowledge industries (Jackson 1999); *heightened flexibility* – workforce flexibility (Atkinson 1984), de-bureaucratization and organizational ability, and flexibility in time and space; *disembodiment* – the absence of humans is a defining characteristic of virtual organization (Barnatt 1995 cited in Jackson 1999: 10); *boundary-erosion* – within or between organizations such as the design of alliances (Grenier and Metes 1995 cited in Jackson 1999: 11); and as *electronic commerce* – use of IT to blur the boundaries between organizations, suppliers, partners, customers. Thus networking influences actual and available managerial roles.

The Management in Three Movements framework therefore predicts a change from managers' roles being constructed by hierarchy and function towards networking as a prosbook that extends the capabilities of the human (Stone 1995). This therefore suggests that "postmodern managers" negotiate their identities across broader social arrangements where existing boundaries have been removed or extended. As highlighted in Chapter 1, parallel changes in structural configurations in organizations have influenced managers' roles by extending their tasks across wider functional and organizational arenas. Galpin and Sims' (1999) study of the narratives of managers in teleworking offers supporting evidence of these fundamental changes in managers' working lives. Although these authors provide an interesting analysis of the influence of changing structural forms on teleworkers' roles, by adopting a narrative methodology, they theorize identity as fixed. In contrast, following the work of Stone reflects the multiplicity, ambiguity and *fluidity* of identities:

> In the discourses with which we are perhaps most familiar, the self appears to be constant, unchanging, the stable product of a moment in Western history. This seems a rather episcopal view of something that is not only better describes as a process but that is also palpable and in continual flux (Stone 1995: 19–20).

And later in the book Stone continues:

> Such fractured identities call attention to alternatives, always multiple, always in tension (ibid.: 44).

Most importantly for this research the disembodiment and boundary erosion of networking influences organizing and managing identities by problematizing the process of location of both role and self.

From accountability to seduction: from technical to cultural control

Accountability refers to accounting practices where roles and structural relationships are linked to and assist with constructing the "moral environment" which then becomes "the right to manage power and exchange relationships" (Gowler and Legge 1996: 42). This form of control provides middle managers with functional role clarity deriving from task and goal directed behaviours upon which performance is assessed. Earlier it was discussed how the "complete clarity and visibility associated with modernity" (Ritzer 1999) are replaced by the play and illusion which are offered by seduction (Baudrillard 1990). It is expected therefore that accountability via roles, rules and hierarchy become replaced by cultural seduction. Control therefore shifts from structurally related accounting practices to cultural control. This control is seductive and shapes managerial roles, identities and behaviours – what they think, believe and value and how they act. Identity in the seduction discourse will therefore be fluid and multiple and constructed and reconstructed discursively through symbolic processes such as rhetoric and discourse. The cultural control at meta and management levels with an awareness that it importantly influences behavioural issues such as achievement and commitment are discussed in the next section.

A meta analysis of culture reveals how organizations require individuals to possess, display and devote commitment to their organizations beyond any organizational form or structure, department or role. The need to manage cultural change and to regenerate and maintain organizational culture occasioned by restructuring also fuels the need to seduce individuals at the meta level. As Alvesson comments "effort to create change rather than just to reproduce what exists... [requires] Cultural maintenance [and] is an integral part of most everyday activities, talk and structural arrangements in organizations" (2002: 177). My exploratory study supports Alvesson's reference to the activities that prevail for cultural maintenance such as supporting values and morale, generating or regenerating organizational identity and/or departmental and/or professional identity, and image management. Structural arrangements however go hand-in-hand with the cultural ideologies of restructuring such as team ideology (Sinclair 1992). Thus there appears to be a shift from the management of control to the management of meaning.

At a management level symbolic forms of control are particularly salient compared to technical control, although other forms of control co-exist. Cultural theorists that critique cultural control such as Ray (1986) argue that symbolic control manipulates culture including myth and ritual so that the workforce comes to "love the firm and its goals" to increase performance. Furthermore Boje and Winsor (1993: 66–7) comment on how human control replaces technical control. At this level then managers are no longer held accountable to the task and role requirements of their position but they are also symbolically accountable. With "high performance" and "high commitment" teams control is exercised via the social system by peer surveillance (Sewell and Wilkinson 1992; Barker 1993) and self-policing (Foucault 1979b; Parker 1989; Fleming and Sewell 2002). Organizations therefore knowingly *seduce* their members through structural arrangements such as teams, the managerial and professional ethos of roles and rely on intrinsic self-motivation and self-fulfilment as part of managers' achievement which is associated closely with commitment. Managers are thus often recognized for how they appear to achieve as well as for what they actually achieve.

Symbolic means of control are an essential part of contemporary management roles (Morgan 1986; Kunda 1992; Willmott 1993; Fleming and Spicer 2003). The management of meaning (Anthony 1994), rather than the exercise of authority or command, is therefore part of everyday leadership and could accordingly argue that "postmodern" organizations espouse "softer", *feminine* attributes of organization (see for example Rosener 1990; Alimo-Metcalfe 1994; Metcalfe and Linstead 2003 for further discussion of stereotypes of feminine styles of leadership). Drawing on Baudrillard, the feminine possesses more potential to *seduce*:

> The strength of the feminine is that of seduction... A universe that can no longer be interpreted in terms of structures and diacritical oppositions, but implies a seductive reversibility – a universe where the feminine is not what opposes the masculine, but what seduces the masculine (1990: 7).

As a management strategy then "cultural engineering" (Alvesson and Berg 1992; Kunda 1992) can be seen both as part of how managers construct their identities, or what Alvesson and Willmott (2002) refer to as identity regulation, and also determining their responsibilities, those things for which they are accountable and thus churning out the "appropriate individual" (ibid.). Organizations adopt the feminine, in style at least, to seduce the more masculine representations of organization. Language is therefore used carefully. Culture is partly responsible for notions of good management and what managers should do. Thus, culture is something that managers have to manage within the bounds of the cultural ideologies to which they are required to subscribe – to remain "on message". This control is centred around the ideas and meanings that individuals want to embrace (Pfeffer 1981; Smircich and Morgan 1982; Barley and Kunda 1992). Alvesson (2002: 125) emphasizes the passivity of managers' actions but does not explore how managers' are complicit in reinforcing organization and how they are active in constructing their identities within these cultural "constraints". This reproduces organization, cooperation and consensus (Willmott 1993). In contrast with this analysis that focuses on generating a shared understanding of culture, "everyday reframing" (Frost et al 1991) refers to "the actor(s) engaged in everyday re-framing mainly influences the people he/she directly interacts... and involves pedagogical leadership in which an actor exercises a subtle influence through the renegotiation of meaning" (Alvesson 2002: 180).

For managers then the move from accountability to seduction requires managers to construct identities that display more open, involved, committed and dedicated selves. On the surface managers may appear to have considerably more autonomy and enjoy more generic roles but as my exploratory research highlighted managers have increasing pressures for managing their staff and leading in an autocratic fashion. Accountability through cultural seduction is extricably tied up with commitment at a behavioural level. At a behavioural level managers' accountability has moved from financial and target driven measures towards behavioural indicators of commitment that are inextricably linked with the ethos of performativity, centring around professionalism, managerialism and leadership qualities which are discussed in the next section.

From achievement to commitment: the visible and dedicated manager

Achievement refers to control that rests on the basic principles of "getting things done well" (Gowler and Legge 1996: 47) and is associated with "success", "competition", and "performance" (ibid.). So in modernist organizations rewards *bought* loyalty (Ray 1986) to social needs of the organization. The changing context of work where emphasis is placed on performance rather than productivity provides the possible foundation of achievement albeit inextricably linked to accounting practices. Middle managers, as a result of changing roles and performance accountability, are judged on different performance criteria as they account for their achievements. There is also emphasis on what is a "good" manager within the discourse of performativity as the exploratory study suggests. Increased visibility for measuring performance of staff and production has suggested that pressures on managers are more heightened in the restructured organization.

Discourses of achievement have shifted emphasis from extrinsic motivators to intrinsic motivators that assist with the processes of seducing employees. In the postmodern organization then commitment from individuals to the organization displaces rewards as a focus of managerial attention. Measures of performance are therefore designed and executed around task and social need. Job insecurity, intensification of work and role ambiguity are fundamental issues for middle managers in restructured organizations which make them feel compelled to justify their place within the organization (Kanter 1983). To confirm their legitimacy within the organization middle managers draw on contemporary discourses of commitment. This supports organizations' demand for increased cultural control at the level of role accountability. Psychological and employment insecurity and vulnerability are something that organizations can manipulate, using cultural discourses of professionalism and performativity to seduce managers which fuels more commitment from them. The exploratory study (see Chapter 2) highlighted that increased commitment results in the need to devote "excessive" hours to the organization – working longer hours, working evenings (Watson 1994) and weekends, to achieve a sense of self (Kanter 1989b) and this has been raised within the context of work life balance. Inkson (1993) in particular associates the longer working hours culture with the multiple demands of managerial work (Inkson 1993) and is often related to increased job insecurity (Joseph Rowntree Foundation 1999).

The need to demonstrate commitment within the restructured (and restructuring) organization is fundamental to middle management identity. Commitment is equated with visibility and long working hours. The gendered implications of patterns of work, such as working evenings and weekends, imply that the discourses of contemporary management reinforce masculinist notions of organization. Managers need to be "seen to be there", with the exercising of managerial power through informal pressures of time-space surveillance (Collinson and Collinson 1997) and time monitoring (Sewell and Wilkinson 1992) which reinforce the dominant masculine culture of management. For many managers studied the need to confirm and secure managers' sense of status and legitimacy discourses of commitment are equated with "being a good manager". The good manager therefore has high visibility, is contactable at all times, is enthusiastic about working longer, and tolerates the neglect of personal time. So achievement is no longer associated with hierarchical career progression, associated status and authority regarding role, and rewards but tied into subjective understandings of organizational expectations of them and attempting to achieve their own sense of self. The "achieving manager" could be expected to be one where performance is highly related to being a "good manager" – a manager who performs through the "seductive" notions of performance – devotion and commitment to the organization.

To summarize, in this chapter I have extensively discussed Gowler and Legge's research as one of the earliest attempts to introduce postmodern ideas within management. This framework was then critiqued and extended to develop the Management in Three Movements model based on the characteristics of organizational and social shifts from the modern to postmodern introducing the *dualities* of hierarchy to networking, accountability to seduction and achievement to commitment for researching managerial subjectivities. The Management in Three Movements framework developed was used in this research to deductively explore managers' subjectivities in chapters 5, 6 and 7 to explore *how* managers still talk about the "meaning" of management as a major part of their understanding of their identity as a manager. Although Gowler and Legge's work was one of the earliest pieces to mark the beginning of a transition from modern to postmodern analysis of management and the extended model of Gowler and Legge's research incorporates these shifts, to take this move further, further developments need to consider gender and power.

4
Rewriting Power and Gender Into the Management of Meaning and the Meaning of Management

> we are difference... our selves the difference of masks.
> Michel Foucault *The Archaeology of Knowledge*

Introduction

Gowler and Legge's work does not claim to address identity as such, but it examines public claims which managers make about what management is, and conditions where that might seem to be contested or threatened. Their self-definitions then are part of their experienced identity, and intervene in a discourse to which managers are held to be subject. However, Gowler and Legge's investigation is not one which explores the conditions of subjectivity, or subject formation, as it does not focus on specific managers (as subjects) or specific contexts. In this section Gowler and Legge's framework is analyzed by drawing on Foucault's concepts of power/knowledge, to explore how relational forms of power shape managers' discursive subject positions. Power is at the core of Foucault's writings since it highlights how privileged and privileging discourses of the subject determine the creation of selves. Foucault recognizes the "other" in determining subjectivities and therefore a Foucauldian analysis of power that challenges forms of hegemonic domination in society in the pursuit to re-gender management.

From rhetoric to discourse

Gowler and Legge are particularly interested in the ways in which a particular use of language – rhetoric in its broadest sense – is deployed to bridge the social, moral and natural orders through the creation of symbolic representations which sustain ambiguity between the ought and the is whilst giving the appearance of being objective and factual statements. Thus particular social orders, which privilege the interests of certain social groups rather than others, are represented as both morally legitimate and naturally occurring. Gowler and Legge point out that the features of these social orders, such as hierarchy, are rarely referred to directly, but also that rhetoric suppresses or leaves un-addressed certain dimensions of the operation of these social orders, allowing apparent clarity to emerge paradoxically through the creation of ambiguity. For example, they note that hierarchies are usually referred to as hierarchies of tasks or jobs, with associated hierarchies of competence or merit. However, what is also inferred by these discussions is a hierarchy of power, which identifies the relation of the moral order not to the natural order but to the political order. The statements which contain these references can be seen as motivated by a need to defend, in some way, the sovereignty of management, and they are therefore, rather than instances of plain-speaking, political interventions in themselves.

Gowler and Legge adopt a perspective from social anthropology to argue that the core concepts of such rhetorics, such as achievement, become totemic – that is to say, they are regarded as being so much a part of the natural order that they are treated with reverence to the point that direct discussion and certainly discursive contestation of them is avoided. The existing state of affairs, which may have emerged over time as a result of political engagements, becomes the natural state of affairs. As the natural state of affairs is not discussable or questionable, the real political skills that managers may need to effect the outcomes of ongoing political engagements and the emergence and passage of new relations into the social order are effaced. Thus there is a secret lore of management, an "inner world" of skills and even magic, protected by myth and totem and revealed through ritual progression, which managers only acquire through the process of being managers and mastering the rhetoric necessary to preserve the mystery and sovereignty of management – and, of course, establishing and positioning their own identities in the process as *speakers* of this rhetoric. The sovereignty of management is a matter of belief or ideology, but is represented as the natural way of things through the myth-making functions of accounting and the idealization of achievement as totemic to mediate the relations between existing social, organizational and institutionalized practices and the possibility that other arrangements might be equally or even more acceptable. Thus Gowler and Legge argue for greater attention to managerial *talk*, and again although the empirical examples they use are of public speaking in print rather than everyday talk in conversation or semi-public meetings, they interpret talk and speaking in their broadest senses.

Despite differences in terminology, there are considerable areas of common interest between Gowler and Legge and the work of Michel Foucault, whose work has itself been considered as a form of theoretical cultural anthropology. Where Gowler and Legge use an expanded form of the concept of rhetoric, beyond its specifically technical classical functions, Foucault redefines the concept of discourse to extend far beyond what people say. Both, however, in my view, are redefining their terms in order to incorporate a greater awareness of the political and epistemological dimensions of language, and the inseparable relation (though not deterministic connection) between language, symbolic forms, social institutions and individual and collective behaviour. As Parker contends, "the self is constructed in discourses and then re-experienced within all the texts of everyday life" (1989: 56).

Foucault, throughout his work, is interested in the way in which the relation between power and knowledge is changed or sustained through language (and to a lesser extent by other symbolic forms). From our discussion of Gowler and Legge, in the phenomenon of the emergence of an effaced or secret side of management practice, obscured by rhetorical language use, we can see that powerful groups such as managers can use their power to ration and limit the distribution of knowledge about their field. They can also use language to define what counts as knowledge, and can police knowledge creation through accounting and disciplinary practices. Through such surveillance they can identify, capture, legitimate and incorporate new knowledge, and disadvantage, render illegitimate and suppress knowledge which they deem to be threatening or challenging to the existing order. Social institutions such as professional bodies may be set up to facilitate this. Individuals may be examined and tested, formally and informally, as a matter of everyday social practice and their positioning as social and even individual subjects – competent, significant, consuming, compliant citizens or otherwise – is affected by how well they pass these occasions of scrutiny under a gaze which may be that of the state, religion, education, professional superiors, co-workers, parents, partners, friends, subordinates, their own children and even themselves. In Foucault's later work he was particularly concerned with how people police their own self-identity against competing models of the ideal self, and how such internalized imperatives literally inscribe themselves on and affect the physical characteristics of the body.

Foucault argued that knowledge does not evolve incrementally, but according to a set of paradigmatic constraints which constitute a particular historical *episteme*, or regime of knowing. The pre-modern era, characterized by superstition, social heterogeneity and social power vested in the sovereign or his liéges, gave way towards the end of the eighteenth century to a modern regime of rationality and science, greater social homogeneity, and power vested in institutions of governance. Foucault does not account for why this change happened, but seeks to understand the *genealogy* of how specific forms of modern institutions of social governance came to emerge to deal with pressing social problems. He is specifically concerned with the boundaries of social order, and how those boundaries are constructed. For Foucault, it is the epistemology of the boundary which is crucial to the functioning of the social practice, and the construction of the boundary relies upon the existence of a generic discursive form which offers the basis for its legitimation. Thus the nineteenth century featured the discourse of *progress*, which emerged in a variety of fields in different ways, whether the philosophy of Hegel, the industrialism of a Robert Owen, the gunboat colonialism of Palmerston, or Social Darwinism. This discourse remains a characteristic component of modernism, though much changed in its forms, although it retains its dependence on the idea of progress being natural, insofar as it depends on the *revelation* of natural processes by the exercise of *reason*. Supported by a realist ontology which facilitated the development of positivistic, or observation and measurement-based social knowledge in the image of science, it enabled the division of the world up into particular problem fields and creation of social institutions, professions and bureaucracies with which to address them. Additionally, it also necessitated the production of laws and legal systems with which to regulate these new institutions and institutional practices, and the extension of democratic structures to bind more of the population into responsible citizenship which would ensure that the laws could be effectively operationalized and monitored. People were no longer individual subjects of a monarch, whose forms of discipline and punishment were most likely to be physically enacted on their bodies, but social subjects, scrutinized for their ability to fit in to a normalized social apparatus and disciplined through institutionalization – i.e. temporary or permanent removal from society subject to their capacity to be normalized by the punishment process. Thus Foucault (1976, 1977, 1979a, 1979b) is able to examine the historical treatment of forms of "deviance" – such as madness, illness, criminality and sexual behaviour – through the disciplines (e.g. medicine) and disciplinary forms (e.g. the clinic) which emerge to deal with them and demonstrate that the ways in which ideas of the normal and the deviant are constructed are subject to shifting historical understandings which are political, epistemological and linguistic.

Following Foucault, a *discourse* can be any regular and regulated system of statements, and discourse analysis then crucially examines the *relations* within the system. As Parker notes "not only are social relations stressed as social relations as they are embodied in discourse, but we may view these relations as power relations" (1989: 67). Although Foucault's earlier *archaeological* work looked in particular at the workings of language, how words had historically acquired specific acceptations and how the system of rules governing the discourse internally came to operate, his later work – in contrast to most of what we would understand as discourse analysis – examines the conditions of power and knowledge which have influenced not only the form of a discourse, but which have favoured its appearance at a particular point in time rather than an alternative, and its specific *relations* with other forms of discourse as it has changed over time. Foucault's view of power, therefore, is not deterministic but relational. As Linstead argues, what a discourse does is:

> ...structure the rules and procedures by which different forms of knowledge are determined. Further, it defines different fields of understanding as legitimate objects of that knowledge... Within these fields, the discourse will also establish relationships between repertoires of concepts... Determine[s] criteria for the establishment of acceptable "truth" and the creation of "truth-effects", and further delimit[s] what can and cannot be said, the normal, the abnormal, the standard and the deviation and hierarchies the field of these relations... (2001a: 226).

A discourse, however, is also concerned with establishing the position of its authorship, usually so as to appear as naturally authoritative as possible. It creates and characterizes discursive spaces or *"subject positions"* to which it both tries to lay claim (in the case of authorial positions) and offers to recipients through *inter-pellation*, which is an implicit invitation to take them up (in the case of reading positions (Hodge and Kress 1988)). In other words, a discourse is already at the heart of processes of social structuring in seeking to position its readers in relation to an idealized reader, and establish its own authority accordingly. Discourse therefore is not dominated by language alone, and is far more than simply a linguistic phenomenon. Foucauldian discourse analysis is accordingly not trying to claim that words determine reality. What it does however recognize is that "practices which constitute our everyday lives are produced and reproduced as an integral part of the production of signs and signifying systems" (Henriques et al 1984: 99). Practices and what is said about them cannot be separated in such easy terms, and accordingly discourse inevitably also relates to non-discursive practices which must be an important focus for discourse analysis. A *discursive formation*, which incorporates both linguistic and non-linguistic phenomena, can be identified by defining "the system of formation of the different strategies that are deployed in it", by showing "how they all derive... from the same set of relations" (Foucault 1972: 68).

What then is the difference between a discourse and a text? Fairclough (1992) argues that discourse analysis links the systematic analysis of spoken or written texts – such as those which comprise the data for analysis later in this book – to systematic analyses of social contexts, taking into account formative contexts and extra-discursive effects, looking at "the particular configurations of conventionalized practices (genres, discourses, narratives etc) which are available to text producers in particular social circumstances" (Fairclough 1992: 194). To complete the link then to Gowler and Legge's work, rhetoric is a feature of texts, which may or may not be rhetorical. In meeting their rhetorical, or persuasive, objectives, texts will not only draw on a variety of linguistic features but will also draw on one or more discourses which warrant the truth of their arguments (Linstead 2001a: 227). Where Gowler and Legge look specifically at the rhetoric of bureaucratic control these are not the only possible forms of rhetoric, as rhetorics of resistance or emancipation may also exist. In whatever form it may appear, rhetoric is the means by which closure is attempted over the spaces between discursive fields (such as the moral-aesthetic or the techno-social), usually in the direct or indirect furtherance of a political object (ibid.).

What then does a consideration of Foucault's work add to the critique provided by Gowler and Legge, with specific regard to the identity construction of managers? *First, it introduces increased discursive heterogeneity.* It supports Gowler and Legge's identification of contradiction, ambiguity and suppression in managerial discourse, but alerts us to the possible operation of a wider variety of discourses in tension within what managers say. In a context of rapid change, this increased discursive heterogeneity we might expect to be an emerging feature of discursive process through which managers seek to establish their identities.

Second, it expands the consideration of context. It widens the concept of rhetoric, links it to discourse and connects managerial texts to the organizational and social contexts which constrain and enable management processes. It also introduces the consideration of time and historical change, which is significant for our central question of whether there has been any change in the ways in which managerial identities are constructed in the last two decades.

Third, it provides a broader understanding of the nature of surveillance and the variety of the "gaze". It expands Gowler and Legge's consideration of accounting practices and the construction of signals of achievement to consider a greater range of social technologies which may be internally operationalized by the individual (as self-surveillance) as well as externally occasioned (as inspection).

Fourth, it introduces the possibility of relational resistance. It emphasizes the importance of power relations and the political dimensions of knowledge formation more than Gowler and Legge do, but by introducing a relational element to the consideration of power. Power for Foucault circulates, rather than passing down, or even up, a system, and is always two-way though not necessarily symmetrical. Actions of individuals may be prescribed by a discursive system, but there is always room for reinterpretation and manoeuvre. Resistance may arise and circulate from individual levels and itself become incorporated, or alternately institutionalized. Foucault does not theorize resistance, partly because his project is primarily one of subversion, but also because of his awareness that, as Gowler and Legge hint, that power is intimately connected with the unsaid, the secret, and that resistance, to be effective, must also organize, if it is to be organized, around its secrets. However, as far as the investigation here goes, it emphasizes the need to look for *ways in which managers relationally resist* the discursive "subject positions" institutionally prescribed for them.

Fifth, it links the formation of selves and subjects. It makes central to any consideration of rhetoric the processes of subjectivity and subject-formation, and thus expands Gowler and Legge's examination of part of the social construction of managerial identity, linking in the process the private and the public. It underscores the part which individuals play in rendering themselves subject to a discourse, their potential complicity in their own domination.

Sixth, it draws attention to the significance and importance of boundaries. Persuasive language is occasioned where existing social processes are themselves alone insufficient to render the need for persuasion unnecessary. This may be in policing the boundary between managers and non-managers, as in most of Gowler and Legge's examples, or it may be regarding the boundaries between different levels of expertise. However, it may relate to a boundary dealt with in the final point.

Seventh, it emphasizes the embodied and gendered nature of subject-formation. That management may be gendered is not a feature of Gowler and Legge's analysis, but Foucault's later work treats gender as a discursive category as much as a social or embodied one (see Moss 1998). Discursive effects inscribe bodies in terms of requirements for appearance, structure or conditioning but also leave the marks of the consequences of performing as a "good subject" in the managerial role (e.g. heart attacks, injury, stress related mental conditions).

Although Foucault's, as some would argue, poststructuralist orientation and his negation of women have been extensively questioned, his contributions are being extensively applied in management and organization theory (see for example McKinlay and Starkey 1997; Knights 2002) although not without doubt and critique. A major criticism levelled at Foucault by many feminists is his neglect of the feminine throughout his work but conspicuous in his discussions of sexuality (see Sawicki 1991 for further discussion). Similarly, Gowler and Legge's work also neglects gender. In order to develop a poststructuralist feminist influenced approach for studying middle managers' subjectivities, Gowler and Legge's research is now critiqued from a contemporary feminist perspective.

Gender-neutral or gender-blind?: A gendered reading of the meaning of management

> Years ago, manhood was an opportunity for achievement, and now it is a problem to be overcome.
>
> Garrison Keillor *The Book of Guys* (1994)

To conduct a gendered reading of "The Meaning of Management" Wajcman's empirical research (1998) was appropriated from the plethora of feminist accounts on management (see for example Marshall 1984, 1995; Davidson and Cooper 1992; Walby 1997) inasmuch as it provided a recent empirical study in the field of management that considers, as the title claims, "Women and Men in Corporate Management". Wajcman aimed to readdress the balance of women's subordination in the male dominated cohorts of management because "the gender of managers does matter" (Wajcman 1998: 31). In this section of the chapter Wajcman's research is critiqued and applied to

Gowler and Legge's research to highlight the importance of gendering management rather than simply voicing the concerns of women.

Managing like a man?

Wajcman's research germinates from the assumption that workforces have been feminized and this provides opportunities for gender equality, although she concurs that she investigated women's inequality "within an explicit framework of equality" (1998: 1). Likewise Wajcman anticipates that her research acknowledges how gendered identities "have undergone a major transformation" (1998: 2). Drawing on her sociological background and her sample of senior male and female managers in high technology organizations who are committed to equal opportunities policies, Wajcman provides a feminist account of men and women's role changes and their experiences as senior managers. Wajcman's research is a response to existing "women in management" literature (the body of work that she subsequently draws on through all her chapters such as Ferguson 1984; Marshall 1984, 1995; Cockburn 1991; Davidson and Cooper 1992) that is "exclusively about women managers, treated in isolation from men. Quarantining women in this way has the effect of locating women as the problem, and reinforces the assumptions that men are uniformly to the management manner born" (Wajcman 1998: 2). Thus Wajcman's aim is to explore men's responses to the changes of women's entry and progression into senior management careers. She continues by observing that "to study senior women managers is to study exceptional women in an atypical context" (1998: 2).

Although Wajcman takes on an ambitious study her research has several major flaws. From the statement above her aims to explore men's and women's accounts conflict with her sample and their context. Therefore if the senior women managers in her study are "exceptional" in an "atypical" environment then how can her conclusions stand up against the wider conclusions she makes across industrial and managerial sectors? Furthermore the methodological justification and ensuing contradictions arising between Wajcman's research objectives and the methodology adopted contributes to the demise of what offered to provide "fascinating and important (*empirical*) insights" (Joan Acker on the back cover of Wajcman 1998). Rather than engage with appropriate theory that adopts consistent epistemological and methodological orientations to the subject matter (such as a qualitative case study research strategy) that supports the small sample of the "exceptional" in an "atypical" environment of the research, Wajcman extends her theorizing across organizational contexts (consistent with the questionnaire method adopted but without the sample size) and therefore loses the credibility of her original research access in high technology organization committed to equal opportunities policies. Linstead in his critique of Wajcman states that:

> Wajcman attempts only the most rudimentary justification of her methodology. There is no mention of the size of the managerial population from which the matched sample was taken, for example. Although the overall sample size is sufficient for statistical manipulation, albeit that the much smaller number of women in the sample (108) would limit the scope of the analysis, Wajcman... stops at the level of stating the percentages of men and women who identified specific factors at the crudest level of description. Not even simple – and potentially useful in this case – cross-tabulations are attempted... Wajcman did not fully embrace the analytical opportunities it presented (2000b: 1108).

In addition we could expect Wajcman's findings to be consistent with her intentions to "explore gender relations of senior management in a 'post-feminist' age" (Wajcman 1998: 2), to examine the organizational changes from gender inequality to equality and, more academically, to follow through on changes in the study of gender from theories based on sex differences to gendered identities, albeit within the dominance of patriarchal institutional structures. So, we can observe the contradictions and complexities within Wajcman's objectives as she accurately acknowledges the need to move away from traditional feminist analyses of management to consider the changing environment and organizational changes for gendered identities that draws on a post-structralist interpretation of gender, and ultimately fails to deliver. Wajcman rightly remarks that:

> Since masculinity and femininity are inherently relational concepts, with meaning only in relation to each other, this study is then able to analyse the gender regimes of management (1998: 2)

Unfortunately for Wajcman, in her struggles to present women's abject voices, she essentialises the experiences of both male and female managers and rests her analysis on fixed conceptions of the subject which are unable to acknowledge the complexities of identity construction in the changing constitution of organization and management. Linstead invitingly elucidates that:

> ... ironically, despite the fact that Wajcman argues that the book's contribution is to recognise masculinity and femininity as relational concepts, with meaning in relation only to each other in specific contexts, the circumstances in which such conceptualisations mutually arise are inferred rather than observed. Wajcman tends to treat her data as being typifications of conditions rather than exercising what would be more appropriate caution (2000b: 1108).

Linstead continues to warn of poststructuralists' potential discontent, indeed "irritation" (ibid.: 1107), based on their theorizing of the decentred subject, with Wajcman's study which downplays multiple differences within and between subjects. He concludes his review with an expedient analysis of the potential traps and dilemmas of conducting gender research, that is to be trapped by feminism's ideologies. Linstead comments:

> Wajcman's writing style seems to embody many of the traits – authoritative, assertive, argumentative, even aggressive, rational and judgmental, a little mechanical and not very metaphorical – that figure as components of "masculine" style, both in management and text. But maybe, as Wajcman implies, a woman's gotta do what a woman's gotta do (2000b: 1110).

However, the application of a gendered reading of Gowler and Legge's framework draws our attention to the gender-neutrality of their theorizing. Wajcman's research illustrates some of the fundamental issues in writing gender into the "Management of Meaning" and acknowledges to some extent how the "gendering processes are involved in how jobs and careers are constituted, both in the symbolic order and in the organizational practices (discursive and material), and [how] these power relations are embedded in the subjective gender identity of manager" (Wajcman 1998: 3). However, although presenting the voices of both men and women absent in much management and organization writings, her feminist analysis reinforces women's "quarantining" by reinforcing the gender binary. Wajcman creates isolated spaces that position all men as dominant, masculine and fortunate over women's oppression and struggles for equality, although her data does not always support this. At a simple level Wajcman's research homogenizes male and female experiences based on gender difference rather than accounting for the much needed analyses that explores difference both at the levels of managers' roles and that considers the influence of the discourses of race, disability, age, sexuality, and family and the multiple subject positions that managers draw on and take up to highlight how discourses influence each other in shaping, constructing and reconstituting individual subjectivities.

Rewriting the feminine into management as hierarchy, accountability and achievement

Drawing heavily on Wajcman Gowler and Legge's research is critiqued from a gendered perspective. A great deal of feminist contributions in the management field have primarily centred on the feminization-in-management thesis which elaborates the idea of the feminine, that signifies in many cases more fluidity, and is beneficial to developing the subjective constructs of the Management in Three Movements framework for furthering a fluid understanding of management and identity. These feminist contributions will be explored in three phases: how hierarchy infers gender segregation, how accountability stresses heightened discourses of performativity that are themselves gendered and how achievement involves gendered notions of commitment.

Firstly, the *rhetoric of hierarchy* is viewed as gender neutral and feminist writings, especially the feminization of management thesis (see Casey 1995), illustrate women's stunted entry into and slow progression through the management ranks. There is also vertical and horizontal *gender segregation* and discrimination that prevails even though the changing nature of women's roles and work in the labour market have been acknowledged (Reskin and Roos 1990; Wajcman 1998). This inroad into management can be seen as an attempt to implement the feminine in management and this has partially been achieved by recognizing the importance of feminine skills and behaviours (Rosener 1990; Fondas 1997; Tienari 1999; Metcalfe and Linstead 2003; Linstead and Catlow 2004). Therefore the hierarchical structures and controls in a modernist framework are based on structures roles and controls that are inherently masculinist and pose problems for women progressing through management especially at senior management levels (Wajcman 1998). However the lack of recognition of the feminine at a structural level privileges masculinist systems of order and control. Within the postmodernist discourse, restructuring and the associated flexibility and delegation of traditional managerial controls throughout the hierarchy have been seen to offer increasing opportunities for women.

With flatter, and perhaps more *fluid*, organizational structures upward mobility is seen to enable women's career progression with structural barriers dispersed. Additionally the emphasis on feminine leadership styles and skills in contemporary organizations supports the opportunities presented for women. However one can argue that feminist politics further subordinate the feminine by firmly setting up the feminine as the *other* and therefore sustains the gender demarcations and subordination of the feminine, thus failing to destabilize the hierarchical structures and controls.

The rhetoric of *accountability* involves the moral and technical reckoning that enforces the hierarchy and therefore suppresses the feminine by endorsing accounting practices based on objectivity and standardized accounting practices. Gowler and Legge's analysis highlights task and financial accounting practices. However contemporary analysis recognizes that there have been changing forms of accountability based on heightened discourses of performativity. These *gendered discourses of performance* are fashioned around and support feminine ways of managing which may offer increasing opportunities for women. That said, I argue here that the potential of feminine management practices to reconfigure masculinist organizational practices are outweighed by the increasingly masculinist nature of the discourses of management that seduce members. Managers are therefore engaged in legitimizing their roles in keeping with increasingly heightened performance measures and cultural controls. A growing body of research suggests that managers are required to display increasing levels of commitment to their organizations and this is itself gendered (Davidson and Cooper 1992; Dickens 1998). If we take Wajcman's argument (1998) that men and women offer the same leadership qualities although women have to manage their feminine and adopt masculine traits such as objectivity, drive, authoritative, rationality to manage their performance then performing the feminine implies that "men will be advantaged by adding new qualities to those they are already deemed to have, women will continue to be seen as offering feminine dualities" (Wajcman 1998: 77). Overall then feminists that strive for sameness by minimizing difference within and between subjects and subject positionings do not create change because the feminine is perpetually reinforced as other.

The theme of *achievement* reinforces hierarchy and accountability and governs by inserting individuals into a rational natural order. Achievement for women therefore is based on masculinist systems of achievement that many women, and men, find difficult to achieve or maintain. Achievement in the "feminization of management" thesis is the ability to adopt feminine skills to manage the "postmodern organization". These feminine attributes that women naturally possess not only create opportunities for women in management but are now essential assets for any male manager. Women's performance may be measured on the ability to adopt masculine skills and capabilities that in my view exclude many women unable to "manage like a man" from achieving, performing and competing. Thus whilst feminism has gone a long way to raise the concerns of women in management, focusing on the ways "women are disadvantaged by the fact that they are not men" and the outcomes of having to "manage like a man" (Wajcman 1998: 8) it has done very little to destabilize the systems of control that reinforce masculinist practices of management. Furthermore, such feminism not only denies difference between women, it classifies all men as benefiting from hegemony. Homogenizing sameness between and within, men and women (as Wajcman does) reinforces woman as other, endlessly subordinated. Equally new forms of masculinity are emerging that don't benefit all men and may benefit some women (Pateman 1989 cited in Wajcman 1998: 30).

Gender and middle management identities

This book is not solely with providing a gendered perspective on managerial identities but also by progressing theory by arguing for increasingly fluid and relational construction of femininity and masculinity (Calás and Smircich 1993; Collinson and Hearn 1996; Fondas 1997; Alvesson and Billing 1997; Kerfoot and Knights 1998; Whitehead 2001; Linstead and Brewis 2004; Pullen and Linstead 2005; Tyler 2005).

To update Gowler and Legge's research, I have critiqued their model from the basis of power by drawing on Foucault and gender by drawing on Wajcman. The last two chapters makes a theoretical contribution by presenting the Management in Three Movements model as both the framework to be interrogated by the data and the lens by which the data are to be interrogated in chapters 5, 6 and 7. Furthermore to explore identity as project which challenges the unitary subject and notions of causality, truth and the fixed self emphasizing identities as multiple, fragmented, plural, and *becoming*, a Foucauldian influenced perspective of self, power and discourse has been written into The Management of Meaning. At the same time a gendered reading, drawing on Wajcman's research, unveils the gender-blindness of Gowler and Legge's management account as a way forward for researching middle managers' subjectivities from a relational, gendered perspective. I explore dimensions of middle managers' subject positioning, through the shift from modernist modes of achievement, accountability and hierarchy (Gowler and Legge 1996) to postmodern features of commitment, seduction and networking through fluid resistance respectively in three case organizations: Larts, Carlux and Nylons over the next three chapters.

5
"Breaking Up Is Hard To Do": Hierarchy and Networking in Carlux

> Disaster hit with the recession and other outside influences coming in and the company went through a major organizational and culture change. Basically, they got rid of the foremen overnight and introduced a new layer of management called the zone manager and they also introduced these things called team leaders and we were going to work in teams... People were very weary and uncomfortable of what was going on... it was chaos... they reduced the workforce by a rather substantial amount and we were basically told well get on with it, but we were told "this is how it is going to be in the future"...
>
> Bob, Carlux Zone Manager

> After death the heart assumes the shape of the pyramid
>
> Julian Barnes

Introduction

The Management in Three Movements model developed in Chapter 3 was based on the characteristics of organizational and social shifts from the modern to postmodern introducing the *dynamic dualistic* movement of hierarchy to networking, accountability to seduction and achievement to commitment as a frame for researching managerial subjectivities. This model has been used as the basic framework to be interrogated by the data and, simultaneously, the lens through which the data were interrogated. In this chapter I explore how and why middle managers draw on the duality of hierarchy and networking to shape and constitute their subjectivities in Carlux.

Carlux, as will be seen below was a traditional manufacturing company whose practices prior to restructuring were resonant with Gowler and Legge's *management-as-hierarchy*. Until extensive restructuring in 1991 the middle management cohort typified the traditional view of "management in the middle". Relating this back to my earlier discussion in Chapter 2 middle managers were part of the chain in a long hierarchy which supported and legitimized their formal positions, work roles and status in Carlux. Restructuring involved making many middle managers (and an even larger number of other workers) redundant and the surviving middle managers are a newly formed group that has been reshaped from front-line leadership positions, the traditional foreman role, and demoted production managers. Middle managers in the "new" Carlux are therefore a hybridized group that merged the often distinct groups of shop floor supervisors and operations managers prior to 1991. These "zone managers" are a much slimmed down cohort that has less managerial status but they experience more autonomy and decision making responsibility. Issues of control and power traditionally achieved through progression through middle management is now a resource retained for senior management and in many cases the production work *teams* rather than individuals.

In this chapter I discuss the organizational changes that have taken place in Carlux since the major restructuring in 1991 and I pay specific attention to how structural changes influenced the zone managers studied. This chapter is based on data collected from the ten zone managers in Carlux between 1996 and 1997. In this section the fragments of four middle managers are presented to highlight their persuasive accounts as a form of first order accounting. These persuasive accounts reveal the paradoxical nature of hierarchy and networking as features of identity construction in making sense of their working lives. Identities, as will be seen and as discussed in earlier chapters, are constructed in terms of the conjunction of past and future, as an explanation of previous events in a way that positions the constructor of the account advantageously for future episodes. The middle managers from Carlux that are presented draw on hierarchy as a construct that characterized their past roles whilst at the same time accounting for their new roles by drawing on contemporary discourses of networking. Identity is therefore a paradox between managers' discursive positions. It will be seen how managers move simultaneously between reflecting on past experiences of restructuring that were relatively stable whilst at the same time legitimizing and securing their future roles by drawing on discourses of "new" managerial work. Identities are therefore masks that are created as resources in a project of becoming, outfits for participation in an ongoing masquerade – a masquerade that protects and shelters their lack and/or loss. Restructuring at Carlux had thrown the managers researched into constantly questioning, legitimizing or resisting their identities. This chapter explores how the managers studied faced up to ontological insecurity which as we will see forces them into constant projects of restructuring their sense of "self" in a turbulent, ambiguous and insecure environment. The research in Carlux reveals how few managers are equipped to confront their "realities" and we see how all the managers presented don masks, some more rigid and permanent than others, to conceal "self" to enable the performance of their work roles.

This chapter suggests that there is evidence to support some movement from modern to postmodern forms of organizing at an organizational/structural level (see Figure 3.1) as a consequence of restructuring in Carlux. It is important to recall that this shift does not portray a fixed empirical shift between the objective and subjective or an irreversible epochal shift between the modern and the postmodern, rather there is a *discursive* shift between the modernist (objective) and postmodern (subjective) modes of organization. These dualities are therefore relational and legitimize the configuration and reconfiguration of managerial subjectivities. More importantly for this study how the managers selected here draw on the coexisting discourses of hierarchy and networking when *doing* identity work in Carlux, rather than one *or* the other are investigated.

On a methodological note (see appendices 1 and 2 for a full explanation), *fragments* of accounts are selected here and since accounts themselves are produced from fragments I have not deconstructed accounts into further fragments but merely selected certain fragments from a larger mosaic. I have done this because these fragments seemed to me to be significant to the participants, they resonated with each other across the accounts of the particular managers chosen, and which seemed to be an issue across the much wider data set which I had obtained. These data are representative of the wider data set in so far as they are taken from it and reproduce elements found elsewhere in the set. I would not, however, wish to claim that they were representative in any quantitative sense, or that mine was the only possible interpretation of either these or the wider data set. I chose the managers as *representatives* which enabled me to discuss their comments in some detail whilst giving sufficient variety to cover all the necessary elements. I was attracted to these managers selected in particular because, even as I conducted the interviews, they appeared to be articulating elements which other interviewees had raised, but had not so well exemplified or expressed, and had a range of differing work experiences, educational attainments and family situations. These managers were also observed at work which enabled me to enrich my interpretations of the data generated from the interviewees.

This chapter is structured as follows. First the background and fundamental issues surrounding the restructuring that took place at Carlux which influenced the managers studied and in relation to which all the managers raised particular concerns about their roles and identities are discussed. Second, and to introduce the central issue of ontological insecurity, I discuss the experiences presented by Bob and Alan as they account for themselves. Both managers draw on discourses of hierarchy and accountability to legitimize themselves and both don masks of change and nostalgia respectively to conceal self and manage loss and lack. I argue during the third section that role ambiguity and ontological insecurity requires middle managers constantly to justify themselves and they do so by defining and constructing themselves as "co-ordinators" and "boundary spanners", thus creating clarity and legitimacy around their roles. This discussion highlights how Chris uses *control* in both a traditionally *hierarchical* sense and in a flexible and increasingly *fluid* sense (networking) to manage his identity. I analyze the tensions between Chris drawing on co-ordination as both a hierarchical and networking form to indicate the many tensions between the safe and comforting "what we know" of "hierarchy" and the ability to manage within the more ambiguous and floating relationships and discourses of networking. I question the discursive shift from the modern to postmodern by looking at how Chris draws on hierarchy and resists the flow of networking, to make sense of his "new" identity. Here I argue that managers find protection within hierarchy, in order to mourn loss and manage change, even though this nostalgic desire for hierarchy effectively brings forward death by restricting the life-giving and innovative energies of movement, turning away from the future by arresting becoming. In the next part of this chapter, I explore how Stuart, an ambitious "key player" in future restructuring adopts masks of change and performance which draw on both networking and hierarchy in a different way. Stuart feeds off "weaker", poor performing or "dying" managers through a discourse of *"negotiating* with the dead". Chris' dramatic need to perform through more chaotic discourses of networking and team working at the same time as empathizing with the orderly other of hierarchy is equally destructive and kills off the development of the self. This chapter concludes by summarizing how the four managers draw on the interrelated discourses of hierarchy and networking, travelling through the space between them, to construct and maintain a sense of onto-logical security. The managers, albeit in different ways, mourn loss and experience melancholy which influences the ways in which they con-struct their identities. I argue that hierarchy is still a core function of what management currently is and how this desire for hierarchy in projects of modernity and self-identity re-masculinizes working prac-tices through modernist discourses of identity and organization.

Carlux: changing organizational structures

Carlux has a long history reaped in prestige and luxury since the com-pany was founded in 1904, formed in 1906 and in 1995 the company celebrated the production of its one-hundredth thousandth car. This legacy influences the company today, infiltrates the company culture and is a vantage selling point. The company had been financially suc-cessful in the luxury car market until the economic pressures of the late 1980s and early 1990s. By this time the company was losing its competitive edge due to quality problems and low sales. Consequently, the epoch of financial luxury in which two brands were produced by Carlux came to an abrupt an unexpected end. In order to survive at the highest end of the luxury market, Carlux restructured manufacturing and introduced a Total Quality Management program, which included the implementation of teamworking in manufacturing and cross-functional teams across the plant.

The company, part of a larger manufacturing group at the time of the research but now part of a well established car manufacturing company, is located on its existing brownfield site, located in the West of England, United Kingdom. In 1991 the company employed 4,500 people in the manufacture of four models of Carlux cars. The cars were manufactured by craft production which consisted of make and assem-bly operations. The components for the car's engines and body features were manufactured, car bodies were supplied to the company by coachbuilders and the component parts were assembled onto the frame. The servicing, testing and project work for the cars were done in house. In 1991 the "crisis" as it was subsequently referred to struck Carlux. Since 1991 manufacturing changed with the introduction of outsourcing components for the engines; investment in developing core processes such as the development of body assembly and servicing and testing, and implementation of advanced technologies. In this chapter I am concerned with how the "crisis" – the restructuring – influenced middle managers' subjectivities.

The 1991 crisis

The traditional working practices of Carlux had not been designed to cope with changing demands and environmental influences in the UK and USA. The USA introduced a luxury car tax in January 1991 that resulted in reduced sales. Sales plummeted from 3,000 in 1990 to 1,750 in 1991. It was against this economic backdrop that the company embarked on a comprehensive reorganization of working practices. In March 1991 the company and its unions reached agreement on the organizational changes necessary if the company was to emerge from the recession as a strong and competitive manufacturer. Entitled "The Future of Manufacturing", or the Red Book as it became known, the agreement introduced team working and ended all demarcations, while committing the company to maintaining the proportion of skilled employees in the manual staff group at no less than 60% and guaranteeing that there would be no compulsory redundancies as a direct result of the implementation of the agreement. All national agreements were terminated and Carlux withdrew from the Engineering Employees Federation. The company recognized that it would have to pay for the organizational changes and it negotiated a two year deal. On April 1st 1991, when the Red Book agreement was implemented, basic rates were increased by 8.62% with a £150 one-off lump-sum payment from 1st June 1991 for satisfactory progress in the transition to the Red Book practices. An unconsolidated bonus scheme that paid £18 per week was suspended. In the second year, from 1st February 1992, basic rates were to increase by 6%, plus 4% for continuing with the Red Book practices. The sharp drop in orders and the continuing recession led to the halving of the 6% part of the deal. In October 1996 an expected bonus was not paid. Through these issues of rewards staff felt that whilst they were supporting the company through the "crisis" the company was not delivering on its promises. Trust was further damaged when despite a commitment that there would be no compulsory redundancies as a result of the Red Book, Carlux nevertheless had to operate compulsory redundancies. Senior management said these were resulting from the drop in orders, rather than the implementation of Red Book changes to working practices but trust and morale were still affected. Along with voluntary redundancies and early retirement, the numbers employed decreased from 4,500 in April 1991 to 1,700 in 1996. Throughout the company there was still in 1997 a sense of grieving over this enormous loss.

When the negotiations with the trade unions ended in 1991 the company ended the demarcations between groups of employees calling all employees "associates" and implemented team working. In 1996 Carlux had started to re-erect demarcations separating "work associates" and "staff associates". The acceptance of these changes was paid for in a two-year deal which included a lump-sum bonus which was assisted by the company's move to single-status terms and conditions which began in 1988. However, the company was still not fully harmonized since there are remained differences between manual staff and others, such as lay-off arrangements which didn't apply to managers and other staff. Some features of the move to single status included a single status restaurant which was introduced instead of several canteens; the job evaluation scheme was substituted by "associates" writing their own job specification and single status uniforms were implemented in 1996. However some differences between staff and workers were still evident, such as separate car parks for staff and work associates and differences in financial incentives and rewards. These changes were particularly problematic for middle managers, who were thrown into an "identity crisis" and "caught in the middle" especially since many of them had progressed from the shop floor.

The reorganization

Carlux reorganized its operations in the attempt to remove "slack" in production and staff. This restructuring to some extent supports the shift from hierarchy to networking discussed previously. A major part of reorganization was the introduction of teams across the manufacturing function in every one of the many stages of the complex manufacture of luxury cars, starting with permanent work teams in the linear production system. Manufacturing was organized into ten zones (the idea of a factory within a factory with ten teams of six to 12 people in each, each with its own team leader) to align the processes around the key production processes/car parts. Maintenance and craft workers were integrated into the teams so they became self-contained production units relying on themselves for setting, operating and maintaining machinery to reduce time delays. Engineering was disbanded into project teams. Teams of "specialists" such as experimental specialists, service centre workers and spares are situated outside the zone to service all zones. Flexible problem solving teams from all the teams were designed to combat problems and tackle quality issues.

Team working across other parts of the site followed in July 1992 in a less systematic and complete way, starting with the reorganization of the personnel department including training and employee relations. Administrative staff from the departments were located together in one open-plan office and the specialist managers (pensions, remuneration and benefits) were in another. These staff teams were said to be more "closely allied to a broader team philosophy" than to the working teams on the shop floor. Hence there were different demands placed on different parts of the organization which was a barrier to developing people. In keeping with increased networking across the site, relocating staff into single offices attempted to remove the physical barriers to communication that existed in the former individual office-based culture.

More important for this study was the reorganization of its seven level management structure into five layers with the abolition of charge hands and foremen and the introduction of team leaders to replace them. Production executives, production managers and area managers were replaced by senior production managers and zone managers. The team leaders were working team leaders, which between leaders and zone and was a source of on ongoing rivalry. Zone managers selected the team leaders after an initial numeracy and literacy test and most of the team leaders were appointed from skilled manual workers. The traditional foreman function disappeared and the majority of the foremen were made redundant. The foremen that remained since left or were appointed to zone manager positions. All candidates for zone management were sent away for a one day assessment course run by external assessors who provided profiles of each candidate's individual strengths and abilities. Carlux management interviewed the candidates and 16 were appointed. One week's external training in the team working concept, people skills and process skills followed the appointments. Individual and group based training is said to have taken place as the need arose. All the managers interviewed felt that senior management were unclear about the role of zone managers and many of the managers experienced great ambiguity surrounding their role. There are no female managers or team leaders in Carlux.

Managing through empowerment

The company decided to develop an "empowerment philosophy" for continuous improvement. Empowerment was seen as "creating self-directed work teams, better working practices, commitment, participation and involvement through autonomy" (Carlux Director). In 1992 the company adopted lean principles such as Kanban and JIT and MRP

II manufacturing techniques. Restructuring resulted in fundamental expertise and skills being lost. As a result, to combat this and other problems in 1993 Total Quality training which provided education for all employees was conducted by LEAP (Carlux's equivalent to the quality department). Participating in LEAP training and activities provided an enormous benefit to me to develop trust, commitment and participation throughout a great deal of the workforce. Also, LEAP was perceived as a refuge where people felt they could come to be offered assistance. In 1994 the company went through the Key Goals process which resulted in a Key Goals brochure which communicated the company business goals throughout the organization. In 1995 the foundations for the future new organization and investment in new models and manufacturing facilities took place, such as reorganization of manufacturing layout, new production systems and technologies. In February 1996 the "Vision and Values" benchmark was launched. The visions and values were produced by natural work teams with the objective to roll it out to the rest of the company. The Vision was that "together we will make Crewe the worlds best workplace". The Values were "trust, respect, opportunity, fulfilment, equality, commitment and freedom". In parallel to this, other natural work teams were focusing on "identifying behaviours that bring to *life* the values set to underpin the vision". At the same time as developing the corporate culture, contractors were brought into the company from 1994 onwards to replace expertise lost in the restructuring which resulted in 23 contract houses being used in 1996.

Transforming the unions

In October 1991 Carlux decided that the company's representative structure was out-dated and no longer suited the plant in light of the changes in the organizational and management structure. It still had a traditional union structure, with the AEEU, TGWU, MSF, and GMB/APEX represented wherever members worked, and was split clearly between workers and staff. There were also separate negotiations for the shop floor and staff. The company wanted to introduce single-table bargaining and reduce the number of union representatives, who would represent all the employees in their work area rather than just their union members. This would, they thought, simplify bargaining and facilitate a better relationship between union representatives and management. After union and company bargaining, Carlux secured an agreement that is known as the "Yellow Book". The Yellow book involved a reduction in the number of union representatives from 120 to 47. These employee representatives were elected by all the employees in the zones and were able to cross union boundaries within the zone. Employee representatives had direct access to zone managers and were therefore able to establish personal relations with them. In turn, the zone managers had industrial relations responsibilities devolved to them by the company, which abolished industrial relations officers. From the 47 employee representatives, 7 were elected to join the joint works-staff negotiating committee as senior employee representatives, and from this group 1 senior site representative was elected. The Yellow Book which was implemented in March 1992 was seen by Carlux as a fundamental change in industrial relations, which gave it, in effect, a single-union deal.

The future

Carlux continued to face further upheavals to remain competitive in the high pressure car market that became increasingly innovative and cost orientated throughout all of its sectors. In 1997 when I departed Carlux there were plans for the "new organization" to support the manufacturing strategy. Whilst the plans and development were confidential at this time, the manufacturing strategy and structure that emerged moved towards being more flexible, cost effective and with an emphasis on faster production. The changes occurring at that time included new methods of manufacture by outsourcing the manufacture of engines and focusing on assembly, high technology production lines, investment in new products and facilities, greater flexibility through using contract/temporary associates, and a stronger emphasis on business performance measures. A project manager involved in these developments commented:

> We need to build better cars quicker to stay in business...we need to be more competitively aware as managers and try to encourage this. About one third of our machinery is not core competence and we need to just keep the core competencies.

The curiosity surrounding the change at the time contributed to feelings of mistrust and uncertainty throughout the workforce. The imminent changes to organization and work design were faced by a mixture of excitement and enthusiasm for those involved in new project work, combined with fear and uncertainty for those with little knowledge of the changes. In summary then, traditionally the company was dominated by hierarchy and an "over-the-wall" mindset. The company changed to a team-based structure driven by a quality and empowerment philosophy with a major focus of the organization being "to sell the best motor car in the world" (Company Documentation). Although significant changes throughout the company occurred during the period 1991 to 1997, sadly the company, and its legacy, was sold to a large international car manufacturer in 2000.

The demise of middle managers as they knew them: ontological insecurity

The above shows how Carlux restructured its workforce. There is some evidence to support the shift from a bureaucracy characterized by du Gay as having the ethical attributes of "strict adherence to procedure, acceptance of hierarchical subordination and superordination, abnegation of personal moral enthusiasms, commitment to the purpose of the office" (2000: 29) to more fluid organizational arrangements that focused on creating flexible working, team working and increased internal and external networking. In this study I am concerned with the restructuring of management in particular. In Chapter 2 I discussed how the pessimistic studies of middle management have highlighted how managers have been downsized and how managers as a result of radical restructuring experience job insecurity and "survivor syndrome" (Cameron et al 1991; Heckscher 1995). Scase and Goffee's study (1989) reported how managers were reluctant to give themselves to their organization. The massive restructuring and downsizing that took place overnight in 1991 and subsequent changes since 1991 took their toll on the zone managers. As Burrell comments "where the 'liposuction' of middle management tiers takes place [it] threatens morale and encourages political resistance" (1992: 68) and this resistance certainly influenced the data generated in the research engagement. The research process was a site for instability on the one hand and self-promotion on the other for the managers in this study. During my visits to Carlux (1996–1997) it was evident that the managers studied still mourned the loss of the workforce that departed in 1991. This loss I argue here is also for them – they have lost their sense of self. Along with downsizing and restructuring, managers have lost the managerial sovereignty associated with the traditional middle management position. This sovereignty may often be used as a mask for many managers to cope with the loss of authority and status of management work:

> faces... assume predictable expressions viewers **know how to read** – the mask of tragedy, the mask of romance (Kleege 2000: 47 emphasis added).

Around every profound spirit there **grows a mask** (Nietzsche 1997: 29 emphasis added).

The mask does not just protect and conceal the face but over time takes the shape of the face. The natural features of the face die and give way, dissolving into the permanence of the mask. We become, we live, our masks. As will be seen in the case of Alan, his extract highlights how some managers in Carlux have adopted rigid and perhaps permanent masks with which to perform self. These managers I suggest here do so to cope, manage and avoid *loss* and *lack*. Loss and lack revealed itself in many and varied ways between managers but all the managers faced overwhelming insecurity regarding their being – who they were and who they were going to be allowed to be. Even though the following piece from Bob (a foreman in 1991) is lengthy it illustrates how unexpectedly the change occurred and the ambiguity surrounding the zone manager position. Managers' sense of being therefore was in many cases thrown into flux and the evidence of their ontological insecurity dominated the managers' accounts:

In 1991 they did away with foremen and introduced team working, there were 124 in the machine shop then. We thought it was a **safe, secure** job working with Carlux. I'll explain how I found out... I was at my mother's funeral when the phone rang.... it was a friend who said "I don't know what has happened at Carlux they have got rid of all the foremen".... I came into work the next day and well they hadn't got rid of all the foreman but they had introduced team working, it would be a different set up altogether... that was quite a **traumatic** period...because nobody knew what was happening... and we had no indication that it was going to happen that quick. Some took voluntary redundancy, some went onto other work.... but there were interviews for zone managers... There was so many of us there to apply I didn't hold much hope. We all went through the interview process... and there were two of us out of the machine shop that were offered zone managers positions. The following weekend we were sent to Southport on a week course... so we were sat there as new zone managers not knowing what a zone manager was and not knowing much about team working... It was a crash course... [laughter]. It was new... Imagine training at my age! We came back and were given an area of the factory to look after, these were called zones, the factory was split into 10 zones... It was on an area we hadn't worked before, it was interesting really, we had to form teams and choose team leaders because it hadn't happened before. And, that is how it started off. It was very exciting at times [lots of laughter]. We were told to get in there and do what needs to be done and if any senior manager comes and interferes then to let him [consultant] know and he would find him something to do.

Restructuring also has symbolic implications for managers as they could not be seen to label themselves or manage in the ways in which they had known. Managers needed to construct "new" identities, albeit superficial ones, and had limited time to rehearse their new roles, their new ways of knowing, in unchartered territories. Subsequently, managers are constantly questioned who they were in the company; they were ontologically insecure. In the next section how "zone managers" – Bob and Alan – confront, manage or negate their ontological insecurity are discussed to reveal how they discursively *restructure* and legitimize self. However it must be noted that the managers involved in the study varied in their degrees of openness when discussing and displaying their insecurities. Some managers such as Alan *mask* their insecurity by drawing on contemporary discourses of the "new organization" to salvage some sense of credibility, security and safety whilst refusing to engage with the past or future, which represent moments of insecurity. On the other hand, other managers such as Bob were concerned with the changes to middle managers in general and pragmatically drew on both past, current and future episodes – the "old" and "new" organization – to make sense of their experiences. As a means of providing introduction to the rest of the chapter, this section uses fragments from these two zone managers to explore more closely how ontological insecurity influences their identities. Both Bob and Alan discuss how the nature of control for them has changed. For them hierarchy here is associated with "old" Carlux and networking with the "new" Carlux.

Confronting the past and managing the future: Bob's mask of change

Bob was responsible for a one of the largest zones in the company which involved engine assembly, axle assembly, subframe assembly, small part assembly, heat treatment, radiator assembly, polishing (metal), and plating shop. He started working in Carlux in 1951 and had been with the company 45 years. He began his life with Carlux as an apprentice machine setter in the machine shop. Since then he had done numerous jobs including pay grade restructuring, productivity study establishing incentives schemes for indirect labour, work study in the aerodynamics shop, a foreman in the foundry until 1980 when he became a foreman in machine shop assembly until 1991. In 1991 he became a zone manager. He is married and has a family. In 1996 "the nature of the job he is in and the stage of production mean there will be a lot of changes for him and his job remains unsure" (senior manager, Carlux).

Extract 1   "Prior to 1990... we had manufacturing director, senior production manager, then area managers, then under the area manager would be the foreman, then the people working but not in teams... We have come from the stance of having a foreman, charge hand, leading hand, superintendent and that was the old hierarchical structure to the system where we now have a more relaxed approach to the hands on side of management such that the teams which are considerably more *flexible*, the individuals are more flexible... that has helped the role I've got now because you could get people to do things before in the old set up but it was difficult because they were always victimised... because they are always singled out by those from the old school of 'I'm a coach builder, I'm an electrician, I'm a fitter.... and I don't do anything else'. So now we still have people who maintain their core abilities and their old trade... but they are quite prepared to *cross the boundary* to the fringe activities that they are required to do that support their core abilities".

Extract 2   "Ownership is now very much on the individual, whereas in the old organization, *authority* lay with senior management... When the role changed some were a little bit *afraid* of it so they decided to take voluntary redundancy. I was very concerned about it but you have to put it behind you and *move on*. It made me *question* what I wanted and what I needed to do. I've been here a long time and I needed to decide what was important to me and the family. My wife thinks I do too much. I *faced* up to the change and I'm doing OK enough for them not to have any concerns at the minute but my area is going to change very fast and I'll just have to face that when it comes. But, we've *lost all I know* and I've had to move on".

Extract 3   "My role has changed so much [long pause]. Initially it was taking on responsibility... as a foreman before I did anything you went to see the superintendent or manager, but then you went to making decision with your team and... nobody had been brave enough before to try and change. Now it was if it works it works, if it fails it fails... The teams eventually took it on board because they were very apprehensive about it, we were apprehensive about it, leaving the teams and team leaders to get on with it... We soon realised that their skills and talents had been there all the while and why did we need foremen?"

Extract 4   "... it's a pity they hadn't done it years ago, but it was obviously restricted because of the way the company was structured. You've got the people at the top who only dealt with the next level down, and nobody did anything besides what they were told". I have had to change the way I think about things and how to confront the way I work".

Extract 5   "It's great to work as part of such a close team, but as you realise there are lots of changes going on. Parts are being moved around, people are being moved from one side to the other, so there has been a lot of disruption with our teams, unfortunately... we are having a big move of labour... we are transferring machining work to assembly and that means outsourcing which means more staff cut-backs... It's been difficult because now we are working with teams where half of them are temporary labour and they are incorporated and treated in the teams the same as permanent labour. So, now, our job is what we make it and we won't know what it is again soon".

Extract 6   "My opinion is that we haven't developed, we were given a golden opportunity five years ago and I think from not knowing what a zone manager was or what to expect and what freedom we could have we didn't develop fast enough to what we should have done... For the first twelve months, two years we were into zone managers... there were enormous redundancy exercises which took the focus off team working... The focus was on *struggling and muddling* through because the company was in trouble financially like a lot of companies were. Keeping the teams going, the management going, keeping interest there. That's what our role was then... to keep on going when the world around us was collapsing...We thought that was the end of it and then we heard that hundreds more had to go... zone managers went as well then... There has been a lot of changes in the last five years. There has never been time to sit back and relax and that's a good thing, it's driven us along and it's driven the teams along. It stops you *thinking* you know [long pause]. It's been tough and you have to *not care*, to do the best you can and well Christ there's all the extra work!!!!"

Extract 7   "I'm shattered when I get home. I just feel at times I haven't got enough time to do a job well, because I have got so much to do. I come in here some days to get something done and I just can't there's people back and forth all the time, things going wrong, machines failing... Really you've got to *balance* that with what you need to do... I feel I could do a better job than I have done developing things and spending more time with people. *I don't spend enough time with them*. There are one hundred and fifty people working in the department so man management is crucial, I have seen zone managers fail because they haven't *changed*... I always put myself in the team, so whilst I'm with a specific team I'm part of that team and likewise I would like them to think that I'm part of their team and I think they do".

Extract 8   "I'm in a position where I've tried to devolve control down to the lads themselves, effectively. What used to happen before is.... that the process was so tight and *rigid* the guys always used to take the attitude of tell me what you want me to do and if you haven't told me then I haven't done it and you can't tell that I've done something wrong. Now what I always try to do is give them the broad picture or the broadest picture I can of what is expected of them and then allow them to decide how they are going to do it. So I don't impose upon them any form of control that would impact upon their performance until it was showing me that it was going to be detrimental to the company. Also, if they want to change their process they can do what the hell they like, I don't mind, it's entirely up to them... Some are doing exceptionally well, others OK and others are just not interested because they want to be told what to do and I'm not in that game".

Extract 9   "There is an air of uncertainty mainly over this side [of the factory] because of everything we have been through and it takes a long time to get things out of people's minds... The company is doing very well at the moment and people know that there is no redundancy over the next two years... But it is still at the back of their minds. A lot of people... like to have an air of uncertainty, so it's a case of 'everything is all right but don't forget so and so'... If there wasn't this uncertainty I don't know whether team working would have developed as far as it has and... if it had been *comfortable*, a lot of zone managers would have fallen back into the old way... so why bother. There's *no job* for people like that now. There is *uncertainty* but it becomes a way of life".

Extract 10   "You need to adapt yourself to different areas of the factory... I learnt the hard way... It was a case of figuring out what worked where and *changing yourself* to get what you wanted done... I don't think that it was being a chameleon and *blending in* but there are certain things you have to do in order to gain their understanding and respect. You have to, you could say 'why bother' but you wouldn't last".

Bob's narrative reveals brief moments of grieving as he recalls and mourns the loss of the workforce associated with past restructuring. Bob also confronts how further loss is inevitable in what appears to be an increasingly uncertain and ambiguous climate and he is aware that his area of production is to be radically restructured in the short term. The death of craft production in Carlux and the related mourning for the sacrificed familiar (see Freud 1984 cited in Höpfl 2002a) is evident – for Bob the overwhelming sadness centres on the words that he has "lost all I know". During Bob's practice of retrospective-prospective accounting procedures (Garfinkel 1967) he tries to mediate between past and future to explain the present. Bob uncovers more moments of doubt, uncertainty and insecurity:

> ... It [the downsizing] made me question what I wanted and what I needed to do. I've been here a long time and I needed to **decide what was important to me** and the family. My wife thinks I do too much. I **faced up to the change** and I'm doing OK enough for them not to have any concerns at the minute but my area is going to change very fast and I'll just have to face that when it comes.

This insecurity surrounding his being (compare with Collinson 2003) – which the changes have almost placed *sous rature* or under erasure as Derrida expresses it – stems from the loss of people (as friends, colleagues, associates, mentors), skills and ways of working. Bob's fragment also shows the uncertainty and ambiguity of the situation in which in he found himself. There are hints of nostalgia here as he mourns the loss of those who failed to accommodate the climate (recall the selection process for zone managers). His loss – of managerial sovereignty – is also evident when he recalled earlier "training at my age" when he commented on the processes of becoming a zone manager from a foreman. So even though Bob was *promoted* to the zone manager position there is a sense that he has lost some of the traditional control and responsibility that he had even as a foreman.

The identity work that Bob undertakes within the interview reveals a paradoxical relationship between on the one hand, ambiguity and vagueness surrounding his role:

> The focus was on struggling and muddling through... Keeping the teams going, the management going, keeping interest there. That's what our role was then... to keep on going when the world around us was collapsing...

On the other hand, there is the "freedom", autonomy and decision-making power accruing from better knowledge and information resulting from increased networking and communication through the implementation of team working. Networking enabled people to *"cross the boundary"* he says, by being "flexible" and suggests that control lies with "individuals" rather than structurally embedded. The emphasis on the changing nature of control, from structural to performance driven control, has as we might expect increased Bob's workload and escalated pressures associated with new ways of working. For Bob the uncertainty and the loss of rigid controls, teamed with intensification of work and the struggle to maintain performance was concurrent with increased willingness to improve performance – for himself and the company.

Interestingly then, Bob simultaneously confronts the past at the same time as he confronts the ambiguity and uncertainty that increased networking brings. Whilst he faces his current and future predicament he does not outwardly condemn hierarchy, as many other managers did, because this hierarchy is associated with safety and protection for him, it is what he knows and it was who he was for so many years. Rather he draws on the past to legitimize the journey he has taken from foreman to zone manager – from *his* past to the *organizational* future – whilst patiently assessing the new ways of working (which were presented ideologically by most other managers a great deal of the time). His realism in his conversations with me over the failure of the zone manager role and the lack of interaction with his teams was rare as we will see when we discuss the other managers.

Bob is calm and pragmatic about the personal and organizational damage experienced and confronts this in a spirit of "moving on". Although Bob illustrates the loss associated with the shift from the hierarchy of the "old" organization to the "new" structure and how this has influenced issues of control, management authority and management practice, he does not dwell morbidly on the past. He addresses the changes and the consequences for him and provides a relatively balanced, pragmatic analysis of the new order compared with the other interviews conducted. There is no doubt for me that Bob has faced up to his *personal* reality since he is one of the few managers that uses "I", when referring to the changes rather than drawing on the other ("they", "we", "other people"), to make sense of his identity. Bob was rare in Carlux in that he was remarkably resigned to his "fate" – and here allows us an opportunity to introduce the concept of death in relation to organization, which will inform our further analysis of the data.

The gift of death and its refusal

Linearity, according to Gibson Burrell (1997), kills. Such is the motif that runs through his book *Pandemonium*, and indeed drives him to structure it in a way that tries to resist linearity, so the reader follows a guided tour of a Gothic Alton Towers, setting out following the top half of the page towards the furthest point of the book (what in normal books would be the end) stopping at occasional full page exhibits or perhaps pausing at the library (the *logos* or bibliography placed at the centre), to return along the bottom half of each page, reading from the "back" of the book, to arrive once more at the beginning, or exit/entrance. Burrell is not merely playing clever word games here as his argument is that taking predictable routes on comfortable and predetermined paths kills off our ability to respond to experience, to being, and the impulse to create or be original. His use of Barnes' metaphor of the pyramidal shaped heart, illustrates how "after death the heart assumes the shape of a pyramid" (Barnes 1990: 237). We could infer therefore that as managers draw on hierarchy they move closer to a form of death – though still alive. As Burrell states:

> The classic organizational shape insinuates itself into the place where once a heart moved in its regular but dynamic rhythm... Only when the heart has lost its capacity for life and love does the pyramid coagulate into existence. Only when life and love are finally extinguished does the hierarchy solidify into its defining state (Burrell 1992: 66).

The irony of this growing closer to the sarcophagus of hierarchy is emphasized by Sievers (1992). For Sievers, formal organizations are an attempt by individuals to develop something into which they can invest a part of themselves and on which they can make a mark which will outlive them, so that they achieve a kind of immortality. Organization recognizes mortality by silencing it, by attempting to somehow create immortality as the organization lives on. Unfortunately in seeking to secure the future for the legacy of the individual or collective, it sacrifices the immediacy of the present and dulls the appetite for life and the experiences of exploration, play and risk-taking which make us who we are. Thus there are two forms of symbolic death which managers can experience – one is the death of being separated from access to immortality, through dismissal or redundancy being severed from the organization; the other is the living death, the loss of imagination, the energetic "capacity for life and love" of being trapped in alienating structures.

If there is a way of experiencing some sense of liberation from this situation, it could come from the assertion of sovereignty in acting creatively and changing or breaking with the system autonomously. On the other hand, it may come through recognizing what Derrida (1995) calls the "gift of death", which entails breaking with what Sievers

(1992) calls the futile but compelling "collusive quarrel over immortality" and recognizing and fully embracing the sense of one's own mortality. From this point a more sanguine and redemptive attitude is possible, despite the fact that it may be coupled with resignation to one's fate as far as the organization is concerned. What such a view does recognize is, through acknowledging that death is inevitable and not necessarily to be feared and that organization against it is no defence, death of or separation from the organization is not the death of the self – it is simply a liberation from the false prostheses that sustained spurious identities to allow the development of new, more life-giving ones. Where managers continue to struggle to create their identity props against mortality, to refuse the gift of death, Bob accepted it and aware of his age and the stage he had reached in his career (itself a linear concept), manages this inevitable death, both organizational and personal, by focusing on what he has achieved and accomplished – as one of lucky ones who could adapt. This managerial loss – a loss of future possibility as much as of past achievements – I argue is "managed" by his "chameleon" like behaviours which blend their own identity to accommodate his environment. This chameleon-like quality, which was in high evidence from observing Bob, masks the ambiguity and uncertainty surrounding his future. This *blending in*" as Bob referred to it reveals his relationship with the "other". We could argue that in order to "last" Bob needed to create a climate of sameness but a sameness that preserved difference between different groups – management and staff – which reinforced the demarcations between white and blue collar workers in bureaucracies. This *mask of change* may assist Bob to prevent his insecurities from being revealed on the public stage. This performance to conceal insecurity and loss we could argue fuels and reinforces the discourses of performativity between managers, who in recognizing difference between themselves actively strive for sameness regarding the right way to manage, the good manager and other competitive discourses of "new managerial work" in order to survive. This sameness possibly provides a safe, if temporary, haven for Bob. Teamed with a fluid ontology of the chameleon and a team working epistemology, Bob illustrates how some managers manage their fragilities. His paradoxical identity work is evident when we see him focusing on loss and hierarchy for safety from the unknown whilst at the same time simultaneously engaging with the discourses of networking/team working through his skills to adapt to change and to confront and accommodate, rather than retreat from, the unknown – the fluidity of networking. Bob's quiet pragmatism as he reflects and draws on these to position his "self" conveys, as

Derrida (1995) maintains, the "gift of death". I argue here that Bob is resigned to the fact that death is inevitable for him and the organization as he anticipates future uncertainty. However in the short term Bob's *mask of change* – his chameleon persona – is useful in bridging hierarchy/networking; security/insecurity and self/other.

The melancholic old soldier: Alan's mask of ideology

Alan started working in Carlux as a setter/operator and then moved into a team leader role in 1991. In 1995 he took a secondment to "take time out" and then became the zone manager in 1996. Alan is 49 years old, married and has two teenage children. He has worked for the company for 24 years. He is responsible for 50 people. "A very difficult interview – not really sure what he wants or does. He has not been in the job long and he refuses to and/or can't step back and reflect. Even though he talks the talk he won't let go to explore why he refuses to talk about the past and himself. Alan would only be interviewed in his office" (Fieldnotes 1996).

Extract 1   "My leadership style is open and honest [pause] as much as possible... I'm in a position of *strength* having come from the shop floor, with high flexibility, acceptability and respect... however I have a need to learn more skills and they respect me for this".

Extract 2   "In the team based structure you need to be more flexible and then more opportunities arise. The hands on, *close control* needed by production managers in the old structure is not necessarily needed in the new because if you get the teams to operate right which we did... then you have more time for other things. The old style manager was *close control*, checking on what people were doing, the new manager is to help and facilitate the teams to achieve the objectives, train, develop and facilitate them, encourage and that type of role. They didn't even know what the role was to be... But, now you've got better communication and involvement. We *communicate* much more now than we used to and across *more boundaries*".

Extract 3   "The role then was very much you're the manager or foreman, you make the decisions and you walked round rollicking the shop floor. It was very much an environment of authority... We weren't getting anywhere... It was old hat and it was really frustrating, you couldn't try any-thing different... So it was very *static*, the work depart-ments were all laid out the same, the only driver they had was the productivity level and outside of that nobody was really interested".

Extract 4   "I download everything I know, by doing this I increase trust. They may be over informed but it's a risk I take... It's gone from this 'point the finger' dictatorial type.... to this coach, this guide, this facilitator. To use the word empow-erment, the definition being, the *freedom to act within defined boundaries*, and that makes a difference... I've got a coaching, supporting and supervising role. The role of a coach is to bring out the players... People know their responsibilities and function and just get on with it... I also *co-ordinate* work with other departments... I am an organizer and coach of these people... I'm not there to direct them everyday... I'm here to *plan for the future* and make sure my staff are safe and to try to keep them on the path if the are wandering off. Honesty, helping them make decisions, openness, leading them to make decisions if they want to. Knowing them, treating them as indi-viduals because they all need different ways of managing".

Extract 5   "Management that manages by empowerment works from the same power base... being accountable and taking an helicopter view... where discipline is through nurturing and *control* if needs be".

Extract 6   "Our role is *difficult to manage* because it needs to be visionary, flexible and reactive, but have common-sense and experience".

Extract 7   "Because of what the company has been through there has been a feeling that you can't say things that aren't very *nice*. There's a feeling that even though they say they want to hear your opinions that if you say them you might not be here next week. We are always going to have that *fear* if we don't challenge it... We need to be more open and honest and they [management] need practice what they preach".

Extract 8   "I was totally lost for four weeks... the change was
             absolutely astronomical... a massive change. The change
             in role was totally different than I had imagined, it was an
             imaginary role... I haven't had any managerial training,
             but I think I'm coping... it's more comfortable now...
             Teams are not working well... I am tearing my hair out I'm
             so stressed" [notes taken from informal conversation when
             leaving the site].

Alan was promoted from the shop floor to a team leader in 1991 and
was relatively new to the zone manager post when I spoke to him. In
contrast to Bob he never acknowledged the past or the "loss" associated with downsizing. Alan fixates on the here and now, indeed he
seems blinkered, daring not to face his realities:

> For [he] is passionately attached to [his] present; nothing in the
> world would induce [him] to trade it for the past or the future
> (Kundera 1998: 6).

This focus on the present reveals, we argue, Alan's *melancholia* – the
recognition of the incompleteness or inadequacy of self. We could
argue that he identified with the old order so strongly that the pain
associated with the loss of this order presents itself as a rejection of
(his old) self and he is unable to see where he fits into the "new"
administration. To paraphrase Höpfl (2002a) the ego is insignificant
and "morally inferior" (to the ever changing demands of the superego)
during periods of melancholia. Alan thus recognizes that he can't
repair the ego because the superego which translates the new imperatives of the organization is always ahead of him and can't recoup the
loss of the commensurability and adequacy that he once experienced.
All he can do is *mask* this melancholia by the ideology of his text, the
ideology of networking.

Alan is so acutely insecure about his managerial role that he does not
draw on the past because this would inevitably reveal his insecurities
surrounding his shop floor background and the processes of restructuring and loss that influenced many of his colleagues. Likewise he does
not dare to look forward as the future represents a source of great
anxiety and unease for him, a newly recruited manager struggling with
the responsibilities of the zone manager role (as his informal discussion
with me reveals), and the threat of exposure of even greater inadequacies. As such Alan actively and keenly presents himself as a leader

rather than manager, using descriptors that to him are "nice". Alan sees himself as a coach and facilitator and his text is imbued with the rhetoric of "new management". This we argue here is Alan's attempt to conceal the "bad" – the insecurity, his lack of skills and experience as a manager, and his struggles with meeting performance targets (as his senior manager informed me). Furthermore these struggles can be seen in the tensions in his fragments: "nurturing and *control*" and "visionary, flexible and reactive" and "common sense and experience" which demonstrate the discursive tensions between new working practices and the traditional control practices of hierarchy.

Moreover, observing Alan in work and speaking with his staff revealed a tension between his behaviour and his espoused behaviour in the text generated in the interview situation. One of Alan's team leaders said to me one day:

> He has never tried to fit to fit in with us [he used to be a team leader]. He isolates himself in his room. He never takes the team work things seriously. He's one of the few managers who hasn't tried to make it work (Brian, Alan's team leader).

His behaviour is a stark reversal of his text – he is dictatorial, authoritarian, unreflective and extremely hierarchical in his relations with his staff. Paradoxically his isolation provides safety from within the demarcations of hierarchy even though he uses the discourses of networking to verbally legitimize himself and as such resist the unwelcome probing of the research process. We see in Alan's fragments that when he refers to the discourses of new managerial work he refers to the "I" which contrasts with the collective "we" and "they" when referring to control and the "old" ways of working. Alan's dictatorial style of management provides safety and isolation which protects him from facing difference, change and the fluidity of networking. His fear of fluidity generates strong resistance to it at a behavioural level even though he draws on fluid notions of management to represent himself in relation to the "other". The *mask of ideology* is performed in his text by presenting himself as enthusiastically buying into discourses of networking which involves high interaction, communication, and flexibility:

> Now you've got better communication and involvement. We communicate much more now than we used to and across more boundaries.

Donning this mask of ideology rescues Alan from confronting his insecurities and furthermore safely recouples him from his authoritarian management practices. Alan in his managerial role experiences himself as lacking. His *desire* therefore throughout his text is one of concealing this lack. Alan does not raise the issue of hierarchy, he focuses and perpetually argues for the benefits of the discourses of "new management". Alan's lack seems to surface from issues of skill shortage and training and managerial qualities necessary to do the job. This lack therefore fuels Alan to perpetually justify and legitimize himself as a manager through the ideologies of networking. We suggest that this mask of ideology at one level conceals his ontological insecurity. This mask in my presence was never transparent or removed, Alan presented a fixed and rigid identity to safeguard his insecurities, his lacking, in fear of being disposed. As he states above "you might not be here", and we could add *without this mask*. This reminds us of Bataille's observation:

> Whatever is not useful must be hidden under a mask (cited in Derrida 1978: 263).

Taking this analysis further then, Alan knows that he is lacking and possibly that his skills and managerial performance are disposable in the long term unless he creates and legitimizes a mask of ideology to confront the fluidity that he so fears. Networking becomes a surrogate to mask lack. In his desire to know the other he recognizes difference and his mask of ideology generates sameness. Ideology is therefore a bridge between self and other as he negotiates and contests his identity. Alan is constantly appealing to reduce challenge at the empirical level between the network. Therefore to "know" Alan is to know the other.

Alan only once faced the realities of his situation when we were both leaving the site at the end of the day:

> I was totally lost for four weeks... the change was absolutely astronomical... a massive change. The change in role was totally different than I had imagined, it was an imaginary role... I haven't had any managerial training, but I think I'm coping... it's more comfortable now... Teams are not working well... I am tearing my hair out I'm so stressed [notes taken from informal conversation when leaving the site].

This extract revealed the tension for Alan. The way in which Alan blurted this out and out of the blue, the language is extreme – "lost", "massive", "totally", "tearing", "so stressed". We argue here that the constant pressure of the mask weighing and taking the print of his face – a *mask of performance* – was more of a burden to Alan than a release from his ontological insecurity. This revelation of self during this brief and somewhat awkward moment of melancholy – "not working", "lost" and "difficult to manage" suggest that Alan is mourning self. This contrasts with Bob who mourned the loss of the others. Alan we argue here is *living death* (Linstead 2001b), the living death of ideology. This death is a much preferred state for Alan than to reveal his ontological insecurity in the public domain.

This latent insecurity is reinforced by the permanency of Alan's mask of ideology because rather than simply mask self it *re-forms* self – his face incessantly imprinted with ideology, falsity and superficiality. This is in contrast to Bob who through negotiating past with future, *works his identity* to safeguard himself. Both Bob and Alan have illustrated how they experience ontological insecurity in Carlux and we have seen how lack and loss is inextricably linked with restructuring and the insecurity they face and manage. We could argue that there is a great deal of ambiguity surrounding their role and drawing on the discourses of hierarchy and networking assist in making sense of their vulnerabilities, uncertainties and identities. In the next section, Chris' fragments are explored to illustrate how he draws on co-ordination as a principal feature of both hierarchy and networking to legitimize self. The tensions surrounding this paradox are discussed.

In praise of hierarchy: the drive towards death

Chris, an engineering graduate, joined Carlux in 1986 as a design engineer and then later moved onto project work developing new vehicles. When the "crash" came, as he called it, he said that he decided to stay with the job even though he always intended to go back to his engineering role. The engineering group was downsized from 425 to 120 engineers with only two managers and "a lot" in the team leader role remaining. He was a team leader at the time then he became a manager responsible for 27 people across 3/4 teams. His teams offered a support function to manufacturing. Even though he is not a zone manager responsible for manufacturing the company labelled him one and the company wanted me to talk to him because they felt he was a "high performing manager". I have included him here because he offers an interesting case to illustrate how restructuring influenced specialist functions; how he perceives networking as a high performing manager and how he struggles with and is influenced by the new ways of working. Chris is 36, married and has a small family.

Extract 1   "Product supply has been restructured to reduce boundaries. I am doing things I have never done before, there are more general functions and less expertise... Things were slimmed down to the lowest and perhaps we are a bit too lean now".

Extract 2   "My job is networking between, well negotiating between, project and manufacturing, trying to bring about closer integration but it's hard because some are not equipped, skills that is, to take on the responsibility, so we have structures and ways of working in place but there are gaps. I spend a lot of time chasing the gaps because people can't do what is expected of them with the new structure. The difficulties lie in the traditional boundaries between project and manufacturing".

Extract 3   "I need to maintain internal and external links now... the contractors make it more different... There are power struggles and you need to be very commercially aware because of the internal competition even though we have integrated people. The support wasn't there to develop the processes, structures were changed quickly and some people can't manage it... There is an imbalance of skills, some got and want, some you got and don't want... we need new blood".

Extract 4   "Before team working we did not have contact, they were separate functions that were isolated. Now there is increased *interaction* and teambuilding elements... Areas of specialisms have gone but we knew what we were doing in terms of our responsibilities and jobs. Now we take on areas that we know very little about".

Extract 5   "With TQM came empowering the workforce but they went too far... management [senior] didn't realize the havoc they could reap with empowerment... the *boundaries* disappeared and until boundaries were set up again well, it was hell. Now it is much more open, less protection around job. We had a problem with ownership and authority. As a result problems arising or decision-making were communicated up the *hierarchy* to the appropriate persons, usually senior production managers. There were time delays which led to inefficiencies in manufacturing. Team working has meant better communication, *networking* and increased awareness throughout the organization".

Extract 6   "My role can be summed up as *co-ordinating* actions to achieve objectives and to develop the people. I have an *interfacing* role and that's between management and workers too. You can't get rid of the conflict but it's up to people like me to work between them".

Extract 7   "There has been increased *co-ordination* now because we are structurally nearer... now customers and suppliers are nearer for quicker access, therefore increased *mutual adjustment* improves the quickness in decision-making and problem solving. This happened within areas and across cross-functional teams... The job and function is *unclear*... Our job *stretches* across functions and across the company, for company wide processes".

Extract 8   "My role is one of managing the *cross function* between teams... My role is to manage between departments. It requires checking all the bit that need doing and if they are not done, to get somebody to do it or cover it. I oversee the problems and ensure that the work gets done".

Extract 9   "Managing the *co-ordinatio*n is fine across functions through natural work groups... but it is difficult when you don't know what your are responsible for... I tried to write a list on my responsibilities for my boss but after a day I told him there is too much to list down. I have increased responsibility across the process but you need increased business awareness also to manage the suppliers and customers and this is hard to get used to. Before you just did your bit".

Extract 10   "In this flat structure, *where do you go*? You either go across the company or go out of the company... My role is one that enables me to work across functions and that makes it worthwhile".

Extract 11   "The old ways of working by communicating everything through your manager and keeping your head down and doing just the job that is expected of you, well it wasn't good and we didn't think. Now even though change is here to stay and we have to adapt it is very difficult for some people. They are comfortable with thinking being the managers' job and all they want to do is earn their crust. The old organization was great though, there was no *cloud hanging over us* and in that sense we had more freedom... Now we have to get the job done and get it done well for our sake and the company's. Maybe we have more loyalty now because we *have to make it work, we are in a desperate situation...* The structure used to be top-down and rigid but it helped us see where we *fit* in".

Chris' textual fragments reveal both the processes of restructuring and the associated constraints of hierarchical decision-making and authority and the benefits of increased internal and external networking. However Chris also discusses the benefits of hierarchy. In this section we explore how Chris uses "co-ordination" as a feature of hierarchy and networking. More interestingly we will see how and why Chris draws on and privileges the status of co-ordination as an attribute of hierarchy. However we could argue that this is not surprising given that middle managers have traditionally performed the co-ordination functions vertically and horizontally (Jaques 2000a/b) as Chris illustrates. His specialist role is one of "managing between" traditionally distinct groups: manufacturing and project and this to some extent determines the use of co-ordination (in various forms) in his text. Chris pragmatically raises the problem for him of getting people to change their ways of working and their lack of skills to be able to accommodate and work within a networked structure. As a result he believes that managers have to "oversee the problems and ensure that the work gets done", hence a managerial role of co-ordination (Mintzberg 1973). Furthermore Chris suggests that because of the "conflict" between senior managers and workers, the managers in the middle have a liasing and co-ordinating function.

However, I argue here that Chris draws on co-ordination as a modern and postmodern construct to legitimize himself as a professional. I argue that Chris did this for three reasons: one, the downsizing, ambiguity and insecurity he faces with the change renders him to draw on as co-ordinating to make sense and *stabilize* his identity with the increasing pressures as a person who has a networking role. Two, that

Chris manages the slipping away of traditional forms of control associated with hierarchy to new forms of control associated with restructuring. We could therefore see co-ordination as a *mask of nostalgia*. Three, Chris draws on discourses of networking to constantly justify his identity as "boundary spanner" (Minzberg 1973) or "connector" (Mintzberg 1971) using the words "liason", "interfacer" and "co-ordinator" to illustrate his role as the linking pin (Lawrence and Lorsch 1986). We could question therefore the relevance of middle managers as little more than structural dopes. Chris also highlights how control has shifted and supports Sewell's observations. Sewell (1998) identifies a chimerical form of surveillance for work place monitoring, a hybridized form between the vertical surveillance that is governed by management information systems and the horizontal surveillance of peer group scrutiny.

Chris is particularly interesting because he is seen as an exceptional manager and although he tries to make team working and its associated practices work, he reveals how difficult that is. We see therefore that Chris refers to the old structure and the hierarchical ways of working as a reference point to reveal how "people" find comfort and safety with the known – with hierarchy. Chris draws on the other to legitimize self and we therefore suggest that even though Chris practices networking he too finds safety with hierarchy even though he is unlike others who can't change and practice networking. Fluidity is therefore problematic for Chris' ontological security, a security that he needs to manage his identity. Taking this analysis further then hierarchy provides the structural and ontological support for managers in situations where increasingly fluid structures question "who was I"; "who am I"; "what have I become" and "what do I want to be". At a functional level, increased accountability and less career security also questions who Chris is. He uses "co-ordination" to "fit in" to organization at a time where his identity as a specialist manager is being questioned. Co-ordination is all he knows.

Supporting du Gay (2000) and Jaques (2000a, 2000b) we agree that forecasts of the death of the bureaucratic organization are somewhat premature. The managers in Carlux take refuge from the "procedural, technical and hierarchical organization" (du Gay 2000) which provides the ethical attributes of the good bureaucrat because it represents:

> a moral achievement having to reach a level of competence in a difficult ethical milieu and practice. They are the outcome of a specific organizational **habitus** – declaring one's personal interest, subordinating one's own deeply held convictions to the diktats of

procedural decision-making, etc. – through which individuals learn to comport themselves in a manner befitting the vocation of office-holding (2000: 44).

However in Chris' situation, he adopts a *mask of change* whilst simultaneously drawing on and privileging hierarchy. As Höpfl (2002b), says:

> ... if the required behaviour is to be performed with **authority** and propriety, ambivalence regarding the intention, the direction, the scripting and the framing, needs to be concealed by a mask (emphasis mine).

Thus Chris legitimizes his identity and conceals his insecurities by drawing on a mask that is flexible, ambiguous and ambivalent. At the same time Chris' fragments are governed by co-ordination as a hierarchical weapon – co-ordination is all he knows. Chris is akin to Alan in that through their masks of networking and their negation of insecurity and self they sustain living death. Managers therefore draw on and reinforce hierarchical structures and systems when taking their final breath in what has been for many managers a long process of anticipation within a terminally ill organization. When we are confronted by the death of a loved one, we acknowledge the words of no hope but our coping strategies divert this grief and we engage in last attempts towards managing the palliative process rather than experience loss and confront our lack. I argue here that managers facing severe ontological insecurity draw on the legacy, structure and practices of the healthy organization, using masks of nostalgia, to conceal their insecurities in attempts to resuscitate self. Moreover, it enables managers to suppress their shortcomings, emotions and lack via masks of change and performance. The ontological insecurity experienced by Chris, a high performing manager, is surfaced when we recall moments of melancholy in his text as we experience the demoralization and low-esteem of working with and resuscitating the palliative worker which as such kills self. However saying this, some managers are apt at negotiating with the dead and we see in the next section how Stuart wears masks of change and performance, by drawing heavily on networking, to manage the dead.

Negotiating with the dead: Stuart's dilemmas

Stuart joined Carlux in 1988 as a skilled machinist when he was "put on the job". In 1991 he became a team leader during the restructuring when there was much ambiguity surrounding the role. He is a member of LEAP, the training department, and is perceived by the Manufacturing Director as "the company's shining star". He is called a shift manager (the only one in the company) which is equivalent to the zone manager. He was given this role to secure his employment because there was no zone manager vacancies to promote him to. When I interviewed Stuart he was just taking up a project management role for 12 month project associated with the future restructuring. The company believes that he will become the zone manager of new area of production. Stuart is a very ambitious manager who started studying when he arrived at Carlux. He was looking forward to doing an MBA. He was 32 years and married. Stuart was selected here to show how a high performing manager resists the sameness of the other and uses a mask of change that rests on high performance to negotiate with management and workers. Stuart has high felt job security and his text reveals how this security (which other managers don't have) enables him to understand how other managers draw on hierarchy to manage insecurity and legitimize self. We also observe how Stuart manages, self-promotes and thrives in a melancholic environment. The seductive capacity of the cultural controls associated with a team working agenda is in high evidence.

Extract 1   "There are still *some who just don't understand* why the company is moving in the way it is and *they don't want to understand* what is going on because that is their background, their culture. They don't particularly want to accept the change, they see others who have and are having a good time [the people that have bought into the new ways of working] but they don't... perhaps that is good because they are spurring those who want to do it on".

Extract 2   "You need to adopt a style that can be flexible enough to deal with many many situations... Being aware of people... a PR person, a listener".

Extract 3   "People have been given the chance to respond (to this HR culture change) to what is going on and *the manager is in between*... People are *afraid* to come forward, they want to know things but they won't... now things are changing... I think it is working and I'm a go-between".

Extract 4   "I was so stressed coming from the shop floor and feeling like 'a fish out of water'. Now it has advantages in that they say 'you know what it's like you've been one of us'... I never go anywhere now and say 'I want these by so and so, now its is there any chance or *how can we...?*' Asking about collective ownership he said 'It's got to be we'".

Extract 5   "The hardest part for me at the minute is finding out what the company wants, what the role is and what is expected from your staff... because I know what the company structure is going to be and what is going to happen to manufacturing and what role I have been asked to play *I know I'm going to be OK* but many of my colleagues and past bosses are not going to be as lucky... There will be more outsourcing, machinery being sold off and more cutbacks and redeployment predicted. This isn't a one off, change is here to stay and it is getting people to believe in this and move with it".

Extract 6   "There are some people who feel like, well, change has got to have benefits and sometimes it is change for change sake sometimes. The company has gone through a lot of pain... and a lot of it is the result of that, it's the fact that in the early days we were working 24 hours a day to help to pull the company around... it's only in the last 12 months that the *fears are coming through, those sorts of concerns are coming back.* We did accept them [the changes] under extreme conditions, now that those issues have disappeared and reality is coming back into it, so the old concerns... are coming to the forefront".

Extract 7   "It is very difficult to understand what the new role of the manager is all about.... The most important thing for the manager is to use his personality and communication but I understand why the one's that can't or won't change can't buy into *our way* of thinking".

Extract 8   "In the last three years I have not known what my job is, there is no one else like me in the factory. They created this job because they couldn't promote me to the zone manager position because all the zones had managers. They knew I would have walked if they hadn't done something to keep me. I'm lucky but I would be better off in terms of getting a career [pause], I'm very ambitious, in the old Carlux".

Extract 9   "There are many people here on the shop floor and in management who are more *comfortable with the ways things were*. They have lost their identity 'cos there's no identity around skills or jobs but processes, and people haven't identified themselves with the processes so many of them still work as they used to because it *helps them make sense of things*. But I have moved on and had to make it work, I had no choice and well, *you have to put yourself first*, second and last. If this is at the *expense of someone else* then so be it".

Extract 10   "When I was a team leader it was difficult to get people to change, *I had to change and that was hard*. I had men much older than me with much more technical experience not wanting to move on, it was hard for them and some of them won't change. They used to sideline me and go to the zone manager because they thought it was the old foreman. People loved the foreman".

Stuart's data are attractive as a younger manager who has worked his way to a management post and educated himself along the way. He is a high performing manager who is highly committed to the goals of the emerging organization and extremely ambitious whilst at the same time as being sympathetic to the toils of his colleagues and staff. However his text reveals many tensions. On the one hand Stuart empathizes with the people who haven't changed and developed their roles and skills in keeping with the expectations of the organization. We see in one of the fragments how Stuart conceptualizes his role as working out what the organization wants; how to deliver these expectations; and assisting his staff to change. Thus we see Stuart constructing his role in keeping with the new discourses of management. On the other hand, Stuart is elitist with his allegiance to "our way" of doing things. Moreover Stuart engages in competitive discourse associated with traditional working class masculinity (Donaldson 1991). His recognition that adapting to change is difficult could be viewed as being supportive of his colleagues who face great barriers trying to accommodate change or simply patronizing that he has achieved what others can't. He therefore constructs himself as a high performing manager based on the other.

Stuart at moments in his text refers to the melancholy of the environment in which he finds himself but this, from my observations, does not deter him. Rather he is "spurred on" by his faith in the system and/or the challenge for him. Stuart in our engagements presents unquestioning loyalty to Carlux which seems to stem from his "I'm alright Jack" attitude. He is pragmatic and I would argue ruthless over his support to those individuals around him; he will guide and develop others who are "willing" but those that do not buy into his discourse are cast to one side – to die. Stuart seems to thrive on the decaying flesh of the dead – the others are his feeding ground. Burrell's (1992) corporate liposuction can be taken further into "corporate phalloplasty" (Linstead 1996) whereby the power of the masculine phallus is reinforced by individuals like Stuart, and perhaps more importantly his senior managers, who thrive on eager, ambitious and devoted employees like Stuart, who take the symbolic flesh from one part of the body (the dead, redundant "fat" of the "slimmed down" organization) to reinforce the potency of other parts of the organization – which includes their own power. This is because even where they are not senior enough to be considered part of the corporate phallus, ambitious and narcissistic managers like Stuart provide harsher, more competitive environments for palliative or dead colleagues that feeds, fuels and regenerates their own energies and their ability to thrive and get things done in the interests of their own advancement (for an extended treatment of a different but similar metaphor of the "vampire", see Kemske 1996). Stuart draws on ideas of fluidity and employs masks of change to justify his competitive masculinity (Collinson and Hearn 1996). With resonance, Kanter (1990: 355–9 cited in du Gay 2000: 79) thus warns of the romantic shift from bureaucratic to entrepreneurial forms of management that makes, as du Gay comments:

> forging a career a more uncertain and political affair. It involves the eradication of various formal rules, regulations and procedures and their replacement by informal networks and an emphasis on individual creativity and deal-making. In other words, the contemporary "entrepreneurial subjectification" of the workplace places considerable responsibility on the shoulders of individuals for their own advancement (du Gay 2000: 79).

Structuring masculinity

Hierarchy, as a principal feature of modernism having tendencies of differentiation (specialization, complexity) and organization (rationalization, commodification) can be pulled apart by technological advancements which make it possible to decouple organizational function from structure. The discursive shift from structural order, rigidity and linearity to flexible specialization has to some extent been evidenced in Carlux. Structures of control and co-ordination were broken down and replaced by new and more flexible alternatives (Thompson and Warhurst 1998), supported by advanced technological developments. Boundary erosion between organizations, suppliers, partners and customers both within and external to Carlux has shown that networking influences actual and available managerial roles. Indeed managers negotiate their identities across broader social arrangements where existing boundaries have been removed or extended. Chapter 2 highlighted parallel changes in structural configurations in organizations have influenced managers' roles by extending their tasks across wider functional and organizational arenas. Although there is no doubt that the organizational form has changed in Carlux, we have been concerned here with how and why middle managers in the company draw on hierarchy and elements of networking as core concepts in shaping their identities.

Processes of restructuring and other associated changes have propelled the managers studied into a continuous process of reforming their attachments to their organization. We have argued that this "extra" identity work is an outcome of ontological insecurity. Bob, Alan, and Chris provide examples stemming from their experiences of external loss and/or internal lack in the interviews recalled in this chapter. Bob mourned the loss of the workforce, his former colleagues, with downsizing and restructuring. Chris mourned the loss of skills, experience and managers' personal sovereignty associated with the restructuring. Alan however does not outwardly discuss loss but rather due to his felt inadequacies reveals insecurity over who he now is through melancholic reflection over his inability to manage his identity. Stuart by contrast is ambitious and buoyant stemming from his security in the company as a "rising star". However, despite their different situations, *all* these managers draw on discourses of hierarchy *and* networking to shape their subjectivities in Carlux. We have seen how drawing on hierarchy to some extent could be a process of nostalgic reclamation of a safe epistemological space which provides ontological shelter for protection and safety for them – it is all they know. Networking, in the case of Alan, becomes then a mask of performance, an ideology, that bridges self and other – the performing other. Stuart could and possibly is constructed as part of this performative other. Bob, Stuart and Chris don masks of change to legitimize self. I illustrated that loss of self has revealed itself in differing ways: Bob blessed with the "gift of death" (Derrida 1995), resigned to managerial mortality; in contrast Alan, Chris and to a lesser extent Stuart facing a living death, their self slipping away in their constant competitive struggle to be "other", or to cope with not being "other".

So if we take the structural shift from modern to postmodern forms of organizing for granted we may expect managers uniformly to draw on discourses of networking to justify their new roles and identities. Not surprisingly managers do draw on networking but as an ideological mask of performance, behind which it remains an as yet unrealized or partially realized vision. The desire, from a Freudian position, for hierarchy on the other hand appears abundantly in managers' accounts, as this comforting structure expresses that there is a rationality in operation at some level which fills the lack of a certain knowledge of what the future will be and promises that it will unfold in a predictable manner if the present operates that way. As I noted in my discussion of Burrell and Sievers, hierarchy is reproduced and reinforced both formally and socially in organizations because it squeezes the life out of people to the point at which they lose the ability to be themselves without it: thus they must attempt to reproduce it in order to cling onto some sense of vitality and meaning. When they appear no longer to fit into the hierarchy, they become insecure and must resort to the use of masks to conceal emotion, vulnerabilities and struggles for meaning. But masking self conceals not the self but the death or lack of self. The masks used surface different aspects of self as a form of "face-work" but we can conclude that Stuart and Chris don these masks to buy time to work out *who* they are and *what* they need to do to become it. Combined with the skills and education they possess, these masks assist them in creating a privileged and fortunate position for themselves. In contrast Bob and Alan *become the mask* – they can't perform in the same ways that Chris and Stuart can and because of their vulnerabilities – they can no longer believe in what they were – they have no option but to believe in the masks. This has worked for Bob but even masks inevitably must change – the permanency that they ascribe to their mask is problematic for positioning themselves in the organization as ironically it is *masking change*. These masks provide an opportunity for generating, maintaining and sustaining *sameness*. Alan and Bob in recognizing difference in relation to the other adopt masks of performance, ideology and change to create the same. They fail to compete, they fail to be fully associated with the qualities and characteristics of the mask, the permanency and rigidity of the mask does not transform quickly or cleverly enough and gives them away. Stuart on the other hand thrives on difference. Stuart's masks of change and collective concern conceal his desire for self-promotion; to improve his own performance by living off the (still warm) remains of the dead.

In this chapter we have seen how managers don masks to suppress, conceal and protect their insecurities. These masks create melancholia in Carlux, but masks can also be liberating. For example Stuart reveals how a mask of change that capitalizes on the potential of the fluid can transcend the situations that Alan and Chris find themselves in – that of the living death. Bob's mask of change conceals his contentment with the gift of death. There is some sense then that to create sameness, managers are donning collective, shared masks, or at least taking their masks from the same property box. To survive long term then masks may need to be adaptable, in flux and unique for the individual. These masks promote competitiveness and self-interest that enables managers to outperform others, be recognized and gather the benefits.

Even though we have witnessed changes in structural form in Carlux, the informal and social hierarchies, which lubricate the formal hierarchy, are alive and well. Hierarchy, a principle feature of bureaucracy (Bologh 1990; Morgan 1996; du Gay 2000), is a *masculine* organizational form. Even though networking has been seen to feminize the workplace (Dickens 1998; Wajcman 1998), the managers in Carlux find solace operating through masculine modes of hierarchy in a disturbing context of feminized organizational forms. The managers we have studied here in their unique ways reinforce *new* hierarchical relations. However I am concerned here with the prevalence and persistence of hierarchy as a core function of management. My research then supports Gowler and Legge's assertion that hierarchy is a defining concept of what management is – in its time – and, we argue here, *who* these middle managers are. They construct and maintain projects of modernity and self-identity (see Lash and Friedman 1992) for improving their fragile grip on ontological security. Even though the managers we have discussed have little agency surrounding the restructuring, we have witnessed emphatically that "breaking up is hard to do" and managers depend upon both the social and formal hierarchy for a sense of ontological security. As Stone elucidates:

In the discourses with which we are perhaps most familiar, the self appears to be constant, unchanging, the stable product of a moment in Western history (Stone 1995: 19–20).

Which is to say that as Westerners, *all* the discourses which confront us, socially, educationally, legally and formally, retain this understanding that the self is unitary, and to behave otherwise is to be untrue to oneself, unbalanced and sociopathic in that it makes it difficult for others – individuals, agencies, social gatherings – to deal with the changing of fluid selves. Perhaps the earliest realization of the inter-penetration of work selves and non-work selves was captured by Stephen Fineman (1983). In his study of a large sample of unemployed or recently unemployed managers, he found that the loss of work entailed a profound loss of identity; experience of non-work made it much harder – indeed impossible – for managers to resume their work identity without it being modified in very significant ways. Hierarchy as a self-defining feature of identity work becomes even more problematic, for example poststructuralist thinkers (Bauman 1989, 1993; Burrell 1997) and feminists (Ferguson 1984; Savage and Witz 1992; Billing and Alvesson 1994) alike have long warned of the dangers of the bureau-cratic organization. Hierarchy oppresses, difference is denied. The gen-dered implications of drawing on hierarchy were discussed here but it was not my intention to provide a gendered analysis of bureaucracy (see Bologh 1990). However, Morgan (1996) has raised two central issues which are worthy of our attention: one, bureaucracies are major sites for the development of modern masculinities and two, men are more than likely to be carrying out *managerial* functions in a bureaucratic office. My data revealed how managers in constructing their identities draw on masculinized notions of rationality. The Carlux case has shown how the company, with no women in management positions is both numeri-cally and culturally gendered to favour the masculine. Feminist analyses have already explored not just the lack of women in bureaucracies but revealed that there has been no questioning of the roles of men within them (see Morgan ibid.). Accordingly one of my interests in this book and particularly this chapter is in how modern masculinities are repro-duced. Hierarchy is associated with legitimate power and legitimate power is historically associated with the masculine in Carlux. Hierarchy not only "ungenders" individuals (Morgan 1996: 57) but disembodies them too, in treating them independently of their bodily characteris-tics, as though the maleness of managers is irrelevant (Kerfoot and Knights 1999; Lennie 1999).

During periods of survival, competition and performance are paramount as individual managers vie for power; they too want to be part of and ascend in the hierarchy. Weaving a text from education, performance, age, commitment, and appropriate social networks becomes paramount. We have seen how managers "do masculinity" (after Morgan 1996). Perhaps surprisingly none of the managers in this company talked of their home lives being affected by their work, but the findings in this chapter support Morgan's (1996: 51) analysis that managers in bureaucracies leave their work identity at work, able to compartmentalize their life *only if* the sexual division of labour remains intact. This supports one of the traditional dimensions of masculinity – that of the breadwinner – discussed in Donaldson's (1991) research on working class masculinities. Furthermore, with increased pressures of working longer hours, work intensification, and demands for demonstrating commitment to work our findings support existing studies that work identity subsumes other identities. Traditional masculinity then gives way to a "more complex and less stable one" (Morgan 1996: 51). However the data I have here do not support this, although managers reproducing and reinforcing traditional modes of masculinity seem to be making a last stand against pressures of change.

Management has long been thought of as synonymous with masculinity (Kerfoot and Knights 1993). The relevance of the masks I have identified in use for the managers studied here is articulated by Höpfl, who contends in her analysis of performance:

> The mask is the site of multiple possibilities and, in collapse, of heterogeneity. The apparent coherence and consensus regarding the collapse the definition of the event depends primarily on masking. The dramatic mask conceals ambivalence about the role, about performance and about the production but it is not infallible nor, indeed, irreversible. When the mask fails the performance is thrown into question: becomes ludicrous. For the actor, the extent of his/her degradation [i.e. the dissolution of self into the mask] is revealed (Höpfl 2002b: 266).

The art of perfecting these masks then is of great importance to the managers studied. These masks, masks of masculinities, multiple and competing masculinities, protect the visible "self" from the revelation of its corruption, its degradation, vulnerabilities and insecurities. The dramatic mask to which Höpfl refers, a feminized front, is one of change and networking which conceals the underlying masculine hierarchy. The desire for hierarchy, for order, stability and security, involves the managers analyzed in processes of "fixing". This fixing has masculinist underpinnings and as Kerfoot contends reveals how masks are used to *validate* achievement and performance:

> those for whom masculinity resonates most loudly appear to be so preoccupied with "fixing" the world around them and others in it as to detract from the possibilities of other forms of engagement. As a result, in its concerns to achieve a fixity in social relations and quash the "uncontrollable" elements of everyday existence, masculinity expends considerable energy in the drive for success, and overlooks the possibilities for other forms of interaction. Yet even this success in conquering the insecurity that is itself both a condition and consequence of "the social" and of masculinity, can only ever be so momentary and superficial, such that its achievement requires constant **validation** (Kerfoot 1999: 185, *emphasis added*).

Kerfoot continues to reveal how masculine subjects strive for control, a fundamental element of hierarchy, which I argue contributes to the demise of self:

> Masculine subjects thereby deny the possibility for "play" within social relations – of shifting between subject positions – for masculinity and management necessitate that the other is subordinated to self. Masculine subjectivity is equally unreflexive and unreflective in its unwillingness, or sheer inability, to challenge the conditions of its own perpetuation, however self-destructive or impoverishing the consequences (Kerfoot 1999: 197).

The managerial masks appropriated are masks of masculinity. They paradoxically mask and suppress the feminine by reinstating hierarchy on the one hand whilst masquerading the feminine as ideology in forming their identities. As Lechte (1996: 19 cited in Moodley 1999: 222) states:

> ... the repressed, which can never appear directly in language... always takes a mask like quality. The mask as a virtual object, is also always displaced. The repressed, unable to appear directly in symbolic form, therefore becomes a mask.

Furthermore, for Moodley:

> ...contemporary man-agement practices through the dis-play of multiple mask(ulinities) hegemonic, compassionate, contrary to "mission(ary) and equal opportunity philosophies" – are still subjecting the "other" to oppressive practices and organizational hierarchies. It seems that when the masculine/managerial masks slip, they reveal forms of dominant and hegemonic masculinities that deny the subjectivity of the "other" (Moodley 1999: 215).

Perhaps what we have witnessed in the managers' fragments presented here is the masquerade of masculinities, the desire for phallic hierarchy to perpetuate masculine hegemony. Yet the masks of networking and change barely conceal that managers are propping up their identities through modernist projects of who and what they are. Their sense of identity, which has after all been built up in a social context in which individuality is associated with differentiation, even if that differentiation is achieved via taking a particular role within a differentiated system, is tied up with having a strong sense of their difference from others, yet an equally strong sense of relating to others via a co-ordinating structure. Drives toward networking dismantle the system and put nothing in its place except pure de-differentiated relationality, where structure, however temporary, emerges from the patterning of relations in interaction – there is no way of knowing who you are in this environment until interactions in the network stabilize and define you, however temporarily unless some metaqualities outside and above the chaos can be found to act in this way. But the postmodern shift implicit in the move to networking places these metaqualities, along with the knowledge needed to validate them, in motion as well, and makes them at least partially unstable, shifting and emergent. The mask of networking, where the managers appear to be embracing the networking discourse but are not fully engaging in the practices which should flow from it, subverts the postmodern shift and reproduces and reinforces masculine forms of management. For managers who found the disciplinary gaze of modernist structures a means to avoid the anguish of ontological insecurity, the responsibility for self that comes with postmodern relationality may be too much to bear. The hierarchical constructions which sustained their sense of self were in a literal sense "erections", and as such bound to subside into inevitable detumescence without structural or cultural prostheses sustaining them (Höpfl 2002a). Managers are allowing themselves to be seduced, at one level, by postmodernist agendas whilst finding solace in modernist projects of forming and maintaining self, and being to varying degrees, behind the mask, torn between the two. And so:

> The actors in this theatre are seen as a never ending masquerade, a parody, a carnival of masculinities acting out at the intersubjective level the full range of emotions and behaviours... The masculine masquerade in turn renders the "other" as invisible to the candidature of management and managerial discourses (Moodley 1999: 221).

6
Seduction in Nylons

...we have to keep the people switched on and improve their motivation from where they are in this moment in time. We expect them to do more and do more better, and I'm not sure we can do that with the background and history we have got at the moment. We need culture change (Brian Personnel Director, Nylons).

... Increased competitive pressure has sharpened what has always been a point of difference between companies, namely time, into a strategic issue. Time appears in the business world in many guises: time-to-market, down-time, real time, customer-facing time, fee-earning time, on-time. Some companies realise that these terms are part of a business shift from economies of scale to economies of time. It is the speed and responsiveness of an organization that now gives it a comparative advantage.... It is no longer good enough to have the right product at the right price. It also has to be in the right place at the right time. All factors have to be present to satisfy customers. This changes the rules of the game. (Kreitzman 1999:121–2)

Introduction: from compression to commitment?

In Gowler and Legge's model, achievement and being able to demonstrate achievement, was one of the defining qualities of "management" in the rhetoric of managers. We could suggest that in some ways we would not expect it ever to disappear entirely. But the problem arises of how achievement may be defined and evaluated in a world "which has speeded up so as to make, as the saying has it "twenty-four hours a very long time" (Harvey 1990: 285). Indeed, so complex is this world that the most successful and talented can be made long-term ill by conditions such as "yuppie flu" or myalgic encephalitis (ME), the Epstein-Barre virus, and similar forms of Chronic Fatigue Syndrome (CFS). Why should this happen, and why do managers seem nevertheless so willing to engage in practices which sustain it, even whilst expressing sentiments like Kreitzman's (1999: 134) respondent "Mike Dollar's children will not go into the same business as him. At least, not if he can help it".

This introduction can therefore serve as an introduction to both this chapter and the one that follows. Indeed, whilst the previous chapter concentrated on exploring the possible horizontal shift from hierarchy to networking, this chapter opens up the fact that relations are also vertical – for example between hierarchy and accountability, networking and seduction and seduction and commitment – but also diagonal – for example between seduction and achievement and commitment and accountability. It could be argued that the postmodern shift in sensibilities has set categories in motion, acting not in a linear way, as we noted in the last chapter, but in terms of relations in many directions which are sometimes reversible, sometimes reciprocal, sometimes not. Indeed so close is the relationship between seduction and commitment that it is only justifiable to separate them for the convenience of analysis here.

In this chapter I start from the position, following Harvey (1990), that the phenomena that Kreitzman observes are the result of the latest and perhaps most spectacular phase of historical time-space compression, where the acceleration of the development of technological and informational systems has added a new dimension to capitalism's historical and paradoxical need for growth and further accumulation, even in conditions of over-accumulation and post-scarcity, which produces the need to find new forms of *flexible* accumulation and therefore new "spaces" – geographical and cultural – to exploit. Speed of manufacturing production, speed of information flow to and from markets, speed of flow of capital through deregulated financial and trading systems, speed of transportation which takes advantage of distributing manufacturing around the world and establishing localized partial assembly functions to put together products with flexible features have had spectacular results in increasing the availability and reducing the cost of products, with short time-to-market and rapid modification and monitoring of customers' needs and preferences. Economies are economies of time and space, not just of material value.

Furthermore, as Lash and Urry (1993: 10–11) note, the rapid flow of information cannot be fully organized because there is not time to screen and evaluate all information. The more information and knowledge flows, the more problems and paradoxes and unforeseen consequences occur, and the more such a system depends on individuals who are *reflexive*, aware of emerging problems and committed to coming up with at least partial solutions to them. *Disorganized* capitalism is sustained by *reflexive* accumulation – what Virilio calls the dromocratic condition (Virilio 1991). As Harvey notes, this entails a good deal of risk:

> Time-space compression always exacts a toll on our capacity to grapple with the realities unfolding around us. Under stress, for example, it becomes harder and harder to react to events...the world's financial markets are on the boil in ways that make a snap judgement here, an unconsidered word there and a gut reaction somewhere else the slip that can unravel the whole skein of fictitious capital formation and of interdependency (Harvey 1990: 306).

For managers in companies such as Nylons and Larts (see Chapter 7), these issues may be removed from their everyday experiences, but as Harvey (1990: 285) demonstrates, they carry through and affect managers' ways of thinking, feeling and doing. Most tellingly for this chapter, in a world where unforeseen problems are thrown up constantly and there is rarely time to respond to them in a considered way, how can it be possible to hold people *accountable*? How can rational procedures be followed to the letter when there is no time to follow rational evaluation procedures? This goes beyond Simon's "satisficing" because even though Simon (1960) recognized that rationality is bounded, and we often settle for the best decision that can be made in circumstances of imperfect information, the problem often is a problem of too much information, some of which may be contradictory, none of which is stable, all of which is likely to change rapidly, and where the degree and extensiveness of interconnection and interconnectedness, as familiar from chaos and complexity theories, can mean that a small change in one part of the nexus – *including this decision* – could produce changes elsewhere which might transform the whole. Similarly with the problem of when can *achievement* be demonstrated and performance properly evaluated? We would expect then that there would be, at one level, a proliferation of ever-changing performance measurement and evaluation systems, in many cases a modernist act of faith, but also that organizations would need to be able to know that they had managers who were *reflexive* and *committed* to trying to solve unanticipated problems quickly and in the right way with insufficient time to do so. In a world where time and space are compressed, competence may have to mean not achievement but commitment, signalled by availability – 24/7 in some cases in Kreitzman's 24-hour society. Accountability may mean not following rules and procedures, but having the right values and mindset to respond in the right way, to be a good corporate citizen even in deviating and transgressing existing norms. I should also note, accordingly, from my reading of Lash and Urry (1993) and Baudrillard (1981), that the new compressed economies of time and space need to be sustained symbolically, and responsible participation in and commitment to them consolidated as far as such things can be, by economies of signs, cultural developments where identities can be formed and commitment can be *seduced* into being. Indeed, this is only to take Gowler and Legge's arguments about rhetoric into further symbolic realms. *Accountability* is not so much demonstrated by doing the right thing, but by being the right person, and as we shall see in this chapter, managers are no longer simply disciplined into being good and compliant corporate citizens, although some of this may be still be in evidence; nor is fearful self-monitoring against the imagined gaze of absent authority as a form of internalized self-discipline enough; but they also need to be *seduced* into a corporate culture which simultaneously validates their identity and mandates creative action – but in which they buy both the rules and the values and visions of the future at a cost to their sovereignty over their self. *Achievement* then we should expect to slide into the recognition of *commitment*, which is displayed rather than measured, as managers attempt to ensure that they are defined by their seniors as members of the more or less permanent *core* of the organization, with its attendant privileges, rather than the disposable and ephemeral *periphery*. But seduction and commitment are ultimately inseparable as processes.

In terms of the general processes at work, moving from control by rationality, which underpins accountability, we would expect to be replaced by a more symbolic and fluid control, or steerage, by signs which deliver a state of enchantment. The third movement, which I will discuss in Chapter 7, is driven by a process of commodification, where managers move from being the producers of commodities, or the controllers of commodity production, to commodities themselves, to be consumed by the organization. This argument I will take up in the next chapter, but for this one I will return to the process of enchanting the workplace, which requires managers to represent their activities in new and different ways than traditional forms of accounting.

Management-as-accountability

In Chapter 3 *management-as-accountability* was referred to as the accounting practices and forms of accountability where roles and structural relationships are linked to and assist with constructing the "moral environment" which then becomes "the right to manage power and exchange relationships" (Gowler and Legge 1996: 42). This form of control provides middle managers with functional role clarity deriving from task and goal directed behaviours upon which performance is assessed. It renders management activity *visible* in particular ways. We have seen throughout this book that restructuring middle managers' task roles has to a great extent resulted in a loss of directive functional responsibilities and associated performance criteria, alongside increased autonomous working, devolved management, more generic responsibilities and increased accountability (albeit in a different form). This is no exception in Nylons, a manufacturing organization that has undergone extensive restructuring and as such the ontological anxiety and insecurity experienced by the middle managers germinated within an uncertain and ambiguous environment. For many managers, as we have seen in the previous chapter, increased performance and accountability goes hand-in-hand with increased pressures which manifests in several ways such as stress, the neglect of family life, increasing working hours and managing visibility. However the Management in Three Movements Framework developed in Chapter 3 hypothesized that the control measures upon which managers are assessed and held accountable have discursively shifted from structurally related accounting practices to cultural controls which are unconscious and covert interventions which may be bound inextricably with managerial and professional discourses. Ambiguity surrounding managers' roles in Nylons suggest that managers have more generic roles but experience more *accountability*, albeit under a different guise in the restructured Nylons. The discourses of accountability as we will see are closely linked to the visibility of their performance, and the performance of their identity work, which is conjoined with managerial achievement and commitment.

In this chapter then I explore the hypothesized relationship between the "complete clarity and visibility associated with modernity" (Ritzer 1999) that provided managers with grounds for accountability and ontological security when doing identity work (Giddens 1991) and the play and illusion that are offered by discourses of cultural seduction (Baudrillard 1990; Calás and Smircich 1991). The middle management cohort had, at the time of the study, experienced endless restructuring exercises and we will see three managers drawing on discourses of accountability (and hierarchy) and seduction in modernist projects which attempt to secure and represent self-identities which emphasized certainty and *belonging* to their organization (see Peter's text below). The texts reveal tensions between accommodating organizational demands which infers that individuals are being controlled by seductive forms of workplace control whilst at the same time resisting aspects of the organization, change or individuals (as we will see from Dan's account below). I may wish to argue that verbalizing resistance during the research process may be a response to being seduced (particularly in the case of Steve below). These data prepare the route for our analysis of resistance in Chapter 8 when I employ Alistair's text to demonstrate how refusal to engage with the changes taking place prevents his self-identity being consumed, manipulated and shaped by the seductive discourses at play in Nylons. Alistair engages in a postmodern identity project which is fragmented, in flux and which has the potential to influence others and the organization and bring about change. The power relations of Alistair's "hidden transcript" offer a new way of theorizing resistance (Scott 1992).

Collusion and the willing colonization of the subject

Seduction, from the Latin *seducere*, has been defined as "seducing to wrong", "the process of attracting or charming", "enticement", or "the act of leading aside" (Shorter Oxford Dictionary). To explore the processes of identity construction, seduction is conceptualized as an unconscious, fluid process by which, in this case, an organization entices individuals into embracing a new form of symbolic organizational control which replaces surveillance, discipline, reward and sanction (see Ray 1986; Kunda 1992; Willmott 1993; Casey 1995; du Gay 1991, 1993; Barker 1993) through technical and structural means (see Collinson 1992; Prasad and Prasad 1998; Gabriel 1999; May 1999; Knights and McCabe 2000; Fleming and Sewell 2002) and which capitalize on cultural and social relationships to *gently divert* an individual's effort. However supporting Thompson and Ackroyd (1999) and Fleming and Sewell (2002) the unquestioning colonization of these subjects by cultural control is critiqued since they lack the influence of individual agency, of resistance. Furthermore resistance "is thought of as a purely overt, organised, and open economic practices" (Kondo 1990; Edwards et al 1995; Fleming and Sewell 2002: 4) and we can see this in some feminisms. I am interested here in a micro-analysis of resistance at the level of the individual which are more subtle, unorganized, subjective, fluid and ambiguous. Edwards et al note how overt and organized resistance are privileged in studies of resistance which makes us aware of the shortcomings of feminist resistance and the potential of "feminine" forms of resistance. The authors state how:

> The majority of research studies... focus on the visible, explicit and collective oppositional practices such as output restriction and sabotage... Yet there are also many other oppositional practices that are often more subtle, covert and secretive and frequently less collective and organized (1995: 291 cited in Fleming and Sewell 2002: 10).

In this chapter I explore how the restructuring in Nylons made the middle managers feel vulnerable, detached from the organization and sceptical of current and future change. The interviewing process became the arena in which the managers studied verbalized different subject positions to legitimize what they did (functional role tasks primarily) in the organization. These modernist identity projects were enabled by the managers drawing on discourses of accountability and hierarchy to legitimize self and in Peter's case this became a means of justifying and reclaiming professional autonomy, status and managerial sovereignty during the research. Furthermore these processes of retrospective accounting enable individuals to resist and have some agency within episodes of current organizational and individual change. Dan on the other hand appears to accommodate change and his text reveals discourses of seduction which include being more involved, supporting the change, and creating a sense of *belonging* to the organization, an outwardly committed individual during his identity project.

This chapter reveals how seductive processes in Nylons play out in the formation of middle managers' identities, highlighting specifically the resisting processes of recalcitration and compliance. Conducting a gendered reading of the data reveals how Nylons employed feminine capital to outwardly bring about change and it could be argued seduce its members. Baudrillard (1990) explores the relationship between seduction and the feminine stating:

> ... seduction and femininity are confounded, indeed confused. Masculinity has always been haunted by this sudden reversibility

within the feminine. Seduction and femininity are ineluctable as the reverse side of sex, meaning and power (1990: 2).

The power of the feminine to seduce the masculine, and we may argue destabilize the dialectical structure (man/woman) that dominates the formation of subjectivity, cannot be underestimated. Within the masculine discourses of management and organization theory, woman becomes presented as the Other, necessary to the constitution of identity but always threatening to it (Cixous and Clément 1986). "Woman" is the site of the fluid and relational, those elements of human experience and consciousness which evade definition, measurement, formal construction and explicit expression – which both sustains and subverts rational modes of organization, presenting new creative opportunities but also a destabilizing threat. In Nylons the head office *installed* Nina, the first female site manager, to "turn the South Wales factory around". Subsequently, the management team introduced women on the shop floor to "bring about change" (direct quote from Nia [Site Manager] and Brian [Personnel Director]. The employment of feminine capital as an organizational strategy to seduce managers to accommodate and possibly comply with the new forms of work organization was overt. Thus, following Cixous, after Hegel, the subject (in this case some of the male workers and managers) requires a recognition of an Other from whom individuals differentiate themselves. Yet this recognition is experienced as threatening and the Other (woman) is immediately repressed, so that the subject can return to the security and certainty of self-knowledge. Together with the experiences of restructuring, the recruitment of "these women" (direct quote) influenced and dominated the middle managers' identity projects.

I start this chapter by presenting the Nylons Case Study and discussing in particular the changes that influenced the middle management cohort. In the next section the gendered interventions that Nylons employed through the employment and overt manipulation of women to seduce, create a response from the middle managers, and consequently bring about change in the men are discussed. Seduction in this chapter is firstly explored at an organizational level by exploring the recruitment of women in Nylons as change agents and how this influences its organizational members. Secondly, at a managerial level we examine whether managers draw on discourses of seduction and/or accountability to construct, legitimize and manage their sense of self during their identity projects. We will see how Dan in particular reveals elements of Casey's "colluded self" which suggests that at some level the change interventions at Nylons have influenced his presentation of self, of which he is aware.

I then go on to argue that the texts of Peter, Dan and Steve, engaged in modernist projects of identity in attempts to gain ontological security, resist the feminine other (the other within and the women in the organization) which in turn reinforces their masculinity which further renders the feminine as abject. The chapter draws to its conclusion by highlighting three key issues that future research on identity need to pay further attention to the construction of postmodern identities by employing alternative practices of resistance to subvert organization and which problematizes the resistance and compliance dichotomy (see Alistair's text in Chapter 8).

Cultural change in Nylons

Nylons is a manufacturing organization which produces polyester and allied materials in South Wales, UK which is part of an international conglomerate of fabric manufacturers. The company was the main employer in a run down, working class town. The site was owned by a national specialist nylon manufacturer when it started in 1948 and employed 400 people. In 1966 a British based multinational producer of related products took over the company which employed 7,000 people at the time and made nylon until 1993 when Nylons acquired it. There has been continual downsizing and restructuring from the 1970s until 1993 as a result of advancements in production and technology making nylon yarn and diffused nylon in one factory and polyester in another. The company has reduced in size from two factories to one and employee numbers have decreased from 3,000 in 1990 to 150 in 1998. During this time the plant had several site managers and this contributed to great instability and insecurity for the plant as a whole. Traditionally when the steel works and coal mines were still producing in the area, the workforce was primarily female which is interesting given the sexual division of labour in the area and the role of women as mothers and housewives and men as breadwinners. This has gradually changed over time and in 1998 the company employed men in managerial and shop floor positions. Women employed were positioned in administration. In 1998 a new female site manager Nia, the first one ever in the company's history, had been assigned to Nylons to "bring about change". Nia was in her early 30s, German and was part of the parent company's fast track executive programme. Nia was in herself a culture shock for the company. Her predecessors had all been male, aged between 40 and 50, Welsh, and recruited at the site rather than assigned to the site from head office personnel.

The restructuring involved closing one factory and those jobs whose functions spanned across the site remained employed in the other factory. Periphery jobs were redundant. In 1994 more jobs were cut from 150 to 132 to the "bare minimum" (Personnel Officer). Roles were broadened to replace lost skills, subcontractors were employed to improve numerical flexibility. During the restructuring the company has reduced its hierarchical organizational structure from seven to four levels. Nylons' flat structure consists of a site manager, functional directors, team managers and production staff. To implement High Performance Work Systems (HPWS) the old foreman/production manager's role was replaced by the team manager to encourage team involvement and responsibility, which necessitated a more "hands off" role for managers. However due to the lack of training for team members most teams were operating with "hands on" management because the teams weren't equipped with the necessary skills and resources.

Since 1994 there have been low-key efforts to develop a High Performance Work System, facilitated by newly appointed team managers. However due to limited financial investment team working across the site remains fragmented. The factory operates a 24 hour production system with seven shifts working. The "softer" behavioural aspects of teamwork organization exist in only two out of seven shifts. Amongst the teams there is a general atmosphere of low motivation and job dissatisfaction. Traditional, rigid and inflexible working practices dominate the factory and this poses many problems for managers attempting to implement new team working practices. The ideas of autonomy, participation and empowerment are institutionalized rhetoric. "Feminine capital" was consciously exploited to endorse, seduce and manipulate other individuals to bring about change. The *Privileging of the Feminine* (Metcalfe and Linstead 2003) therefore served to endorse stereotypical views about women's characteristics and skills – their collaborative and supportive work attitudes (Fondas 1997; Dickens 1998). Nylons integrated women into the organisation under discourses of culture change, organizational renewal and team development. These gendered processes are however underpinned and maintained by masculinist ideologies of organization and management as we will see below.

The company promoted first-line supervisors to team managers and removed the production manager role. The team manager therefore incorporated the traditional supervisor and production manager roles.

Senior production managers lost their jobs and one manager (Rob) remained as the production director. These changes resulted in managers feeling they had "more to do" and hence were subject to more rigorous performance measures but the managers experienced a loss in role accountability and professional autonomy. As such there were great problems in morale and lack of respect for Rob who managed technical rather than human resource issues which were openly discussed between the managers and senior management but the problems were never addressed to prevent resistance or outflanking (after Fleming and Sewell (2002)). This outflanking, and associated lack of communication, resulted in the managers feeling detached and uncooperative. As one manager commented "if there is little we can do about it, then there is no point in trying. The first effort they have made is, ironically, bringing someone (the researcher) else in to listen to us. But, it's a good start because we are trying to open up again" (Ray, Team Manager). So, at one level we could argue that the majority of the managers were suppressed by the implementation of the changes and the lack of involvement or consultation. Withdrawing from the organization was a conscious strategy for many of the managers who experienced these changes. To signal substantial change and to disrupt the status quo of staff and middle management, women were used, by adopting a more feminine managerial strategy, to *seduce* individuals and win them over to the new way of working. The process was not communicated and as such management was surprised by the resistance to these changes and to "these women" and to reinforce the problems between management and the managers the resistance was not managed. Consequently, lack of communication and more backstage planning replaced the open communications that the company espoused. It is not surprising that a great deal of resistance has built up for individuals and the interviews were the place where many of the frustrations were voiced to an "outsider".

I arrived at the company in 1997 to interview the managers as an "action researcher". After Nia responded to a letter that I had sent the company requesting entry, Nia and myself arranged that I would interview all the managers on site and observe them when possible for research purposes (unpaid) in exchange for diagnosing and delivering team development sessions (paid). Thus my role was one of managing my urgency for rich, novel and "valid" data within the professional capacity of a team facilitator. At times the data collection process was honest and relaxed because I spent one or two days a week with the company for 12 months. At other times, especially in the early stages of my involvement with the company, the data were heavily laden with rhetoric as though the managers felt that they needed to "play the game". This chapter draws on data that was collected during later stages of the study because it more adequately represents the experiences of the managers interviewed, even though I acknowledge and will discuss the masking and the hidden scripts of the managers in Chapter 8. Nylons developed considerable dependency on me as my time with the company proceeded, so much so that when I finished my study they presented me with a cheque "to assist with my studies" which in my view reflected how desperate senior management were to understand the middle managers and get them on board with future changes. However, this extra payment also reflects how Nylons seduced and manipulated *me* to convey important changes to the managers that they felt unable to transmit themselves. I interviewed all the senior and middle managers (the team managers). I had an office in the building and much data were collected from individuals visiting me in an ad hoc way during their working day. The managers selected for presentation in this chapter were selected because they illustrated key themes that were representative of the larger data set (see Appendix 2 for further discussion of data representation).

Seducing the masculine and feminine: bringing about cultural change?

The data suggest that organizational and managerial restructuring has emasculated the team managers through their loss of sovereignty and autonomy and the lack of consultation and involvement in the change programme. The management of Nylons have deliberately employed and utilized the seductive capability of women, the other, to entice the male managers to bring about change in their attitudes, to support further organizational change. Nylons signals change at two levels – the introduction of the factory's first site manager, Nia, and women on the shop floor. At shop floor level, the organization, including Nia, play on the vulnerabilities of the male workers and managers interviewed, assuming that they would be seduced, though not necessarily with ease. This process of seduction rests on a notion of desire that an individual, in this case the men in Nylons, desires the other for recognition. Regardless of whether the response is positive or negative this Hegelian notion of recognition is desired and required. In Nylons the women represent a negative consequence for the men – deeper anxiety, vulnerability and in some cases heightened resistance which further emasculates them. Before moving on with this discussion, the introduction of female labour in Nylons is discussed.

Feminine leadership: creating sameness or difference?

Nia was an ambitious, 34 year old, German graduate, who arrived in Nylons during the year of this study. She was the first female site manager at the South Wales plant and one of only three women in the site manager role across this international organization. Nia's assignment was to "bring about cultural change" (Interview with Nia and Brian the Personnel Director) and much is made of her subject positions of being a woman and of her being a manager. The company expected feminized ways of working (Dickens 1998) to enable change. Although much was made of Nia's embodied presence of being a woman, Nia's colleagues and staff described her leadership style as masculine and authoritarian which does not support the feminine stereotypes of women's leadership skills and qualities in the women in management literature (see for example Fondas 1997; Wajcman 1998). The following quote from one of the female production employees, although empathetic of Nia's role as a female manager (unlike many of the men), still refer to the masculine assertive and aggressive to express her behaviour:

> She has a very difficult job to do, it's bad enough for us being so few of us. She may be assertive and aggressive at times but I think that's part of being the boss. The men are very aware that their boss is a woman. I say "good on her" she may be more aware of our situation and we may be better off (Sandra, female production worker, age 32).

Not surprisingly, individual views of Nia tended to be gender demarcated. Her male colleagues and staff account for her leadership style by emphasizing her female gender:

> She mixes well with us, she communicates with us more informally than the previous managers. But, she has a detached role (Phil Team Manager age 42, 28 years service).

> She is confident, willing to listen, and she has to get results, and she will, no matter what she has to do (Bob Production Director).
> She wears a mixture of things but she manages to mix her business side with her feminine style (Personnel Director).

Furthermore, and again not suprisingly, Nia, proud of her career achievements, doesn't support her colleagues' views of her masculinist management style. Nia denies her gendered identity:

> I manage this factory in relation to, one, the objectives that have been set for this site, and two, how I've been trained as part of the

corporate management programme. Being a woman doesn't matter. Do they expect me to behave differently? I do what I have to do to the best of my ability. I work evenings and weekends, so it's probably a good thing that my husband isn't around during the week (Nia).

Here we see Nia promoting a leadership image of gender neutrality but continues to highlight that this is at the expense of her private life. Her script emphasizes the public, negating the personal and understating aspects of our femininity at work. Nia consciously downplays being a woman, striving for sameness, suppressing otherness. As it has been argued elsewhere that men and women often conform to the traditional masculinist interpretations of effective management (see Collinson and Hearn 1994, 1996; Billing and Alvesson 1994; Metcalfe and Linstead 2003), the feminine is abject even for her own processes of identity construction. We could argue that femaleness for Nia is something that she needs to manage (see for example Hearn and Parkin 1995) and she manages this by promoting sameness. In contrast, Nia contradicts her text of her own role when she discusses the potential and capabilities of the women on the shopfloor to bring about change. For Nia, the feminine infers difference. This difference, it is hoped, will make *the* difference at an organizational level. Nia comments:

I believe we [women] have different skills, maybe teamwork, definitely communication and interpersonal skills that position us over many men. It's being given the opportunity to get to senior management positions, and then the opportunity to display these skills.

From this extract Nia identifies herself as a woman and acknowledges that women possess different skills to men. The words "position us over many men" are particularly pertinent; women are being privileged at the expense of men and men and women are homogenized thereby dissolving difference. Nia inverts the gender hierarchy by her social actions, not only does she downplay her femaleness (sameness) she capitalizes on the femaleness of female production workers (difference), which support feminist studies of women in work. The contradictions she presents can be seen from the following:

Being a woman doesn't matter. Do they expect me to behave differently? I do what I have to do to the best of my ability.

Furthermore, Nia illustrates the masculinist performance criteria upon which she accounts for herself:

> I am required to manage better than my male predecessor. I have to make the factory work, but I have to build the trust of the workforces that Stephen still has. So, I have to show them that they can trust me and that I can do the job that previously men have performed.

I would argue here that this inversion of the male/female dichotomy prevents the subversion of the symbolic order necessary for bringing about institutional change and possibly praxis for gender equality.

The power of the other: women on the shopfloor

Women on the shopfloor were recruited to "bring about change" and "address the gender imbalance" (Brian Personnel Director). Until this recent, intentional strategy to employ women there was gender segregation of both skill and task and women were employed as administrators. The appointment of three women in production signalled a key change for the company who perceived "these women", as they were commonly referred to, as crucial to organizational development. The feminine attributes that women naturally possess (see for example Alimo-Metcalfe 1994; Rosener 1990 for feminine leadership styles) are seen to be necessary for men and women in contemporary organizations and therefore represents an opportunity for women to address gender inequality (Wajcman 1998; Fondas, 1997). In Nylons women were positioned within the teams to challenge the masculinist and "laddish" (quote by a team member in Production) shop floor working practices and culture. To "change the way we do things around here" (Brian Personnel Director), "these women" were seen to possess the:

> key skills and commitment for productive teamwork which hopefully will be infectious (Bob Production Director age 51, employed by the company for 25 years).

However increased pressure faced the women since the organization had high expectations of them and they were required to adapt to the male dominated environment. These new female recruits were expected to:

> ...manage their environment. We are not geared up to women on the shop floor and they have had to work around that. There is a

shortage of facilities for women but we are investing in new showers and toilets for them and they will be ready soon. The men are not used to working alongside women and so they will have to cope with sexist remarks, even though we have tried to talk to these men (Brian Personnel Director).

And also,

We are expecting an awful lot from these women. Nia heading the site has already brought about changes but with *these women* on the shop floor with the guys, who knows what will happen. I have told them of the company's expectation of them and they are working very hard (Brian Personnel Director).

Here we see Brian reinforcing the gender binary by privileging women and positioning them against the men. Destabilizing the gender dualism through capitalizing on the fluid feminine is necessary to bring about change. The feminine in Nylons is fixed, and it is argued here that whilst the feminine is stable then the potential for change is difficult to achieve. Femininity is homogenized as we can see by the ways the women were utilized to exploit their femininity. Thus "the gender distinction based on biological sex differences illustrates how the gendering processes served not to privilege the feminine but instead favour the masculine; veiling feminine subjectivities within masculinist team practices" (Metcalfe and Linstead 2003). Traditional hegemonic masculinity (Messner 1992; Kerfoot and Knights, 1993; Collinson and Hearn 1996) and traditional working-class masculine identity (Donaldson 1996) continues to prevail and thrive by the reinforcement of gender difference.

The gendered subtext of the change processes in Nylons and how it dominates the agenda has been discussed. I now move on to discuss how middle managers' identities are constructed and will analyze the gendered discourses involved. I noted earlier, the introduction of women into the company during organizational restructuring and the loss of managerial sovereignty as a consequence of these changes inform the re/construction and legitimization of middle managers' subjectivities through their retrospective and prospective accounting practices to explore the discourses of accountability and seduction during their identity projects.

The vulnerable self: masks of managerial sovereignty

Peter is 58 years old and has been employed by Nylons for 31 years after spending a few years working at a nearby factory. He started with Nylons as a production worker, received in-house training and was subsequently promoted throughout the organization. Peter is married with a grown up family. Peter is representative of the ageing middle management cohort that management refer to as contributing to "the stalemate culture". We will see in the following fragments from several interviews with Peter that he is unable to move on in the organization and accounts for himself and his work role retrospectively. The future represents the unknown and he is fearful, anxious and uncertain about it. To build up ontological security during his engagements with me, we see Peter situating himself in the past, the management role of the old organization that he knows all about and we will see him accounting and legitimizing his identity through discourses of managerial sovereignty. This mask conceals the ontological insecurity that poses great threat, risk and ambiguity for him as he conducts his identity work.

Extract 1   "To drive through the high performance system they [site management] agreed that everyone would get £800 bonus and then afterwards we would get £800 consolidated into their salary to start off the high performance work system. This backfired... They still say about the £800 and will continue to say about it in 20 years time. They are very bitter because all the promises have been broken... our jobs came to grow and got bigger... people were going to be more flexible and had to do more work. Because we were doing more, we also expected the people below us to take on a broader role and take on the things that were dropping off the edge because we didn't have time to do it... The biggest effect is that people have had to become more autonomous because the managers at whatever level haven't got time to hold hands as much as they used to. They coach and support now. There's an expectation that people have to get on with it... At my level, managers used to be in the driving seat, they used to turn the steering wheel, and operate the valves when they were in a crisis. He would be involved in the day to day rather than in the forward thinking. The change there was intended for the shift managers to step back from that whilst maintaining the responsibility for making sure it happened but not doing it themselves. We fell down a hole there because we did slip back to because we didn't think thoroughly how we were going to stay in control. So now we have a situation where they say "I used to do that but now we have passed that down to the team". But the problem is they have to make sure it's done properly. When you go in and ask whether its being done properly it may have been, it may have not been, but there were too many don't knows... We are stretched".

Extract 2   "This lack of structure... perhaps you're expected to have interactions with everyone. I've got such a broad role... That's another problem, not enough people know what's expected of them, they don't know what their responsibilities are. They need to be defined. Going for this empowerment scenario will mean that unless jobs are well defined then they'll have no idea they'll do what they like. We suffer from lack of control because people are pushing that trust thing. We try to build trust but letting them do as much or as little as they want to but they take advantage. Where we are heading needs to be underpinned by training and knowledge of what is expected of them. But, it hasn't worked and I have had to make sure that I take control. I was a good manager and my way worked and I have had to trust that this is what I do best. This is what managers do in a crisis isn't it. With no direction, I have had to become accountable, and too make the men accountable too but this may not be the right way these days... There is a lack of control and this will be a bigger problem as we grow".

Extract 3   "They are not being told to do it [their jobs]. Well they say it's the Nylons way of directing and guiding them, but it doesn't get done. People know that they are not being held accountable and they are not chastised or chased by anybody so it doesn't happen. I've got a feeling that I'm being treated differently to everybody else, where I feel that I do the majority of things on site and feel that I'm pressured if I'm not doing what I'm supposed to be doing. I guess it reinforces my own sense of responsibility to get it done and that's what I do".

Extract 4   "Since our senior managers have left there has been a lack
of direction so what's happened was that everyone had
some reality check so they knew where they were going,
and we were changing very fast. Now the change has
stopped we are back to where we were six or seven years
ago... the communication channels are, well [pause] poor
and there's no reporting through us. So it becomes easier
not to bother than try to sort things out... Under the old
structure there was a different structure of management
and we were always informed about a lot of things. So, we
had more involvement".

Extract 5   "I was a good manager, we had direction and now we have
to make our own way. I'm a manager that takes control
and does what needs to be done to make sure that my men
perform. As a manager, I must do this and I have to work
harder now to get it done. The problem is that the men
don't always follow, they have been empowered and
without monitoring them they won't work. They have to
work or it makes the team look bad".

Extract 6   "I'm a manager that communicates and manages the men,
I co-ordinate, lead the men, do all the bits that fall between
the cracks".

Extract 7   Peter: "...some managers are better than others, and some,
two in particular are quite good. Three of them are worse,
one of them is older and doesn't really care too much. Two
of them are just pissed off and not switched on to the
concept... they tend not to work as one team. They are
always looking over their shoulder to see what the others
are getting in terms of benefits. They are not working
together as a single cohesive team".
Alison: "Where do you fit in, you keep saying 'they', what
about you?"
Peter: "If I'm honest, well, [long pause] I just don't know.
I think I perform well but I think I'd be classed as someone
who just isn't linking with the concept, I mean teamwork,
empowerment. The sad thing is I'm doing the job I've
always done and doing it well but the game's changed and
it takes a lot to change. How can you change everything
you've worked for and really enjoyed?"

In the first fragment we see Peter referring to the £800 bonus that Nylons used as an incentive to initiate change. Peter was seduced by this money into believing that the company was genuinely intending to change its management style and that this gesture was symbolic of its valuation of the managers' efforts rather than simple remuneration for them. He was prepared to change, he trusted the company to do the right thing during the crisis and was disappointed when the company didn't deliver their financial promises. This event is closely linked with Peter's existential anxiety which as Whitehead, drawing on Giddens (1991) and Bauman (1992), comment arises from "being in an environment characterised by risk, disruption and lack of trust" (2001: 95). Peter acknowledges his lack of trust in the company but his text is saturated with the discourses of being a "good manager". Although he seems committed to being a good manager in his text he is unable to become the "postmodern manager" that Nylons desperately need taking initiatives, supporting the changes and being autonomous and able to deliver in ambiguous and difficult times. He repeatedly comments "as a good manager" and "as a manager" in extract five to emphasize his managerial role in the company. In performing this script Peter displays vunerability and resistance to the restructuring and current changes and avoids, throughout my interactions with him, confronting the future – the unknown and uncertain. This reminds us of Ford et al's "resigned background" as a mode of resistance where as a result of historical failure in the organization individuals adopt a position where regardless of what they do "This probably wouldn't work either" (2002: 110) and as Ford et al continue "when people encounter failure, they blame the failure on factors outside of themselves... characterised by having given up trying... [and] a sense of despair, apathy, hopelessness, depression, sadness, and listlessness" (2002: 111).

When asked about his current role, Peter drew on the past and described what he did, and continued to do, which endorses a modernist conceptualization of identity (Giddens 1991). The functionalist rhetoric of management work seen in "I'm a manager that communicates and manages the men, I co-ordinate, lead the men, do all the bits that fall between the cracks" reveals that even during his verbal performances he is locked within a functionalist framework of managerial work (Mintzberg 1973, Stewart 1989). Peter refused to engage and discuss his private life during our interview sessions. Peter's mask is one of managerial sovereignty to cope with the daily pressures of being unable to accommodate the demands, change his outlook and manage the changes. We see Peter finding security by fixing, locking and securing self by drawing on masculinist notions of management work – rigidity, control and accountability. He is critical of the new ways of working – flexibility, autonomy and empowerment.

However in one private encounter with Peter we see him reveal the hidden text that was negated during his public performances of self:

> Without my hard hat on I would be unable to come into work and face the troubles that await me. The men look to me for guidance because the technology and the customer have changed. Management look to me to improve performance but the performance is all metric…. we haven't developed the people, including me, to deliver on this. I have so much to do that I can't be the manager they want me to be but I have to. **I have to perform and it's so frustrating**.

Sadly for Peter he cannot perform the leadership role of "guiding, coaching and facilitating the teams" (Brian Personnel Director) expected of him post restructuring. He is unable to "play the game" either verbally or behaviourally and loses credibility in the organization. Frustrated by the ambiguity and lack of direction, he turns to what he knows – hierarchy and accountability (which supports my findings in Chapter 5). This supports Jaques' work which re-appraises the positive benefits hierarchy: "we need layers of accountability and skill" (2000a: 127). Peter without the skills and training to work within the "new" organization, is unable to transgress the past. He constantly constructs his work subjectivities within a modernist project of identity (Giddens 1991) – the functional role that he performed/performs – to mask his ontological insecurity. Ontological security we could argue informs the quest for a stable identity and enables us to "standardise our existence" (Beck and Beck-Gernsheim 1995; Giddens 1991 cited in Whitehead 2001: 97).

Like many managers in Nylons, we could argue that Peter's effort to construct a competent managerial self is partially because he is driven by masculinist discourses of performance and because "management… is a *seductive* site for such identity work" (Whitehead 2001: 96 *emphasis added*). Organizational change fuels managers' pursuits of their identities and the ambiguity and ever changing dynamics of the situation and their associated vunerabilities and insecurities reinforces the hegemonic masculinity of being a manager in Nylons. In the final fragment we see Peter confronting the frustrations of being trapped by what he knows and the destiny for managers like himself that lack the transferable skills and within the increasing expectations of the post-bureau-cratic organization (du Gay 1996; Garsten and Grey 1997). His texts reveal the tension between flexibility and control, and between sta-bility and fluidity. As Garsten and Grey comment: "the narrative of the self involves finding a balance between what can be controlled and what is contingent, fickle and more difficult to control" (1997: 218). Peter locates his subjectivities within a hierarchy that holds him accountable (to himself and the organization) which provides meaning for his managerial role and managing the meaning of his existence in the restructured Nylons. Peter's retrospective accounting practices and the "accountable role" that he constructs during his public identity work enables him to resist and hold back from fluidity, from seduction. The accountability of managerial work therefore provides reference points (see Bauman 1992) to "achieve" episodes of security within a postmodern environment of high risk, insecurity and ambiguity (Hirschorn 1997).

The consumption of self: managerial and cultural seduction

Dan is much younger than his middle management cohort aged 42 years old. He is an engineering graduate and has worked in Nylons for 19 years after starting as an engineer. He took his management diploma on a part time basis, is married and has a teenage family. Dan's interpretation of his role in Nylons varies starkly from his peers which may be influenced by his education and age. He is an ambitious manager who on the surface appears outwardly committed to the new ways of working. In contrast to Peter he focuses on current and future episodes to construct his identity. His personal life is neglected at the expense of his public space. In Dan's texts we see him drawing on dis-courses of seduction to construct and legitimize his role. I am less interested in whether or not he has been/is seduced by Nylons but rather that organizational change has influenced, shaped and con-sumed self. Casey's notion of the "colluded self" could easily be applied to Dan since aspects of his identity are consumed as he per-forms the "committed manager" as part of conducting "good work". We see this within Dan's fragments where he uses rhetoric associated with new forms of managerial work such as "committed, flexible, empowered and leading" to justify his role (extract 2). Although Dan is using "postmodern" rhetoric to legitimize his managerial role, his identity project is underpinned by a modernist agenda – the role he conducts and the functions and responsibilities he performs. Further-more, there are tensions and contradictions in Dan's text which we argue is part of his "playing the game" – the game of being seduced and on-board with the change that needs to be played to belong to the organization and construct his work identity, and the retrospective and pragmatic consideration of the change that took place and how it has influenced his identity project.

Extract 1   "I think that I have a good idea about what my role is but I'm not sure that that applies to everyone on site... We are trying to grow and we need to get things in place. Shop-floor recruitment is taking place, but I don't know what plans there are for middle management and whether it's to be restructured when the new machines come in. How we grow concerns me. Middle management seem to be doing all the work and the pressure seems to be around that group at the moment".

Extract 2   "I've *created* my own role even though the boundaries are not clear. However, how much you go outside this role depends on the individual. There are lots of opportunities to help people out and this depends on the workload at the time. My boss would expect, he wouldn't not stop me going off and helping else where, but where does that stop. You have to maintain your responsibilities and go that bit extra to grow, but there's a tension there. It's about being committed, flexible, empowered and leading, not managing".

Extract 3   "We step back now because our role is increasing. When the change took place we changed as well. Whereas our change took place and we *embraced* the change, the change for everybody else stopped but we were expected to continue which we have done".

Extract 4   "The people that I'm working with have been here well in excess of 25 years, so they know what they are comfortable with doing. The question is trying to change the hearts and minds of them to accept that unless we get better quality, better safety then we are always going to run the risk of this plant losing numbers or eventually closing. I'm one of the few people who believe that the changing the hearts of mind of people is what is needed... we are not speaking the same language which means we are not pulling in the same direction".

Extract 5   "There was an identity crisis with the change but I think I handled it better than the other managers because I had more idea of what was going on. The managers didn't know what was happening and they started going in different directions... So, because jobs were not defined people had identity crisis dealing with changing environments, and this resulted in the people who should have been supporting not doing so. This has continued. They look for support from me rather than supporting me support the day to day heart of the plant".

Extract 6   "The other managers are really dragging me down. This week it's been terrible because they are uninterested and I've been trying to help them do their job and do my job, and, hum, they need someone there to guide them... communication on site is virtually non existent... we don't work together".

Extract 7   "Reorganization is great, it's crucial to making the plant work. Improved communication, changing management styles, responsibilities defined and understood by everybody needs to occur is what we need and it's working. Although my team size has been reduced by half it was necessary... I've not got satisfaction from my job because I can't do it as well as I would like to do it. As well as do my job I feel that I fill in the gaps that others don't do because they don't go that extra mile with their own role. As long as I know that what has been expected of me has been done I'm happy, but when I haven't done it to the standard I would have liked to do it then I'm very nervous, uncomfortable rather".

Extract 8   "Nia has come in to shake things up and I think she's doing an OK job. We need new blood to change the way we do things around here. I must say that she has had some negative reactions but as long as I do what's expected I think I'll be OK. They want younger people that don't know what went on and who can't move on. They brought in women on the shopfloor too but the men aren't buying it...
Alison: What about you?
Dan: I don't mind who does what, I've just got to get the guys working together with these women. As long as my

team performs that's all I want. The other teams are not performing as well and that's because of the poor leadership".

Alison: Do you consider yourself to be a good leader?

Dan: I coach and direct them and when they are stuck I get involved but we need to stand back and let them carry on, a more detached role. I think I'm good at what I do compared to the others but then I'm fortunate to have had the training and the experience... I do what I need to do to secure my career. I am a committed manager and I know I can perform better. With the bigger role to perform and all the extra things to be getting on with, I have little time or energy for anything else. The shift responsibilities also cut into my family life. Work is everything to me"

Alison: "At the expense of your family?"

Dan: "No, but you have to provide and if your not around who would know whether you are needed or not. I have to be seen to be doing more and better."

Alison: "But when should you say enough is enough?"

Dan: "That's difficult, perhaps when the change slows down".

In Dan's script we see him reflecting on the impact of the changes for him and more specifically his role. Akin to Peter he engages in a modernist project of self-identity, he focuses on what he does, unable to penetrate his public mask. Dan's mask of performance was fixed and he was unable to reflect on the private, indeed we could argue that Dan's private space is consumed by his public role of being a manager and an outwardly committed manager at that. He knows the game has changed and the interviews and informal conversations conducted with Dan were part of his public performance of displaying commitment to the organization. He must show that he is meeting the company's expectations and his self-serving ambition allows him to prostitute himself at least on the public stage. Dan's case supports our premise in Chapter 3 that the changing forms of accountability based on heightened discourses of performativity are fundamental to postmodern discourses of organization. These *gendered discourses of performance* are fashioned around and support feminine ways of managing. As such, on one level Dan is confronting the feminine other within by addressing feminine management practices. However, at a meta level Dan is seduced by the cultural controls in place as he reveals his hegemonic masculinity which makes him more vulnerable and a target for more seductive practices in future. Dan conforms to the stereotypical masculinist discourses of managers, legitimizing their identities to keep up with increasingly heightened performance measures and cultural controls, which requires Dan to display increasing levels of commitment to the organization and this is itself gendered (Davidson and Cooper 1992; Dickens 1998).

The fragments we have used here from Dan's texts are infused with the discourses of new managerial work. His texts are saturated with talk of change and cultural change. The rhetoric within his text such as "the heart of the plant" and "changing hearts and minds" reveal that he has been seduced by the Nylons employment of culture to bring about change. However at several junctures we see Dan more reflexive that he is indeed playing a game which we argue is *narcissistic gaming* which revolves (as he admits) around the self-interest of his career (we will discuss narcissism further in Chapter 8). Even though he negates his personal/familial space, indeed he sacrifices them for the sake of his ambition and hopefully and ultimately his managerial career. Moreover, as Whitehead in his profeminist analysis of women managers in Further Education states "[individuals are] largely assimilated and co-opted into a work culture which promises material reward and a sense of belonging in return for *visible* dedication and a readiness to identify with the corporate culture" (2001: 87 [insertion] and *emphasis* added). Managing this visibility and the commitment to the organization is an inherent process of doing "the interview". Furthermore, managing resistance to the organizational changes also runs through the text and is a central constituent of doing identity work during the research engagement.

During the display of high performativity we see tensions and contradictions within Dan's text moving from discourses of culture change which takes a collective and cohesive orientation to the organization (note his anxiety and frustration at the other managers and the lack of integration) and the individual self-interest that drives his mask of performativity. We can see this from the way he excludes himself from the other managers, constantly referring to "they". There is a tension between the "modern sensibility highlighted [by] individualism" (Hirschorn 1997: 17) and the collectivism often endeavoured by organizations managing culture (Peters and Waterman 1982) which reproduces co-operation and consensus (Willmott 1993).

Dan, like Peter, is also avoiding the "other within" during his identity construction. Dan's discussion of "these women" and Nia is particularly revealing in that confronting the feminine emphasizes his neglect of the feminine within and also the masculine project of identity construction, Dan has been consumed by the organization. Although the evidence remains partial, it seems he must maintain his public identity through the employment of masks. Moreover, even Dan acknowledges of his loss of self-identity (Höpfl and Linstead 1993) and as Brewis and Linstead (2001) contend in their analysis of sex workers the loss of self-identity may "require the... [individual] to engage in the emotional labour necessary to maintain a sense of self-identity which is distinct from that involved in the business arrangement" (2001: 84). Dan has rehearsed and rectified "the display of expected emotions" (Ashforth and Humphrey 1993 cited in Noon and Blyton 2002: 176) as he publicly constructs and legitimizes his identity to respond and manage cultural expectations (Kunda 1992; Alvesson 2002) necessary for organizational regeneration. Dan's construction of his identity during this research was typical of Ray's argument (1986) that individuals come to "love the firm and its goals" to increase performance, even though it may only be a mask of performance characterized by love, belonging and commitment. Managers are often recognized for how they appear to achieve as well as for what they actually achieve. In this section we have discussed how Dan responds to the increasing pressures he faces and the ways which the seductive influences of the new ways of working have played their part with Dan. In illustrating this point I have overlooked how the seductive discourses of management are inextricably tied up with the cultural discourses. I argue then that the seductive ontology of management drives Dan's identity work (which may appear ideological at times), particularly his prospective accounting practices which are stimulated by ambition, career and the nature of management itself.

Resisting change: resisting the other

Resistance to organizational change is not surprising given the Nylons context and the subject has been well documented to explore the effects of such resistance on the labour process (e.g. see Edwards 1979; Reed 1997). Furthermore, from radical and revolutionary feminisms (see Weedon 1999) to studies of women in management challenges and resistance to phallic power have been extensively debated. Treatments of resistance from constructionist (Ford et al 2002) and postmodern persuasions (Foucault 1980) are less rehearsed in the organization field (with the exception of Collinson 1992, 1994; Gabriel 1999; Knights 2002; Fleming and Sewell 2002). Following a poststructuralist line of inquiry, our conceptualization of resistance after Foucault is "where there's power, there's resistance" (1980) and therefore resistance is central to researching identity and will be discussed in this section and continued in Chapter 8 since it disrupts the predicted linear shift from accountability to seduction and reveals the tensions between accommodating organizational demands which infers that individuals are being controlled by seductive forms of workplace control whilst at the same time resisting aspects of the organization, change or individuals. I will analyze from Steve's text that verbalizing resistance during the research process may be a response to being seduced.

To explore the construction of managers' identities, I draw on the work of Ford et al (2002) that analyzed, from a social constructionist perspective, resistance to change as a "function of the ongoing background conversations that are being spoken" (2002: 105) to problematize resistance (which predominantly assumes an objective and homogenous quality) within its social context and consequently appreciate its heterogeneous and fragmentary nature. As such the interview texts produced are woven displays of constructing and legitimizing power (as we have already seen by Peter in his performance of managerial sovereignty and the discourses of careerism in Dan's text) and resistance to the other, to change. Resistance is socially constructed and as Ford et al (ibid.) maintain:

...resistance is a function of the socially constructed reality in which someone lives, and that depending on the nature of that constructed reality, the form of resistance to change will vary... Accordingly, change, and resistance to it, is a function of the constructed reality; it is the nature of this reality that gives resistance its particular form, mood, and flavor (2002: 106).

Although Ford et al's social constructionist orientation is refreshing it overlooks the fluid, ambiguous and relational nature of resistance; the interdependency between individual and organizational resistance; and reinforces the resistance-accommodation dichotomy when theorizing agency. Commenting on Bourdieu, McNay comments:

Bourdieu is critical of the dichotomous logic of domination-resistance which tends to simplify the complex nature of freedom and constraint in capitalist society and instead employs the term "regulated liberties" to denote a more complex relation between the dominant and its subjects (Bourdieu 2001: 102), (2000: 58).

Bourdieu warns us above of the dangers of reinforcing the resistance/ compliance dichotomy as either/or and cause and effect. Much research on individual agency has been dominated by either studies of traditional forms of resistance or compliance to new organizational controls as we discussed earlier, with the exception of poststructuralist informed researchers (for example Knights and McCabe 2000; Fleming and Sewell 2002) that have problematized the resistance/compliance or accommodation dichotomy (which will be discussed further in Chapter 8). However, during the processes of making sense of the individual agency and writing an interpretation of agency resistance becomes objectified and we would not wish to support this since texts are "ephemeral and have no existence or permanence other than when they are being spoken (Berquist 1993)" (Ford et al 2002: 107). However the intertexuality of text supports my analysis that resistance runs through all the managers' texts but I pay specific attention to resistance here because Steve overtly discusses it but following Ford et al I "locate [s] resistance in conversational patterns... rather than 'in' the individual" (2002: 108). These conversations constitute an organization's culture (Schein 1997) and Nylons is struggling to overcome the culture of resistance characterized by *complacency* (we'll be OK again), *resignation* (whatever we do we won't make a difference) and *cynicism* (which I will discuss in this section more closely) (see Ford et al [2002] for their use of these generic resistance giving backgrounds) at the level of managerial identity. In this section I am interested empirically in how an individual, and in this case Steve, draws on the language of resistance during his identity work which at some times indicate resistance to the seductive forces that try to consume self and resistance at the recognition that he is being seduced rather successfully by the feminine.

Steve is a middle manager, age 56 that has worked in the company for 35 years. Steve is typical of the majority of managers who have incrementally been promoted through the system. Steve however has been selected here because unlike the other older managers his managers believe that he has managed the change well and is a high performing manager which offers us an interesting analysis. Although the changes in Nylons has threatened the status quo for the managers (Spector 1989 cited in Ford et al 2002: 104); increases fear, anxiety and ontological insecurity; confidence in the ability to perform (O'Toole 1995 cited in Ford et al 2002: 104), Steve is not typical of the resigned or complacent manager which we would expect to reveal high levels of resistance. Change as Ford et al comment:

> threatens the way people make sense of the world, calling into question their values and rationality (Ledford et al, 1989, and prompting

some form of self justification (Staw, 1981) or defensive reasoning (Argyris, 1990). Or... when people distrust or have past resentments toward those leading change (Block, 1993; Bridges, 1980; Bryant, 1989; Ends and Page, 1977; O'Toole, 1995), when they have different assessments of the situation (Morris and Raben, 1995), or are protecting established social relations that are perceived to be threatened (O'Toole, 1995), (2002: 105).

Studies of resistance in management work support Ford et al's study but I am not interested in whether or why Steve resists but rather how Steve draws on the language of resistance to construct and legitimize particular subject positions at particular episodes. Steve is also particularly interesting because he verbally resists the gendered interventions taking place and he was one of the few middle managers who would openly discuss Nia and the female production workers.

Extract 1   "Remember we've been highly unionized since the 1950s, and anything that takes the trade union away from their collective roll they worry about it. I can understand that because we've got ageing work force, and they work on an 'all for one and one for all' principle, and to take them out of that structure they worry about whose going to be the blue eyed boy... It's getting an element of regeneration through the organization. We have to get them to understand what it is we need to do to put things permanently right... managers need to do more in terms of ownership and this is a weakness... When we were in survival mode there was more ownership then. There was a need to survive and a need to go the extra mile".

Extract 2   "The main effect is the shopfloor... it is a very *old* factory. When we went into the high performance system the bulk of the operating group were mid forties and they were very perceptive to change, they were in tune, and saw opportunities to change, they saw the need to change and there was a want to change. To secure their futures it was the right road to go down. From that day to now, the majority of that group are now in their mid fifties and as they say they are in their life boat and they don't need to change. Now we are taking on younger people, the opportunity to change may present itself. These managers are *resisting change* and who can blame them".

Extract 3   "In an organization which is looking to be, to advance, to improve quality and safety, to change, then to motivate to accept change is difficult. They are stuck in the ways of the past, and we find that the ways of the past are more comfortable... I'm demotivated because of the divide that appears to be coming in on the site [senior managers and middle managers]... There is no teamwork in my organization. We are not asked our opinion anymore, we used to. We went through a stage when we were called in afterwards. Now we are not even called in. Five years ago that was different".

Extract 4   "I run my shift the way that I run my shift, and my colleagues do the same thing, and because of lack of guidance and general direction, we run our shifts the way we think is right which can have problems because we can go down one road on one shift and the other shifts find out. So we are not all going the same way... We need direction, re-establishing the ways and where we were five years ago. We were part of a management team... Before [the change] the managers at different levels spoke the same language so you never needed to jump the reporting layers. It's protocol we never go beyond our next manager in line".

Extract 5   "Nia has been brought in to shake the place up. She's OK and she is committed to change but we don't know what's going on. We changed, we had systems in place. It was ripe for change. Now it's gone. It's not an issue but surprise because not just because she's a woman but because she's so young as well. We didn't *know* the other plant manager that much and I guess she'll be the same. These people are looking for promotion and use this place as a stepping stone. I'm not opposed to the changes and Nia but I'm not supporting them either. They are *using* the women and I don't think it's right and they are doing it to upset the men that have been here years holding the place up. I'm *not getting involved*. I'm sure you already know and I'm sure you'll buy into this being a lady. We've taken on three ladies which I'm personally delighted about, but the feedback we've got from the guys out there has been appalling. It's ranged from disgraceful in terms of diversity issues to well 'we think you've got a problem here'. We haven't had a lady on shift for many, many years and most of these guys have been brought up in an all male environment on shifts. Some men are in their fifties etcetera. There is a distinct *fear* that you've just brought ladies in to work along side us and that's a problem... I don't blame them, it's not what we're used to but I must be seen to be holding my tongue, you know what I mean?"

Extract 6   "I don't like what's happening to us and the organization that means so much to some of us older managers, so I try to stay out of things but you can't and you voice your concerns about the changes to management and to the union representative. When you need to you need to *do* something about what's happening or otherwise we should just roll over. Our expertise isn't valued and I don't like that. We are sidelined and I don't think that's right. I know I must follow the new procedures but they don't benefit me and I just do my own thing but why shouldn't I and who stops me".

Extract 7   "I feel that we are being taken over. We have to be seen to support the changes, even when that means we are being disloyal to all that we are and know"
Alison: "Taken over?"
Steve: "We need to show that we are all working in the same direction, being committed, following the new procedures even when it's all bullshit and we are all working against each other".

Steve in the first extract illustrates the changes in the role of the trade unions in Nylons and how individuals are responding to try to protect themselves. The shift from collective to individual accounting practices may contribute to the ways in which managers feel the need to safeguard themselves which may take the form of traditional forms of resistance against management control. Steve also goes on to indicate the urgency for middle managers to support the restructuring to "survive" and this contrasts with the resistance from the middle management cohort. Senior management at the company saw the ageing workforce as part of the problem of resistance to change. "Resisting change" (extract 2) seems to stem from the threat of "younger people" and the need for managers to protect themselves. This retreat from change and the unknown renders Steve into a modernist project of self-identity (Giddens 1991) accounting for himself through the past. He comments: "They are stuck in the ways of the past, and we find that the ways of the past are more comfortable" (extract 3). Although Steve constantly refers to "they" when referring to the changes and the loss of managerial sovereignty (extract 3 and 7), the need for ontological insecurity runs through Steve's text as he reveals fear, anxiety and ambiguity.

Steve overtly discusses resistance in extract 2 and in extract 6 Steve whilst acknowledging the need to "try to stay out of things" and not resist the changes taking place in Nylons he can't as he says he has to "do something". Although Steve's texts does not say what he does his resistance from observing him and speaking to the other managers revolves around cynicism (Ford et al 2002). This behaviour is also compatible with Fleming and Sewell's scrimshanking where he actively resists the role that he is accountable for (extract 6). At times Steve disengages from the politics of the situation but only after preparing others to speak and act on his behalf. Without cognitively or emotionally withdrawing (Prasad and Prasad 1998) Steve disengages in way consistent with Fleming and Sewell's active disengagement where the individual retains "the ability to comply without conforming" (2002: 12).

On one hand Steve's text can be interpreted as him resisting the change and the implementation of women (extract 5) but on the other hand it can be suggested that Steve is resisting the fact that he is aware that he has already been seduced and it is as a "seduced man" that he finds difficulty in coping with the knowledge that he is an easy target to be seduced in the future. Insecurity regarding his age and the knowledge that finding another job at his stage in the career life cycle contributes to his compliance to be seduced. Furthermore his "fear" (extract 5) of the other, the women, and the unknown is also a source of resistance. It may argued here that Steve is one of the lucky ones who can verbalize his feelings and resistance which enables him to reflect and manage when to disengage and accommodate the changes. He accomplishes this by presenting himself as a resigned and complacent individual when is he actually much more cynical and mischievous. In this way then resistance has positive benefits for Steve and it assists in managing his existential anxiety. Steve's text highlights for me how resistance is complex since resistance against seduction and resistance as a response to being seduced cannot be separated.

Seduction and the feminine

To summarize this chapter, the rhetoric of *accountability* in Gowler and Legge's framework which involves the moral and technical reckoning which enforces the hierarchy and therefore suppresses the feminine by endorsing accounting practices based on objectivity and standardized accounting practices. In Chapter 2 I argued that contemporary analysis recognizes that there have been changing forms of accountability based on heightened discourses of performativity which are themselves *gendered* which are fashioned around and support feminine ways of managing. It could be argued that the postmodern shift in sensibilities has set categories in motion, acting not in a linear way from accountability to seduction, as I noted in the last chapter, but in terms of relations in many directions which are sometimes reversible, sometimes reciprocal, sometimes not.

In Nylons it was revealed how the organization used women to signal change. Drawing on Baudrillard, the feminine possesses more potential to *seduce*:

> The strength of the feminine is that of seduction... A universe that can no longer be interpreted in terms of structures and diacritical oppositions, but implies a seductive reversibility – a universe where the feminine is not what opposes the masculine, but what seduces the masculine (1990: 7).

The power of the seductive capability of the feminine to initiate change cannot be underestimated, indeed it is dangerous and it has been seen through the texts of Peter, Dan and Steve how they draw on the discourses of accountability and seduction to construct and legitimize their identities. The feminine then, women employees in this case, challenged the working norms to "change the ways we do things around here". The rhetoric of culture change was imbued with the power of feminine capital. Dan in particular employs a mask of culture change to protect himself from the feminine, from the fluid and the unknown. The managers in the Nylons case signal change where there is no going back to the good old days of ontological security however much they attempt this by constructing themselves through discourses of managerial sovereignty. These managers are instrumental in constructing modernist narratives of management. Being a manager has changed and the measures by which they are held accountable have changed long term. The stakes have changed in the game – no certainty, no security and more accountability but this accountability is subjective. Furthermore the game is one of high risk, risk to themselves. As individuals become enchanted, and therefore controlled by the discourses that govern them, and the vulnerable self becomes victim and open to the colonization by the organization. Individuals as it has been seen in this chapter have little choice than to collude and become treated as a commodity. As seduced commodities performances of commitment are inevitable, as observed in the next chapter.

7
"Why Not Take All of Me?": Achievement & Commitment in Larts

> ...there's a feeling that you have to be in this place, not only to get the job done but to be seen to be doing extra... (Wayne, Larts).

Introduction

In the previous chapter, I outlined the relationships between accountability and achievement, and seduction and commitment. My argument was that being accountable no longer means following the rules, but being the right person, and seduction acts as a new form of discipline over self-identity which involves the manager actively in the construction of their own "iron cage". As I noted then, our Management in Three Movements model leads us to expect that under postmodern conditions achievement morphoses into the recognition of *commitment*, a performance appreciated rather than measured, involving the further use of masks as I have already identified, as managers struggle to establish their identities as *core* to the organization, with all its professional and social advantages, rather than the more temporally vulnerable and potentially throwaway *periphery*. Seduction and commitment are ultimately inseparable as processes, but having examined the move from rational control to control by enchantment in the previous chapter, I will now turn to look more closely at the commodification processes – where managers move from being the producers of commodities, or the controllers of commodity production, to commodities themselves, to be consumed by the organization – entailed in the movement from achievement to commitment.

In the management and organization literature, the need to demonstrate commitment within restructured (and restructuring) organizations is equated with being "seen to be keen", predicating long working hours (Collinson and Collinson 1997; Dickens 1998). The gendered implications of patterns of work, consequent upon the continuing gendered division of labour, such as working evenings and weekends, imply that the discourses of contemporary management reinforce masculinist notions of organization. Managers need to be "seen to be there", with the exercising of managerial power through forms of surveillance which reinforces the dominant masculine culture of management through informal pressures of time-space surveillance (Collinson and Collinson 1997) and time monitoring (Sewell and Wilkinson 1992). Discourses of contemporary organizations inform the middle manager that s/he is disposable and must constantly prove her/his value added. To confirm and secure their status and legitimacy, therefore, discourses of commitment (time-space) are equated with "being a good manager". The good manager therefore has high visibility, is contactable at all times, is enthusiastic about working longer, and tolerates the neglect of personal time. In this chapter Jackie argues that this is what being a manager is all about in contemporary competitive organizations. The presentation of the self here is one where management work is promoted to be of primary importance, demanding the sacrificing of all other spheres of life. These sacrifices serve as confirmation of one's status as an "effective manager", thus securing identity and purpose.

This chapter presents accounts of four middle managers, drawn from interview material, to illustrate and explore issues of identity construction in one organization. I chose these managers because the masquerade in which they were participating, though having many different scenes, was the same one in organizational terms and many of the displayed perspectives of the organization were shared by the participants. I could have chosen four other managers as our representatives here, four being a number which enables us to discuss their comments in some detail whilst giving sufficient variety to cover all the necessary elements. A female manager is included not simply because of her female status but because she illustrates the demographic predominance of males at middle management level being the only female manager in the company. I was attracted to these four managers in particular because, even as I conducted the interviews, they appeared to be articulating elements which other interviewees had raised, but had not so well exemplified or expressed, and had a range of differing work experiences, educational attainments and family situations.

Restructuring at Larts

This company has a manufacturing facility, located on a brownfield site in Kent in the UK, and a strategic centre based in London. The factory makes and assembles Rotary Diesel Fuel Injection Pumps for agricultural, industrial and marine use, and the van and truck market. The production process consists of manufacturing the different components of the pumps and also the final assembly of the pumps.

Larts, during the period of this research, was under tremendous pressure to become competitive, cut costs and become more efficient. In 1984 John Parnaby (consultant and author of Just-in-Time [JIT] production systems) advised the company to drive ownership and accountability to the lowest level, by cutting out as many tiers of management as possible. Parnaby started the structural move to mini-business units, focusing on the main areas of the production process. Subsequently, another group of consultants was brought into Larts which centralized and reincorporated the units into its traditional manufacturing layout. These persistent traditional manufacturing systems remained until environmental influences caused the need to change to become prominent. The consequence of this series of events was that the organization seemed to be going through continual cycles of change where one sequence overlaid and blended into another.

The company had restructured every couple of years since the early 1980s, by downsizing and restructuring manufacturing as a short-term survival strategy. They went through a number of unsuccessful change initiatives in an attempt to deal with competitive environmental pressures throughout this era. More recently unitization and teamworking (as part of a Total Quality initiative) had been introduced to ensure financial survival and to increase its competitive advantage in the market place. In 1993, the structural reorganization into units over a two year period was initiated which in combination with other down-sizing initiatives reduced the number of employees from 3,000 in 1985 to 1,800 in 1995. Unitization entailed all peripheral staff being made redundant, such as electricians and maintenance; central engineering was surplus to requirements. Trade union membership also fell as restructuring dramatically reduced their potential membership, disillusioned others and placed in question their existence if they could not protect members' jobs. Consequent to the downsizing process, there was an increase in demand for contractors (such as electricians and building maintenance) to supply the extra skills needed to replace the expertise lost in the downsizing on a project by project basis.

Changes in the management structure were part of this process, reduced from seven to three levels. Middle management – now confined to one tier – consists of both specialist and support managers and newly created team manager roles in production. These team managers have replaced the production manager position in the old structure. The "new", reduced middle management body is comprised of some "old" production managers, and some newly recruited team leaders, which produces some tensions (see Smith and Wilkinson 1983 for a classic example). In the following section, data extracts from four managers from this tier, whom I will call Wayne, Jackie, Terry and Justin are discussed. I highlight the gendered discourses of increased masculinization produced by the resulting behavioural emphases on commitment and performance, whilst simultaneously revealing the insecurities and fragilities of being a "middle" manager in Larts – no longer just "a cog in a wheel", but a product on the shelf.

Managing in the middle

In what follows each individual manager's account is interpreted to highlight the ways in which they use identity as a first order construct to construct their subjectivities; the idea of identity as paradox to legitimize self; and the negotiation of past and future episodes when positioning self into the unfolding organizational story – the masquerade. Within these processes of identity construction common themes of performance and commitment are revealed which have gendered implications for all the managers concerned. The four managers are Wayne, who has worked his way up to middle management since joining the firm as an apprentice; Jackie, a career manager; Terry, a grandfather who is finding that he no longer fits into the company to which he has given his life; and Justin, a graduate manager who although successful and still young, is becoming disillusioned.

The male breadwinner: killing the father

Wayne is in his early 30s, married with 2 small children. He has worked for Larts since he was 16, having joined as an apprentice. From our engagement with Wayne it was evident that he is a very ambitious manager who is keen to go further in the organization. Having progressed from an apprenticeship with the company, he sees the gaining of more formal qualifications as an "insurance policy" to secure himself against further restructuring:

Extract 1   "It's changed so much since I started here. A lot of my mates haven't survived the changes... they were good guys but they weren't in control of what happened to them. I've been lucky, of course I have, but I've worked for it, I've never sat back, I've always tried to get more paper behind me... you've always got to keep up, but it's getting in front that gives you the insurance."

Extract 2   "I get very, very stressed with some of the responsibilities I've got. I'm sitting at home, it can be ten o'clock at night and I've got to come in. I live ten miles away... I'm contracted 37 hours, but I'm expected to do the necessary hours to get my job done. We have 24-hour responsibility but that doesn't mean we have to be here 24 hours a day (laughter)... The job is bigger because there are less guys to get more done, and it's different work, not just the production stuff. It's the other stuff that takes the time..."

Extract 3   "...there's a feeling that you have to be in this place, not only to get the job done but to be seen to be doing extra..."

Extract 4   "My wife doesn't work so she looks after the kids, I try and see them at weekends, but at night they are usually in bed. I think to myself, what am I missing, but what would their lives be like without my job?... I'm just lucky my wife is at home, she provides stability for the kids, but sometimes we argue like mad... If I didn't work here we wouldn't be able to live in a good area, on a nice estate, then things would be much worse."

Wayne's account deploys some elements familiar from traditional working-class masculine identity, such as that of self-sacrifice (Donaldson 1996) but with a contemporary twist provided by the industrial context of the late 20th century and the conflict with the idea of the "New Man" (Knights 2001). Wayne sees himself as ordinary enough in his abilities and gifts, but with a determination to make the very best of them. As a man he is supposed to be, on the one hand, part of the collective of other men and connected to them in fraternity, and yet ready to do whatever it takes in a dog-eat-dog world to survive or to get one better than them. Masculinity in this sense is already a mask, as men share and even create collective identity whilst keeping their secrets and protecting their advantage. Thus Wayne's first extract rests on a justification of the situation that working hard and getting ahead is demanded by both circumstance and by who you are, and being a "good guy" is not enough as you have to master the situation. Wayne sees this as achieved through qualifications, but these perhaps function as a sign for other activities that he does not mention. He also evinces a degree of paradoxical guilt that he is a survivor, that he is marked out as different from those men he was close to once, although this is precisely what his actions were intended to do. He is genuinely distressed that his friends lost their jobs, but has to remain hardened to this, to keep his sentiments masked, as he knows he could be next. So he is also proud of what he has achieved, despite the tinge of guilt that it has isolated him, internally and psychologically, and materially, from his former friends.

Wayne is struggling in his account to reconcile and justify the past, and to try to read the future from the present in order to guarantee it. His experiences of restructuring and the redundancies that came with it are clear drivers for his behaviour that barely mask his ambition, and his need to establish a secure future – not just for himself, but for his wife and family – is the rationale for the regime of self-sacrifice which they all endure. Wayne is stressed, facing the demands of being on call 24 hours. He feels that he can never be "his own man" but always the servant of another and at their behest and whilst being reassured that he is needed through the demand to work long hours, he is also anxious that the work itself is changing and he worries about his ability to keep up, to manage the "other stuff" that makes the manager's job so different from its traditional variant. The contemporary economic situation that confronts the organization, and indeed the middle management cohort, combined with longer term insecurities reflecting his reflection of himself, serve to accelerate notions of insecurity.

Yet Wayne is not the only one who sacrifices or is sacrificed. His wife sees little of him, they have lost some of the ease of their relationship and fight under the stresses, his children have a weekend father. He worries that they have lost what was on the one hand an element of traditional masculinity, the good father, but also that he is not able to respond to the demands of being a New Man, ready and able to shoulder some of the domestic burden to allow his wife the space to be herself, and not just "wife at home".

Wayne's mask, which amounts to one of "this is what you have to do to be a manager" externalizes some of the responsibility he might feel for being in this situation, and some of the guilt he does feel for being powerless to change it for the better. This guilt involves the sense of being an accessory to a crime – the killing off of the domestic side of his nature, the good father that he could have been. Commitment here is more of a death sentence than something driven by desire, as weighed down by responsibilities to the company and to the family, neither of which he is able to discharge without it being at the expense of the other, he is torn between the two, and to cope, one must be sacrificed. Stability is not produced by this sacrifice, however, except in a temporary fashion, and Wayne's account has a promissory dimension in that it tries to imply that the future will indeed be more stable as a result of present sacrifices. Wayne's mask then, is also one of the good manager as guardian of the future as well as saviour of the present.

In contemporary management accounts, discourses of commitment frequently mask a paradoxical relationship between the need to do more for the organization versus the need to provide for his family. He legitimates this by occupying and reconstructing a male-breadwinner discourse and although dissatisfied with working longer hours he actively rehearses his commitment to the organization. A good manager, therefore, is one that associates effectiveness with that of present sacrifice and dedication to Larts, to securing its future. They are even supposed to accept that they may have to sacrifice themselves literally in a future round of restructuring in order that Larts, the greater good, can survive, and this awareness plays around the edges of Wayne's words. The presentation of the self is publicly constructed and verbalized to reveal how sacrifices have to be made in one's private life and in Wayne's case the gendered mask as main family provider, the "male breadwinner", is used as justification and confirmation of having become a committed and dedicated manager – the family has colonized work ontologically in this formulation, despite the reality of work having colonized the family's private time and space materially. These legitimizing acts that reinforce one's status within the organization over discourses of familial and home life are suppressed and subsumed under the dominant discourses of the organization, survival and market competition and thus we see an assertion, reinforcement and extension of masculinist career patterns and working practices.

A better man than you?: killing the woman

Jackie has worked for Larts for 10 years. Jackie is single, 34 years old, and the only female middle manager at the plant. Jackie's text illustrates how she privileges her work commitments over personal commitments, despite having no husband or children to worry about. She professes to be extremely ambitious and regularly works 60 hours a week, together with weekend working and frequent attendance on residential in-house training courses. She says that "her life is Larts" and downplays life outside work:

Extract 1   "I do the best job I can (long pause). I have the skills and I get the job done whatever I have to do to get the results..."

Extract 2   "...I don't think I manage differently to my colleagues... I work very long hours, evenings, weekends, holidays but then this is my decision. I don't have family commitments... I don't have a partner, I get to see friends when I can, but most of the time I'm just glad to chill out when I get home and do nothing. By the time I've done the things that need doing, like feed the cats, it's a bath and bed, even then I can get called in if something goes wrong".

Extract 3   "If I didn't work the way I do I wouldn't last one minute. fit in and I manage to get good results but that takes effort and some of 'em won't do it. I'm lucky I'm better educated than most and I have the experience which is more than a lot of the lads out there. The difference is that I can manage my staff and develop them at the same time which is why I'm in a better position than the rest".

Jackie actively constructs a "competent" self and she is outwardly ambitious and aggressive. Her expressions downplay her femininity, her difference in terms of managerial style as a woman, and construct her self in terms of generic qualities possessed by either sex. She is not different, just better. She is not in the grip of insensitive or hostile forces, she has chosen a path and it was, as she says, her decision to do so. Whilst there may be a hint of nostalgia in her account of her day ending with a hot bath, if she's lucky, it is very muted. Indeed, there is none of the tone of self-sacrifice in Wayne's account, and in most other respects this account has the hallmarks of a more bourgeois form of masculinity.

Jackie shows an extremely dedicated side, but does not express this as being particularly to Larts, but rather more to the job and her own sense of professionalism which downplays the value of her personal life. Her success at work was confirmed by her line manager who suggested that she outperforms most of her male peers both in terms of hours worked and in her actual performance. Jackie's justification of her "sameness" – she pointed out that she "fits in" – can be interpreted as an acknowledgement of securing her participation in future episodes in Larts, a committed worker regardless of her experiences as the only female manager there. Jackie knows there is a risk to her job, and she does not want to make this situation worse by introducing a gender dimension and encouraging her colleagues to recognize her difference. Indeed, she is creating a self-identity which is durable and transferable from one work situation to the next – that of a de-gendered professional manager.

This gendered mask is potentially limiting to all individuals in Larts. Jackie's eagerness to promote what she sees to be the gender-neutral nature of performance measures within the organization may actually preserve the dominance of control systems which are masculinist and patriarchal in their nature and effects. She confessed that she can see how her working patterns may set a precedent for other managers with children and those people who are unable to work the hours that she does, but she believes that she has made her choice to devote her energies to her career and that such a choice is an inevitable aspect of modern competitive organizations. Again, as with Wayne, she devotes some effort to constructing the dedication of time and self as part of what the good manager does, and in an even more professionalized way deploys this to function as a stabilizing concept in her account. She copes with the past and present in the same way that she will cope with the future, a formula for success that nevertheless is not constraining and leaves her fluid and flexible enough to accommodate the ever-changing expectations of Larts.

Jackie has resisted the discourses of femininity that promote more passive identities, choosing to present more masculine images in order to "fit in", and performing self as indisposable, committed, dedicated and "better than the men" attempts to secure her future role in Larts. Restructuring in Larts for Jackie has, and may in future, lead to increased levels of expected performance amongst her middle management colleagues which escalates the internal competition between them. Jackie seeks to secure her future by remaining more competent than her colleagues, by being ahead of the game in skills and attitude, although with the possible exception of her ability to develop others these skills are not characteristically gendered. Jackie's gendered masquerade is problematic, as feminist literature suggests, for those males with familial responsibilities such as Wayne (see Davies 1990; Hochschild 1997) although many studies highlight how women still have the major responsibilities for the home child care (Davies 1990; Bailyn 1993; Wajcman 1998) stemming from a gendered construction of the separation of "work" and "home" spheres (Duncombe and Marsden 1995; Sullivan 1997). Jackie's justification of her "sameness" presents not only a level of performance that individuals with families find hard to manage but also a rehearsal of the constant negotiation of managing being "different", "woman" and "manager". Jackie suppresses the woman in her identity, but not completely – it is ironic to the point of paradox that her only managerial characteristic that she singles out as being different from those of her colleagues, the ability to develop others, is one which the "women in management" literature suggest that women managers are particularly strong on (Wilson 1995).

The old soldier: killing the past

Terry is 55 years old, married with children and grandchildren. He has worked with Larts for 39 years since he joined the company at 16 as an apprentice, working his way through the ranks to become a production manager in the "old" system, and has held this post for approximately 20 years. Restructuring into units resulted in a loss of responsibility for Terry resulting in insecurity and self-doubt. The threat of losing his job as an older manager is a real one now that Larts that has introduced "new blood".

Extract 1   "I have given my life to this company, working, giving it my all, and when it comes down to it decisions are taken that affect everything I've worked for without my involvement. I have devoted my life to this factory, and for what? Now I have less power and responsibility, and unless you're prepared to conform to the new requirements of you then there's nothing left... but if you don't and more important, you show it, then you won't be here".

Extract 2   "I still have a lot to give, you can't lose all those years of experience, working with the people... but we still have worth especially as older, long serving managers, we have value.... I understand that the company needs to bring in new people to change the stalemate culture, but there's a place for us too...".

Terry expresses feelings of above all, betrayal, and at a personal level. Where Jackie and Wayne take a fairly impersonal view of the company, and their commitment to it is not constructed as reciprocal or as one of "loyalty", Terry does not see it that way. He has given, and the implication is that he gave freely, not just his time but his "life", an investment that was as much intangible as tangible – ideas, feelings, effort and increasingly experience. Yet the past did not in Terry's case guarantee the future, and the self-accounting he produced to establish a durable and serviceable identity failed him as things changed. Now it is felt that the loyalty was not reciprocal, and that rather than the company giving back something in the way of consideration for all that its older managers have given in the past, they are making no concessions at all. Terry is now working longer hours and managing larger workloads and feels bitter and resentful that, at his age Larts expects increasing levels of performance and present the threat that he might be replaced by a younger manager – someone perhaps like Wayne or Jackie. The need to perform in exactly the same way as the others increases his insecurity and vulnerability underscored by his demotion of status, which he resents, as a "new" middle manager in Larts.

To compensate for these retrospective experiences Terry secures a point of reference that he uses as a resource (Parker 1997) to ontologically position and secure himself, finding a place in the future. He does this by drawing on his experience and skills to secure a sense of self in an organization where loyalty and commitment to long serving members is a "thing of the past". The loyalty which the traditional managerial fraternity implied may have dissolved under competitive pressure along with other sentiments, but Larts still expects loyalty of a sort, although it now seems more like political correctness. If you voice any sort of disquiet, you risk being seen as not "on board", not part of the new way, or not up to the job, and move yourself to the head of the queue for the next restructuring. Terry then protects his future role by keeping up with current demands, suppressing his unhappiness, and arguing for the continuing value and worth of older managers to the company in terms of experience and know-how. Yet despite its usefulness as a survival strategy, ultimately all this seems to do is to underline the exploitative nature of today's Larts, and offer the older manager up once more in the tradition of self-sacrifice of the working-class male, as someone who has still "a lot to *give*" because worth is only measured in narrow performative and transactional terms. It is the past itself that has been sacrificed here.

A hired gun on the road to burnout: killing the manager

Justin is a 32 year old, engineering graduate who has recently married. He has no children and his partner has a career in retailing. They depend on their dual income to manage their financial commitments. He has worked as an engineering manager in the company since graduating from university at the age of 23 and reveals some of the pressures that a younger, well-qualified manager faces in the company. Wayne is reflecting on his educational attributes to position himself as "manager".

Extract 1   "I'm lucky you know, I have my qualifications to support my position here and to get me into somewhere else if I need to... I probably will have to move, there's no security here nowadays not like the older managers they knew what it was like to experience a steady job...".

Extract 2   "...I'm lucky I have no children, so no family commitments, and my wife works so we can manage our life style, but we rarely spend any quality time together".

Extract 3   "I get so tired, there's no shutting off since the redundancies, we are all working harder... My job here means that I have to be at hand 24 hours a day, production is 24 hours and so are maintenance and all the support functions. Being on call, pagers, mobiles, the phone at home and at the office means there is very little free time. I am always coming in when I think it's unnecessary... No weekend, there'll be divorce".

Extract 4   " ...The thing is if I just worked long hours and there was no stress that would be something, but you can't do this job and stay stress free, it's the constant pressure... we have to keep putting more in. The fear for me is that I'm pissed off with the job, being a manager, and I'm only at the start of my career".

Comparing himself against his middle management colleagues Justin immediately expresses difference. Justin has no loyalty to the company and sees himself as mobile by virtue of his qualifications. This can be contrasted with Wayne, who is a Larts man and hopes to remain so; Terry, who is a one-company man and even if made redundant is so unlikely to get employment at his age that he has indeed given his life to the company and Jackie, who has invested so much in suppressing her gender difference and fitting in successfully at Larts. Unlike Wayne, Justin's qualifications will not give him so much a future *in* Larts, as a guarantee that he will have options elsewhere, perhaps to trade if necessary. In some sense, then, Justin's model of masculinity is more akin to that of the traveller, the "hired gun" of the American West (see Simon 1997). If settling becomes problematic and insecure, he will have the option to move on. Nevertheless, just as the hired gun constantly has to demonstrate his ability and is only as good as his next gunfight, so Justin constantly has to demonstrate his own performance. Just as a hired gun cannot afford to have family commitments, Justin has a marriage to another career professional which gives them no time to put down roots, or even spend much quality time together.

Justin shows how intensified working patterns, commitment via longer working hours and increased expectations for performance influence his role as manager at Larts. He now questions his position, role and identity since he believed that being educated was a route for having a better standard of living, a route for protecting himself from the unhappy experiences of others in the past. Justin's account positions himself for his future role whether inside or outside Larts, in that he is competent enough to do the job well and simultaneously flexible and transferable enough to leave, and is not weighed down by any sentimental, social, familial or ideological commitment to the company. However, he does this by exerting more effort and at the same time being more "pissed off" with the gendered performance expectations he encounters, and wonders whether he will be able to do this, for whoever the employer, for the rest of his life. Behind the mask is the constant worry that the hired gun may be killed by a ricochet from his own weaponry.

Commodified selves

As I have argued in this book, there are epistemological and ontological limitations with existing research that presents middle management as a genderless and homogenized body. The processes of identity construction of four middle managers within Larts were explored to illustrate how these individuals draw, implicitly and explicitly on gendered masks to construct and legitimize their generic roles and identities as managers, regardless of being male or female. The four managers revealed in their persuasive accounts the paradoxical nature of their identity construction in making sense of their work experiences in Larts.

The masks used by managers in their performance of the self may actually enable the managers to be and say what they would fear to otherwise. The paradoxical nature of masks suggests that masks may function to both conceal and perform the natural. This masking initiates the re-creation of managers' identities. Jackie's mask – "a better man than the men" – is one that aids the construction and reconstruction of the other quite explicitly and therefore offers the potential to conceal difference, assist praxis and re-theorize the abject. The gendered masks, masks of masculinities, not only conceal but reveal individual subjectivities and serve to reinforce the masculine signifiers of organization. Discourses of commitment to the organization disguise other middle managers' subjectivities from the organizational gaze. "New managerial work" fuels the masking of individuals' subject positions and therefore legitimizes and reinforces the dominant masculine discourses of management and organization within an image of gender neutrality. The boundaries between public and private are increasingly blurred as organizational identities colonize the spaces in the manager's life, subsuming it under the "greedy" discourses of management and organization. Masking not only bridges the past and present but the public and private.

Within this chapter, Wayne can be seen to have great difficulty in adopting the mask of "breadwinner", because some aspects of this traditional male identity are being stripped away whilst simultaneously being valorized by discourses of new masculinity. Thus the role of good father, present if not dominant in traditional breadwinner discourse, is being rendered almost vestigial at Larts whilst men in general are being exhorted not only to fully embrace their fatherly roles but to share it with the more caring roles traditionally associated with motherhood. Terry's masculinity is itself under assault as he has been demoted, and is forced into a rearguard action to establish his continuing credibility and value for the company. For Terry, behind his mask of the loyal and battle-scarred "old soldier", masculinity is presented as a matter of survival, which he is hoping will not be reduced to a survival of the fittest but that other considerations will be taken into account. He has to continue to profess and display commitment to the company he feels has betrayed him, whilst struggling to find answers to the questions "what was it all for?" and "who *can* I be now?". Justin, at the other end of his career, feels a similar disillusionment behind the mask of bravura competence of the "hired gun". There is no loyalty either way here, no vision of a shared future, just a job of work to be done.

Just as the hired gun – who is also frequently masked – gets no second chances, Justin knows he must perform whether he believes in the employer's cause or not. Behind his mask, the loneliness and emptiness which he shares with us may be discerned.

The analysis presented in this chapter illustrates increased feelings of fragility of identity amongst the middle managers discussed in Larts, with the middle managers experiencing and revealing great uncertainty and insecurity over their role and status. Organizational restructuring has fundamentally challenged the recourses to legitimacy of these middle managers. Therefore, these fragmentary social texts illustrate how, in their engagement in the research process, each manager draws on various discourses and their associated images as a linguistic resource in creating their "self". Each text illustrates the ways in which some middle managers seek to confirm, create and legitimize their role and purpose within the organization, reflecting on and negotiating the personal aspects of their lives with their working lives. Within each text it can be seen that, due to a range of different factors, middle managers are feeling great uncertainty and insecurity over their role and status, extending to the point of ontological self-doubt. They highlight some of the different reasons for this and illustrate how and in what ways middle managers attempt to secure an identity, however temporarily as a staging post to the future or lifeline to the past. In seeking to secure a sense of purpose and belonging, middle managers are increasingly sacrificing their personal lives to satisfy the levels of commitment required by the organization.

Analyzing middle managers' identity construction, I argued that the gendered masks adopted serve to legitimize their identities, revealing a range of tensions between work, home and ultimately self. Middle managers face struggles to accommodate intensified working regimes that involve longer working hours and escalated pressures for commitment to the organization, at the expense of commitments outside work which effectively leave them insufficient room to be themselves – not only are they unsure about their work futures, *they don't know who they are any more.*

To return to our Management in Three Movements framework, it can be seen that commitment itself is not what it appears to be, that the seduction which underpins it as part of the postmodern structural-representational-behavioural spine of networking, seduction and commitment has not worked in that the managers are only differentially seduced. This, I argue, is first of all a result of the operation of masks, which has already been discussed, and second, a result of the workings of the commodification process. As Featherstone (1991: 14) argues:

> If from the perspectives of classical economics the object of all production is consumption, with individuals maximising their satisfactions through purchasing from an ever expanding range of goods, then from the perspective of some twentieth-century neo-Marxists this development is regarded as producing greater opportunities for controlled and manipulated consumption.

The original value of products, for Marx and others, lies in their use-value, in that people pay more for what they need most, or what meets their most important needs most. But because consumption is not evenly distributed in terms of economic power, in that some have more resources than others, and material and technical resources which can include skill, are not equally available, the picture becomes complicated because products acquire differential values related to other considerations than their utility. Eventually, this exchange value displaces use-value altogether in the advanced consumer society. As the memory of the commodity's use value fades, however, it means that the commodity may be freed to take up a third, symbolic value through cultural associations and illusions. Advertising and the media particularly create and proliferate these, but the process is embedded in everyday life. For Baudrillard, for example, it is the process of reproduction of the commodity in these symbolic systems which is more important than the commodity itself, because the potential endlessness of this process of reproduction of images, signs and simulations destabilizes meaning and social regulation in everyday life (Featherstone 1991: 14–15). Organizations which we might consider to have been originally set up to produce commodities to satisfy particular needs now engage in a more complex set of activities, creating and sustaining symbolic value for their products, differentiating their products through symbolic means – but also themselves being subject to the endless redefinitions of consumers and the market. Even the organization itself may become a brand, and come to have more value in terms of its brands and their identities than the value of the actual machinery and premises it uses to create them.

All of the managers studied in this book found their work to some degree affected by these processes. For this chapter, it is the way in which managerial work and skills have become revalued and differentiated into commodities themselves which is of particular interest (see

Casey 1995). Put in these terms, under the original conditions where products were produced to meet needs – transportation (Carlux); producers of Nylon yarn (Nylons); and mechanical components (Larts) – labour was controlled by management to make sure that the necessary tasks were performed in the correct manner, in the correct time frame, at the right quality and cost, and that problems which arose developed transferable solutions. As the shift to exchange value became more complete, the *differentiation* of value spread to managerial work and effectively, the control systems applied to measure managerial activity and render managers increasingly *accountable, commodified* and *quantified* managerial work into such elements as "achievements". In a postmodern world such measurements depend on a chain of significations that are increasingly separated from the reality they represent. Carlux, for example, although it produces a vehicle which is highly technically sophisticated, depends on its immense brand image to sustain its market position, and this has in the past prevented it from going under. The worth of managerial activity may become subject to a battery of technical metrics and attempts to represent it symbolically, such that management becomes the production of reports and accounts about itself to demonstrate its own value as though it were a continuing use-value, and not, particularly in the new public management a socio-political matter. Here the measure and terms employed become a world of circulating signs of their own increasingly disconnected from the satisfaction of real need as a defining quality of management. Management itself in these processes, is increasingly commodified. However, as seen in terms of seduction, achievement and commitment, it may move from the measurement of activity, managerial work, to the regulation of managers as persons, by intervening in identity formation and self-construction. The managerial self becomes a *commodity* – what matters is how much the manager is prepared to give of themselves to the organization which is valued symbolically with a loose relation to material reward in exchange. The managers in this chapter have illustrated the hidden costs of this commodification for the selves they are expected to sell, and have enabled us to identify how these costs are differentially distributed across genders.

8
Disrupted Identities in a Still-Organized World

Introduction

This book began by raising the question of whether the criteria through which managers, especially middle managers, define management and shape their identities have changed over the past 20 years as new organizational and social forms, sometimes labelled postmodern, have changed the context of their practice. Gowler and Legge's seminal paper on the meaning of management became the starting point and assuming the rhetorical formation of identity in this paper to have been modernist, I used my reading in organizational, management and social theory to project the directions in which change could be expected to occur under conditions of postmodernity. The criteria developed related to underlying questions of *structure*, where the shift of process from differentiation to de-differentiation should have led to a corresponding shift from hierarchy as core to identity, to networking as a major shaping feature of identities; to questions of *representation*, where shifts from rationality to enchantment should have led to demands for accountability being displaced by processes of seduction; and finally to considerations of *behaviour*, where shifts from commodification to consumption should have led to concerns for achievement being displaced by concerns for commitment.

In chapters 5, 6 and 7 of this book I have been concerned to interrogate these shifts, with a particular emphasis on the gender dimensions involved which were raised by our data from three companies. The data provided qualified support for the shifts being in process but incomplete, for a variety of reasons, but three key factors seemed to intervene in the process – gender, narcissism and power and resistance. The first, gender, I discussed as I progressed through each chapter and will summarize in what follows; the second, narcissism, I will discuss in full; the third, power and resistance, was introduced in Chapter 6 and I will expand upon that discussion. I will then return to the second model of subject formation introduced in Chapter 1 – the model of "*Modes of Subjectivity Formation*" and identify the modes which were in operation across the interviewees in the three companies as discussed in the previous three chapters and the present chapter. I will then return to my observation from the data, as noted in Chapter 6, that the shifts in the model were not simply horizontal, but vertical and diagonal relationships between the characteristics were also in motion – indeed I have tried to indicate this fluidity by the circular two-way arrows on the diagram (see Figure 3.1). This is attributable to the incomplete satisfaction of the conditions for heterarchy to occur in the companies studied. To conclude this chapter, and the book proper, I will argue that managers' identities have always been a matter of negotiation and contestation, but against a background of relative stability and significance. Their experiences provide us with some direct evidence of the impact of postmodernization processes on not only their work, but on their identities. These processes are never finished, and continue in motion – they involve changing individual subjectivities, shifting power lines, and challenging gender assumptions.

Gender as an obstacle to change?

Gender has been a central feature in my analysis of the modern and postmodern criteria of middle managers' identity work. To summarize, a gendered reading became a way to appreciate difference within and between individual middle managers; acknowledge how masculinist discourses dominate management practices with the feminine positioned as abject; and explore the gender mask that middle managers employ when doing identity work. In the last three chapters the gender mask has been analyzed to account for the ways in which middle managers restructure their sense of self. Data from managers in Carlux, Nylons and Larts has explored the intersections of modern and postmodern features of managerial identity construction – hierarchy and networking, accountability and seduction, and achievement and commitment respectively. Throughout the three chapters, as managers draw on modernist projects of identity this remasculinizes discourses of identity, management and organization. In Carlux I concluded that hierarchy is a core function of management and this desire for hierarchy in identity work further masculinizes working practices and identity construction. Indeed, as I have argued, hierarchy is a masculine organizational form (Chapter 5) and managers draw on modes of hierarchy to disturb feminized forms of networking, finding news ways of reinforcing new hierarchical relations and therefore masculinity. Hierarchy oppresses, ungendering and disembodying individuals in the process too (Morgan 1996). For Wajcman (2004) flexibility and technological advances emancipates women from this oppression, using technology as a medium to reconstruct their identities beyond the limitations of their bodies.

Interestingly, in the case of Nylons (Chapter 6) feminine capital was employed outwardly to bring about change and as I have argued to seduce the masculine thereby masking modernist organizational forms and working practices. But even in this case the feminine is consumed and cast out as other. Accounting practices based on objectivity and standardization suppresses the feminine and managers drawing on modernist forms of accounting enforce hierarchy. I proposed in chapter 3 that accountability for managers are fashioned around and support feminine ways of managing but the discourses of performativity are themselves gendered (see Thomas and Linstead (2002)). Managers are both consumed and commodified whilst simultaneously resisting the power of the feminine, the fluid and unknown, by donning masks through which they can construct their identities. As seduced commodities, performances of commitment become inevitable. In Larts I was concerned with the *performance* of the self. Seduction underpins commitment as part of the structural relations of networking. I explored the gendered masks that conceal and initiate identity work, and as I revealed through the discussion, these masks are masks of masculinities that serve to reinforce the masculine signifiers of organization. Achievement is inextricably tied up with commitment, and it is these displays of commitment – the discourses of being a good manager – that fuels the advent of masculinity in managing their identities. However seduction and commitment has not worked in that managers are only differentially seduced, the result of the complex workings of the operation of masks and as an outcome of the commodification process. Managers, in part, have sold parts of the self in their identity work.

Regardless of whether managers employ modernist or postmodernist identity criteria throughout their narratives, the masks employed by managers throughout the chapters reinforce and perpetuate masculinity. Thus managerial masks are masks of masculinity, unable to capture and confront change. Managers paradoxically mask and suppress the feminine by reinstating modernist forms of organizing whilst mas-

querading the feminine as ideology. Masculinity dominates the formation of managers' subjectivity and the power of this as we have seen
cannot be underestimated. In Chapter 6 it was demonstrated that
resistance to the other, to the feminine, is central to some managers'
modernist projects of identity in attempts to gain ontological security.

Totally devoted to self: narcissism in identity work

No sensible career was good enough,
Only a hero could deserve such love.

W.H. Auden
(Collected Poems in Mendelsen cited in Kets De Vries 1995: 13)

Disillusionment... may not occur until middle age, when recognition and reward in an ascending scale are no longer forthcoming...
Tartakoff (cited in Kets De Vries 1995: 14).

Narcissism is the term given in psychoanalysis to an obsession with self,
whether with the strengths or with the weaknesses of the self, or
whether the self is used to dominate others or is constantly realigned to
meet with the approval of others. It has become an important concept
in organization studies in recent years for it connects with some important managerial concepts such as leadership (Downs 1997) and organizational culture and power (Schwartz 1990) through its concern with
problems of identity formation at both an individual and a collective
level. As Schwartz (1990: 32) puts it, our sense of identity is tenuous
because many of us cannot be what we are, or cannot allow ourselves to
be what we are. We are said to have "made something" of ourselves, or
to have "become somebody" or even a "has been". Identity is not something that can be taken for granted and is an achievement that will
evaporate unless it is maintained. There is accordingly an imperative to
become something that one is not – or is not naturally or automatically
– and the sense of emptiness that accompanies this signals the need for
what Schwartz (1990: 32) calls the *ontological function*. This is a meaning
function which tells us who we are, or whom we should be, and we
look outside ourselves to find it and so locate the criteria of our identity.
For Schwartz, and for different reasons for Foucault, social institutions
are created to perform this function, for telling us who we are or should
be and fashioning and disciplining subjects and selves. People may find
their identity so located in these institutions that their behaviour is dis-
torted to extremes – for example believing the organization can do no

wrong or cannot make mistakes – adopting a mindset which Schwartz, following Shorris calls totalitarian, where the organization defines people's happiness for them, and may become the only arbiter of that happiness. Schwartz's examples are General Motors and NASA, but small organizations may provide this function just as effectively, depending on the individual. The other side of this coin is where individuals seek to manipulate organizations to determine others' happiness in ways which particularly benefit them, and is the sort of behaviour which particularly fascinates Downs (1997) and is most relevant to our data. The key point for Schwartz is that narcissism is based in a fantasy world rather than reality, and at some point the distance between the two will cause at least a degree of organizational or personal collapse unless attended to. Narcissism may therefore accelerate or impede broader social or environmental trends, and it in this capacity that it seems to disrupt some of the tendencies in the data. Managers who feel their identities are under threat may consciously or unconsciously employ narcissistic behaviours to confirm their status, to themselves and others, as confident, significant, valued and committed organizational performers.

The origins of these approaches lie in the work of Freud, whose development of the term narcissism (although Havelock Ellis, the sexologist, was the first to use it in the 19th century) has been hailed as one of his major contributions to the social sciences as a whole by such as Adorno, Fromm and Bettelheim (Carr 1998). Freud thought that narcissism was rooted in the primary relationship between mother and child – after all, Narcissus in Ovid's version of the myth was the progeny of the rape of Liriope by the river-God Cephisus, and his relationship to his parents was always therefore problematic. Mother-love gives the infant the impression that it is the centre of the world, but as it grows it becomes aware that it is not, and that there are rivals – particularly the father – for its mother's attention and its place at the centre of things. The infant's experience of its own *attraction* for others therefore decays with time as it becomes displaced. Similarly Narcissus was so beautiful from birth that those who encountered the child questioned whether he could live very long, on the principle that such a fine creature must, like the butterfly, be transient (Holmes 2001: 21). Tiresias, the hermaphrodite seer, in reply to these concerns, first articulated the ironic problem of the narcissist – as long as he remains trapped in self-love, unable to see himself, or others, as he really is, not at the centre of the world, then he can survive. Once he gains self-knowledge and realizes that beauty is ephemeral, he can celebrate his beauty only as a transient phase in his life, part of the passage towards death (Holmes 2001: 22). Thus without what I noted as the "gift of death" in Chapter 6, which is the recognition that they and their position relative to others inevitably will and must change, narcissists are unable to move beyond and transcend their own self-obsession, which arises from either an over-acute awareness or a blanket denial of their own frailties and inadequacies. Narcissistic managers may displace their sense of such vulnerability, and seemingly re-establish themselves as central to their evolving organizational situations, by behaviours which take two broad forms.

Classic male narcissism, the active "thick-skinned" (Rosenfeld 1965) or oblivious (Gabbard 1996) form, tends to glorify itself and attract flatterers and fawners. Such people do not see the impact of their actions on others, at least not clearly, or discount them, breaking hearts and betraying those who give them their affections and loyalties. However, the alternate feminine, Echoistic, passive "thin-skinned" (Rosenfeld 1965) or hypervigilant (Gabbard 1996) form is only too aware of its fragilities to the point of losing its own voice, living only by pale imitation of others, as was the case with the wood-nymph Echo who pined for Narcissus in the original myth. For both, the lost object is one with which a relationship is truly possible only through a retrieval which displaces or re-places them – for Narcissus, one in which the sound of the voice of the other can blend in with and become the sound of his own more responsive and inclusive voice; for Echo, one in which her own voice can be raised to play an equal part in the multiplex voice of the Other (Holmes 2001: 24).

For Freud, it was the social civilizing process which forced human beings out of their classical self-centredness and into relationality. In Holmes' condensation of events, Copernicus decentred man cosmologically from the centre of the universe; Darwin toppled man from the pinnacle of his authority over nature and revealed humanity to be an unfinished project, still unfolding; and Freud argued that psychoanalysis ontologically decentred the will, revealing consciousness itself – Descartes' *cogito* – to be a slave of *unconscious* drives. Postmodernity, it could be argued, in further deconstructing identity and individuality, shows how any remaining sense of who we are arises not from originary qualities but from our relationships with others in the world. Thus the progress of civilization could be argued to be an accumulation of attacks on narcissism, yet so effective are narcissistic defences that it perennially assumes new forms in response. So resilient has it proved that it has even been argued to be the characteristic state of postmodern culture (Lasch 1979).

How then does this connect with the lives of the managers in our study? Kets De Vries considers the relationship between fantasy and reality in executive identity work:

> [In an environment] ...of inner fears, anxiety and guilt, as well as affiliative, dependency and aggressive needs, executives have to come to terms with their own narcissism and thus place limits on potential conflicts between fantasy and reality in their leadership styles. Recourse to fantasy, however, will remain important as a way of mastering disappointments, instead of becoming a way of arresting human development and growth (Kets De Vries 1995: 186).

Kets De Vries captures adroitly the pressures and responses that has been seen in the lives of the middle managers researched in this book. I will now briefly explore firstly, how the concept of narcissism helps us to understand how narcissistic behaviours arise and secondly, how individuals employ narcissistic behaviours as a response to ontological insecurity and existential anxiety. These narcissistic defences affect and may derail any development towards postmodern forms of management, especially insofar as they are more relational, as they constitute a direct attack on narcissism.

Organization and management studies have primarily drawn on psychoanalysis in their discussions of individual and organizational narcissism (Brown 1997; Carr 1998), but Lasch (1979) employs the term sociologically to refer to its negative, destructive sense as a collective pathology of the whole society. Nevertheless, the elements and definitions of narcissism in all approaches involve identifying narcissists' "preoccupation with themselves or their own interests" (Carr 1998: 87). From a poststructuralist perspective however most psychoanalytic perspectives on narcissism offer too much of an essentialist fixed view of self, even as a relational construct, that is rejected in this book. Narcissism as used here therefore refers to the *continually changing processes of narcissistic behaviour that individuals consciously and unconsciously perform.*

Brown's analysis of narcissism at the individual level highlights how "identities... are preserved through individual and social processes of self-esteem regulation" and "self-esteem is narcissistically regulated through ego defence mechanisms" (Brown 1997: 643). I agree that "individuals have a need to maintain a positive sense of self, and they engage in ego-defence behaviour in order to preserve self-esteem" (Brown 1997: 845) as in the research reported here managers employ narcissism as a tactical process to convey and establish themselves as self-confident, secure and committed *organizational* members. Brown identifies six psychological/behavioural categories that characterize the narcissistic personality: denial; rationalization; self-aggrandisement; attributional egotism; sense of entitlement (or "epistemic narcissism" – Britton 1998) and anxiety which were distributed across the managers' texts in this book. However to explore how narcissistic behaviours arise and how individuals employ these behaviours as a response to onto-logical insecurity and existential anxiety more closely I will use data from Larts (which were presented in Chapter 7) to illustrate how the Company Director Randle's narcissistic displays influenced the ways in which one middle manager, Timothy, performed his identity work by viewing narcissism as an essential component in managing his public self. The adoption of narcissistic behaviours then, I argue here, is imper-ative to managing performance and success in Larts. As Downs (1997 cited in Fulop and Linstead (1999: 192)) states: "narcissistic behaviour produces a dearth of values, careful image management, an absence of empathy, loyalty or any deep emotion, and an obsession with personal gain" which will be seen with both Randle and Timothy. Downs con-tinues "The narcissist, as leader, creates problems for organizations" and I have seen this working in Larts. Although I am not interested in defining individuals as narcissists or otherwise, Randle's very public displays of narcissism set the stage for others, wishing to impress and succeed, to follow without reflecting on the negative consequences of his behaviour for the organization as narcissistic values and norms become institutionalized. On the other hand, although Timothy is annoying to his colleagues, he uses narcissism in a positive way for himself to manage ontological insecurity and anxiety. He is driven by the abject (Kristeva 1982), as he confesses.

Narcissistic displays in Larts: is Randle setting the scene for the rest?

I am a man in full control of the company, I know where it needs to go and I will get it there no matter what. I expect a lot from my men, they need to work hard and carry out my instructions so that I can keep control of everything, otherwise things will unravel. Of course I consult them – they need to show me that I can trust them and that they can do the jobs I want them to do. But at the end of the day I know what I want and where I'm taking the com-pany. It's not a job for the light-hearted. Times are tough and I have to be hard on them because I expect a lot.

I understand all my managers – I've been there and I know the busi-ness – and they are in full support of what I do. My company is my life. It's when others get involved that things go wrong. I am a man with ambition, I don't want to slow down and if others don't like what I do then they know where the door is. I know the price of failure, I've seen it… I was here seeing the changes happen and seeing senior management leave, it all fell on my shoulders and I'm the one that turned the company around.

Randle's inward looking behaviour seems prominent in these short extracts, and his seeming discursive obsession with who he was and is seems to underline that he is the product of an image that he has created for himself. Several other interviewees commented on the difficulties they had with Randle, and yet Randle had no idea that his management style and personality might be major obstacles in developing the company. He dwells on his own ego, and his own certainty that he is right, at the expense of needing to be reflexive. Indeed, although these extracts are short, Randle demonstrates all of Brown's criteria for narcissism, in particular, what I have called oblivious narcissism: denial (*they are in full support of what I do*); rationalization (*they need to work hard and carry out my instructions… otherwise things will unravel*) self-aggrandisement (*I am a man in full control of the company*); attributional egotism (*I'm the one that turned the company around*); sense of entitlement (*if others don't like what I do then they know where the door is*) and anxiety (*I know the price of failure, I've seen it*). Notice how Randle repetitively and almost invariably uses the "I" form, placing himself at the centre of most of his utterances. The necessity which he experienced for personal gain and his unacknowledged need to impress his colleagues, even junior colleagues and, I felt, myself as an interviewer in this situation, which were apparent in his general behaviour both reveal Randle's existential anxiety, his underlying sense of the fragility of his self-worth, and how he energetically performed the confident self in public to legitimize himself for the preservation and maintenance of his identity.

Striving for recognition: Timothy in Larts

It is important to me that Randle thinks well of my performance. Nobody wants not to be liked, don't you think? What do you think? Well, I think I'm doing my job properly anyway and I'm keen to impress not only my boss but also others around me. It's good to make your mark and stand out from the crowd. I might not have as much experience but I think I have more to offer than my colleagues, I have the background and education to outperform them.

I want to do the best job I can. You have to make the most of what you've got. I have to present my confident side. I need to show them that I'm knowledgeable, it's important to me. I'm also one of the busiest people with the most responsibility but Randle knows that I can do it and he trusts my ability.

Sometimes when I'm at home and I think about the day I've had, I wonder why I do it all. I also feel that I'm being watched and I need to manage this. I put so much into managing my career and whether I am getting on can be questioned. I guess I try harder and harder but I don't know why. I have to try to keep up with the things my colleagues are doing, so I have to spend a lot of time talking to them and networking, sometimes it spills over and occasionally I'll invite them round to tea at the weekend, just to make sure I'm not getting cut out of any loops. I don't really like them or have anything much in common with them, but you don't get to the top without keeping up your contacts.

Timothy used strategies that were chameleon in nature in order to get closer to his colleagues to impress upon them his competent self. At times we see him knowingly presenting an identity that is consistent with Randle's displays of narcissism, and which is consistent with Downs' observations of how narcissistic behaviour affects others. Timothy's narcissism is echoic, as he behaves in the way that he thinks is what Randle expects and wants. He responds by mirroring Randle's behaviour. Timothy demonstrates Brown's criteria in the following statements: denial (*Well, I think I'm doing my job properly anyway*); rationalization (*I have to try to keep up with the things my colleagues are doing, so I have to spend a lot of time talking to them and networking*) self-aggrandisement (*I need to show them that I'm knowledgeable, it's important to me*); attributional egotism (*I'm also one of the busiest people with the most responsibility but Randle knows that I can do it*); sense of entitlement (*I think I have more to offer than my colleagues*) and anxiety (*I wonder why I do it all*).

Timothy's vulnerability, beneath his self-centredness, is typical of echoistic narcissism. He also displays a degree of reflexivity in his awareness of his identity work. Together, these factors enable his colleagues to admit to some sympathy for him, where they would be more critical or rejecting of Randle. But Timothy is, they report, Randle's man. Unfortunately Timothy concentrates on the self that he

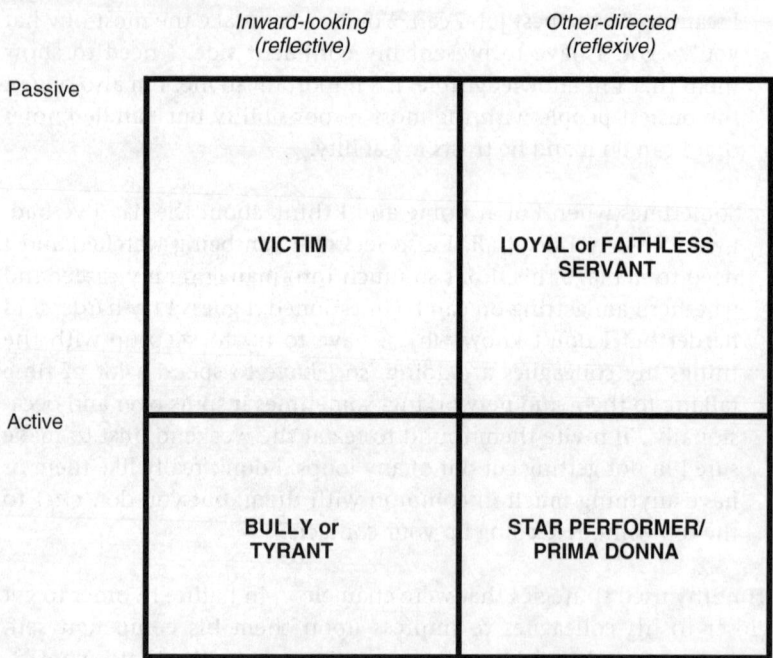

	Inward-looking (reflective)	Other-directed (reflexive)
Passive	VICTIM	LOYAL or FAITHLESS SERVANT
Active	BULLY or TYRANT	STAR PERFORMER/ PRIMA DONNA

Figure 8.1 Archetypes of Narcissistic Behaviour

creates to satisfy the fantasized other at the expense of the real others who constitute his colleagues. So despite his desire to be liked and to stay in the communication loop, the manipulative nature of his networking contributes as much as does a Randle to an environment of mistrust and political game-playing amongst his peers and staff.

To summarize, many of the managers throughout the three companies presented in this book displayed narcissistic behaviours and/or masks of narcissism at particular moments of their identity projects. The following model was accordingly developed to reflect the dimensions of whether an individual is reflective or reflexive of their narcissistic behaviour and whether they are passive (echoistic or hypervigilant) or active (oblivious) in the process.

If we consider narcissistic behaviour as discussed above it can be seen that it varies along dimensions of the more or less active (in the classical myth the masculine or feminine), against the more or less reflexive being aware of self or others (thin-skinned or thick skinned). Regarding the former, I can construct a scale of active–passive; regarding the latter, the key difference seems to be between being reflective, capable of reflecting on one's own thoughts and feelings but not of relating them to others, and being reflexive, where the desire to situate the self amongst others and in relation to others can, for good or ill, produce a calculating and strategic approach to self-identity. I have chosen to label the dimension inward-looking versus other-directed to try to capture this. On the passive side, the inward looking quadrant is the classic echoistic melancholic, the victim of circumstance and their own inner failings, obsessed with them and powerless, apparently to do anything about them. The active form of this inner directedness is more aggressive and becomes the bully or the tyrant. Interestingly, this behaviour is not about the controlled or tyrannized others: they are merely incidental to the bully pursuing whatever are their own concerns of the moment and the others are unfortunate to be in the way. Less active forms may take a less direct and more surreptitious approach, but will be about advancing the narcissist's narrow agenda. The more outward looking passive form results in a situation of apparent sublimation – the narcissistic self fills its own lack by performing service for others. This may appear admirable, but it can have negative consequences for the self's own genuine development (consider, for example, the butler, Stephens, in Ishiguro's *The Remains of the Day*). A servant, also, may be either loyal or disloyal, and if the reassurance and recognition the narcissist craves is not forthcoming then more dysfunctional behaviour may take its place (we might wonder about the motivations of several former servants of the Royal Household in recent years, both in the Press and in the Old Bailey). The active form of this narcissism in its positive form gives us the star performer, driven by the need to perform for others, to gain recognition by moving people and giving to them and creating, being an overachiever and often in a team setting (Ted Turner, Olympic yachtsman and founder of CNN would fall into this category). A more negative form of this self-centredness would be the prima donna (Madonna seems to walk the fine line between the two) and the most extreme and negative would be the delusional Hitler figure, for whom country appears to take the place of ego with ultimately disastrous consequences.

In my data I have not seen any of the extreme examples of these forms but certainly the forms were present in milder varieties. All the managers were to some degree self-oriented, and for some this was clearly driven by a deeper self-hatred which underlay their outward self-focus. Randle, however, seems to exemplify well the active–reflective quadrant, with his often bullying need to dominate others, whilst Timothy is active–reflexive, displaying a need for the admiration and approval of others. The overriding need to serve others of the passive–reflexive can be seen in the case of Bob (he's the good servant in Carlux), whilst in the same company Alan shows the depressive resignation of the passive–reflective.

Personal identity processes clearly had organizational effects in our case studies. More generally, the recent rediscovery of narcissism's relevance to mainstream management theory has offered some powerful insights into the psychodynamics of managerial interactions, and emphasizes the extent to which micro-processes can affect strategic changes in organizational direction. Narcissistic processes are not necessarily oppositional to such changes, but by the fact that they are centred around personal rather than organizational need, may be *frictional* in diverting or resisting the smooth passage of change. In the next section, I will return to the consideration of resistance initiated in Chapter 7, looking more closely this time at *social* micro-processes of frictional resistance which occur alongside individual narcissistic behaviours, which affect and divert the movement towards more postmodern managerial forms.

Resistance and the hidden text

Resistance, as Clegg (1994) has observed, is often more effective in its deployment of the power to subvert the dominant, rather than to invert it. Resistance in practice is often barely recognizable as resistance, being more subtle, unorganized, covert in practice and secretive than organized opposition (Kondo 1990; Collinson 1994; Jermier et al 1994, Edwards et al 1995; Gabriel 1999; Fleming and Sewell 2002; Fleming and Spicer 2003). Figure 8.2 shows the range of practices of resistance and relates them to the relative degree of organization of power relations in the institutions under study. In the case studies I have examined, there is a shift from apparently organized and structured power relations to a much looser degree of structure characterized by greater empowerment, but the extent to which the grip of top management has slackened and middle managers are empowered is under question. In several of the accounts of our respondents, resistance from the left-hand column of the diagram surfaced – the more subtle, subversive, less visible modes of frictional resistance which are often not recognized as such.

Even the most extreme form of silent relations – which Figure 8.2 calls withdrawal or non-involvement – has power because, as a form of

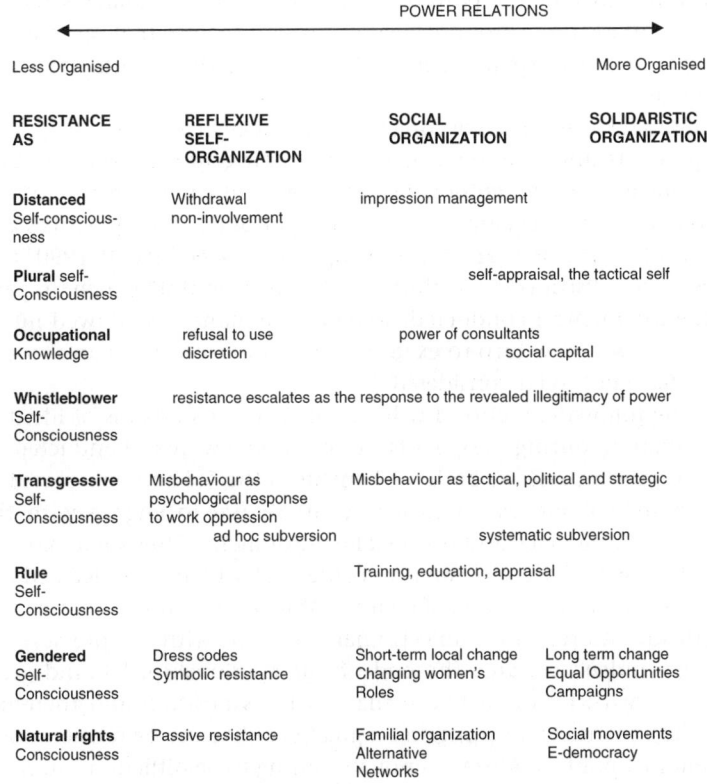

Figure 8.2   Power/Resistance Matrix

Adapted from Stephen Linstead's modification of Stewart Clegg "Power Relations and the Constitution of the Resistant Subject" in John M. Jermier, David Knights and Walter R. Nord (eds) (1994) Resistance and Power in Organizations. *London: Routledge p. 298. Reproduced in Simon Lilley and Edward Wray-Bliss "Organizational Control" in Stephen Linstead, Liz Fulop, simon Lilley and Associates (2003)* Management and Organization: A Critical Text. *London: Palgrave/Macmillan.*

abstaining or dissenting from social interactions it dissolves the organizational power relationships which must be maintained on a daily basis to unmask the "ideological absurdities that shore them up" (Fleming and Sewell 2002: 859). Scott (1990) goes further in arguing that all confrontations where there is a significant imbalance of power are laden with deception in which the powerless feign deference and the powerful are usually sensible enough to assert their mastery with subtlety. Those without power are never fully free to speak their minds in the presence of the powerful, and this goes for managers too. In order to resist, these groups "create a secret discourse that represents a critique of power spoken behind the backs of the dominant" (Scott 1990: xii).

Simultaneously, and reflecting the fact that even amongst the powerful power is unevenly distributed, and their grip on power is never absolute but always vulnerable, the powerful, or those within the power structure, develop a private dialogue about "the practices and claims of their rule that cannot be openly avowed" (Scott 1990: xii). These secret discourses constitute a "hidden transcript" which, in parts of the interviews I conducted, some of the managers allowed me to glimpse. I will now turn to examine an example of this in an account that I have not so far considered.

In the following section I will explore Alistair's process of identity construction during fragments from interview text conducted at Nylons. Alistair assesses both the benefits of the old and new organization and then moves on to justify his refusal to engage with the changes taking place and his social environment. After some months of talking with Alistair he finally "confessed" why he had decided not to engage with the process of change. At first, I had noted that he was a difficult and resisting subject, unable to cope with the pressures of change. Indeed towards the end of our relationship, I found great empathy with him and found that Alistair's position and therefore how he constructs meaning was a great deal like my own orientation to feminist politics. Alistair is not abstaining to be difficult or to resist the institutional order, rather by refusing to engage as a subject from the process during work (note his "confession" was outside of work) he felt that he could have more influence and maintain loyalty to his identity. Refusal was a way of not being shaped, manipulated and consumed by the cultural controls in Nylons. It is particularly interesting that Alistair is the only manager in Nylons that does not place his personal life backstage. Performance for Alistair is underpinned by a modernist – work, role doing. His refusal to commit to the system that *marginalizes* individuals means that he is free to transgress it and reveals potential to *subvert* dominant symbolic order. Alistair's refusal strategy therefore has a postmodern capability which reveals itself in the flexible, fluid and playful way in which he performs his identity (Baudrillard 1990) and the power of his dormant voice, the hidden script.

Alistair is not typical of the average manager in Nylons, being much younger at 40 years old and unlike Dan who is a similar age is not ambitious and self-directed. Alistair has a small family and is not formally educated, having worked himself up from the production line. Alistair seems not to be "playing the game" but rather has a belief that his hidden text has more influence and power than any role he might adopt. A strategy of desisting rather than resisting means that he can manage his identity in a way that he is in "full control" (quote from Alistair) of his identity project – he creates what Scott (1990) would call a "space for dissidence". Alistair is also considered to be a high performer because this protects him – as Brian (Personnel Director) states "he manages to perform and we can't take any fault with him but he doesn't get involved. We can't work this one out". This commitment *without* seduction is a characteristic dilemma of postmodern change identified, inter alia, by Linstead and Chan (1994).

Extract 1   "We changed what they [shopfloor] knew and trusted and we managed it badly. I feel bad for the people that can't cope with the situation they are in and there's no way out for them or they will be out of here. I have had to rethink my position but more importantly what I want to do and I guess what I want to do in the future. I have *withdrawn*".

Extract 2   "Managers have their own agendas and their own ways of doing things... I'm just not getting involved. Perhaps that's wrong but I just don't care anymore, well I must care, don't I? We are less involved in things now with the changes but I wouldn't say that people were switched off... There are things that I'm frustrated about, such as only being able to do my job to a half satisfactory factory level because I'm dragged away from it... We used to cascade all the information down through management to the shopfloor and now its being done via the trade unions. So now the communication here is really poor... It used to be good, but its gone down hill over the past few years because I can see them slipping further and further back to how things used to be. I used to get very frustrated and depressed".

Extract 4   "When I used to let it [change] affect my emotions I used to say 'I just can't do it any more'".

Extract 5   "Now I have created a space in which I can perform the job that they [management] want me to do and I can manage not being happy with that by not reacting and doing *my* own thing. Some of the managers are not happy and do what they [management] want and that makes them feel demotivated and worthless. For me I hit my targets and they can't bother me, they need me. But when they need the extra stuff, well I just won't do it but I make sure that me and them know I'm well within my rights so they can't and won't touch me... You can sometimes make more *impact* by not saying or doing anything. They think I'm *quiet* but I have influence with the men and they know that when the time comes I'll stand up for them. Until then, well [long pause] I'll keep well out of it [laughter]".

Alistair's behaviour reminds us of Scott's (1985) depiction of "footdragging, false compliance, feigned ignorance, dissimilation and so forth that are conducted below the veneer of legitimacy; covert and seditious acts carried out in the silent spaces of everyday life" (cited in Fleming and Sewell 2002: 859–60). The important words here are everyday and silent, beneath the surface and acts. These are detached processes for Alistair, he is not emotionally driven or involved. Fleming and Sewell refer to this as disengagement "whereby the self is detached from the normative prescriptions of managerialism through irony and cynicism" (ibid.: 860). Alistair refuses to be seduced, but as Baudrillard notes:

... seduction and femininity are confounded, indeed confused. Masculinity has always been haunted by this sudden reversibility within the feminine. Seduction and femininity are ineluctable as the reverse side of sex, meaning and power (1990: 2).

The corporate attempts at seduction therefore may themselves be undercut by their reverse side, by using subtler strategies against them than by outright opposition, subversion through the micropolitics of everyday life and interaction (De Certeau 1984). Alistair's success in maintaining his identity outside the corporate discourse highlights the importance of these quotidian minutiae in sustaining non-dominant forms of subjectivity, and is, with few exceptions, a process which feminist research and research into women in management have neglected. The more mundane, elusive, more "feminine" strategies have been overlooked in favour of giving attention to the more dramatic acts of suppression or abjection. Grounded in such methodological approaches, it is hardly surprising that feminism has tended to reproduce dichotomous accounts which reinforce the gender binary which feminist politics sets itself to reverse. Or conversely, grounded in dualistic epistemologies, it is hardly surprising that feminist research chooses methods which will reproduce evidence to support them. But as Alistair demonstrates, individuals do not necessarily act in a dichotomous manner and do not automatically take their subject positions up on one side of the binary or another, but can cross the line in their behaviours in order to refuse the incorporation of their identity into one set of assumptions or its opposite.

Alistair uses a mask of competence to preserve the space in which he reflects, reconsiders and reconstructs his sense of self. His subjectivity then, is adaptable and fluid, and perplexing to his superiors – he does the job very well but without buying all the ideological trappings that come along with it. He was and is not seduced, but there is nevertheless a sense of betrayal about his tone. Alistair's use of this space is as a space in which he can *not be*, where being or becoming exist purely to evade those attempts at fixture and refiguration that are thrown at them by one organizational change after another. Whatever Alistair is, he is so by virtue of *not being what he is expected to be*, even though his behaviour is exemplary. He responds to the rapid change and fragmentation of identity by not revealing his identity at all – indeed his hidden transcript is more of an inner conversation, a debate without a resolution, a set of at times unconnected reflections and visions of the future. Yet it is also an embodied space, because Alistair, although detached in his public practice, is nevertheless emotionally involved in his dissident space, and he feels sadness, guilt, regret and occasionally reveals frustration through a passion for human potential. So Alistair is not simply epistemologically postmodern, but he encapsulates a sense of embodiment which postmodern analyses often neglect.

The forms of narcissism and resistance that I have discussed can be viewed as features of and responses to the fragmentation of identity experienced under increasingly postmodern social and organizational conditions. In the section I will look at the ways in which people may seek to construct their own sense of subjectivity against this background, and illustrate the model developed by identifying examples of these processes from the empirical data.

Fragmented identities and modes of subjectivity

[The postmodern form of narcissism] is the effect of the disintegration of an individualistic experience whose only meaning was the project of modernity, of self-development. The narcissistic condition in the world of modernity is one where the subject continually strives for others to create and support his existence (Friedman 1992: 352).

Identity continues to be the problem it was throughout modernity, though it has been problematized anew in the contemporary orgy of commodification, fragmentation, image production and societal, political and cultural transformation that is the work of contemporary capitalism (Kellner 1992: 174).

For Friedman, narcissism is closely linked to the changing nature of identity formation in the shift from modernity to postmodernity. Kellner somewhat wryly observes that identity has always been experienced as a problem, and has not just recently been problematized by the postmodern, although the postmodern condition has accelerated and fragmented the processes of identity formation. For Kellner, what is left may be a disaster of instability, a totally "fragmented, disjointed life subject to the whims of [managerial] fashion" or it may be a new set of opportunities for reconstructing the self. Friedman sees that postmodern narcissism accordingly cannot be one where the narcissistic seeks support for their existence in any coherent or unified way, but in which the whimsicalities of that existence, seen almost as a *game,* conscript others into supporting or subordinate roles which shift as the rules of the game themselves shift. In considering how subject formation may be said to occur, especially in the accounts I have gathered, I can identify five categories, or modes, through which the "game" may be said to pass:

1. *Mode of Incorporation* (the ways that individuals accommodate organizational goals in a climate of change and restructuring) – The question here is how individuals align themselves with new organizational goals and objectives and accommodate visions which may be at odds with what they previously held. These may range from enthusiastic embrace to attempts at avoidance, examples being; vision/advocacy (seduction); acceptance; accommodation; consent; citizenship; and "knowledge management".
2. *Mode of Disciplined Subjectivity* (how individuals fit themselves into gendered organizational social systems/discursive structures) – The question here is how individuals identify with new systems with different requirements of them and different means of controlling and

Table 8.1 Modes of Subjective Identity Formation

	Mode of Incorporation	Mode of Disciplined Subjectivity	Mode of Subjective Identity	Mode of Resistance	Mode of Autonomy
Bob	Pragmatism	Learning	Mortality	Sanguinity	Chameleon
Alan	Ideology/Leadership	Authority	Melancholy	Masks fragility	Autocommunication
Chris	Accommodation	Professional competence	Connection	Reflexivity	Nostalgia
Stuart	Change Agent	Hypercompetition	Career	Gaming	Reward
Peter	Acceptance	Good Management (failing)	Inadequacy	Resignation	Apathy
Dan	Commitment	Hypercompetition	Multiplicity	Gaming	Player
Steve	Compliance	Political subject	Collective	Counter-seduction	Cynicism Active disengagement
Alistair	Collusion	Professional competence	Personal	Subversion	Dissidence
Wayne	Commitment	Professional competence	Breadwinner	Reflexivity	Conflicted
Jackie	Change Agent	Hypercompetition	Career	Androgyny	Self-negation
Terry	Acceptance	Rejection	Experience	Passive	Apathy
Justin	Commitment	Professionalism	Materialism	Discursive	Skill

evaluating them as organizational members. Examples are social subject/team player (surveillance); leading subject; political subject; professional subject; "acting subject" (performer of a role or roles).

3. *Mode of Subjective Identity* (the means by which individuals position, or see themselves positioned within/identify with wider social discourses) – The question here is how the individual weighs organizational discourse to other wider discourses of which they may be a part. Examples may be personal; familial; professional/careerist; ethical; aesthetic.

4. *Mode of Resistance* (how individuals resist, transgress and establish discursive structures or change and create new ones) – Here the question is how individuals resist being colonized by discourses of which they do not approve or believe, how they resist having unacceptable identities inscribed upon them. Examples both individual and collective can include political opposition; non-cooperation; subversion; symbolic/discursive; counter-seduction; transgression; reflexive critique; dissent.

5. *Mode of Autonomy* (how individuals convert identity into agency and how praxis can be enabled and realized) – The final question is how individuals are able to create identities which they can use to establish some sovereign epistemological space which can become a resource for change and development. Examples are political agency; emancipation; empowerment; networking and alliances; bricolage; play; and managing boundaries.

The modes may be seen to be themselves involved in deploying masks, at a tactical level, whilst simultaneously cohering to form different dimensions of a larger mask. If we turn to the interview data over chapters 5, 6 and 7, the different dimensions in play can be seen as follows (see Table 8.1).

New meanings of management?

If we return then to consider Figure 3.1 in which I extended the work of Gowler and Legge, moves toward postmodern conditions of networking, seduction and commitment have not fully arrived at their postulated destination. I have noted that three factors – the existence of gender discrimination and gender politics, narcissism, predominantly of the negative kind, and tactics and strategies of often unvoiced resistance – have interfered with this smooth passage. However, an alternative perspective which suggests that this is not the full story could be offered.

One instructive term that has been applied to the new world of net-working is heterarchy. Seeking to bring the foundational work done at Columbia University, New York in the 1950s by Blau, Gouldner, Lazarsfeld and Merton on forms of bureaucracy up to date with recent developments, the Andrew W. Mellon Foundation funded a seminar series between 1999–2001 at Columbia's Centre for Organizational Innovation (COI) and the Santa Fe Institute to explore the nature of the new phenomenon. The series concluded that heterarchy rests upon "patterns of distributed intelligence, collaborative structures, and lateral co-ordination as organizations move from economies of scale, scope, and speed to economies of increasing returns and network external-ities... as they confront conditions of radical uncertainty". Furthermore, empirically observed "patterns of flattened hierarchy, collaborative structures, and horizontal accountability" are enabled by "complex digital ecologies consisting of the Internet, intranets, extranets, web-sites, and virtual collaborative work spaces. Extended connectivity and ubiquitous computing do not simply allow organizations to perform existing functions more effectively; they also present opportunities to radically redefine their mission and redesign their operations." These twin developments have given rise to heterarchies, which are character-ized by the *lateral coordination of organizational diversity* and a *distributed intelligence* negotiated across *multiple evaluative criteria* (see http://www.coi.columbia.edu/heterarchy_whatis.html accessed 12/03/05). Whilst alternatives to hierarchy are not new in organization theory, the com-bination of collaborative structures with enabling technologies pro-duces a qualitative difference in the nature of the organizational relations which emerge.

David Stark, Director of the COI, has worked extensively on the question of whether there are some types of organization that are more likely to be able to redefine, redeploy, recombine assets, working on start-up and digital economies in Silicon Alley (Manhattan) and Eastern Europe (see Stark 1999, 2001; Beunza and Stark 2004; Girard and Stark 2003, 2005). He observes that "organizations with a capacity for reflexivity...." managing the "active rivalry of coexisting principles – the organization of diversity" are most successful in these settings. This, in effect, is heterarchy – heterarchic organizations operate with *minimal hierarchy* and have *organizational heterogeneity*. There is uncer-tainty and self-organization, which requires that management becomes the art of facilitating organizations that can perpetually *reorganize themselves* (http://www.santafe.edu/sfi/publications/Bulletins/bulletin Fall99/features/organizationDiversity.html). The organizations Stark and his colleagues have studied are actively experimenting with new forms and are conscious of the bricolage in which they engage, the diversity on which it thrives and the learning which ensues.

It seems clear that the companies in which I studied do not operate in these economic conditions and do not have the full features of heterarchy. They lack diversity, the lateral communications are not yet properly formed, knowledge and learning are not being properly managed and intelligence distributed and redistributed. They are not reflexive at the organizational level. Perhaps the most telling absence is that of the empowerment that is required if the parts of the organization are to become autopoietic. The organizations themselves have not sufficiently relaxed their higher level control structures in order to gain the full benefits of heterarchy because they are not willing to take the risk of failure. Managers are asked to make the new structures work, but they are not told that they will not have all the necessary tools to do so. Because something is missing, and the shift from hierarchy to heterarchy (essentially the focus of Stark et al's research) is still, in effect, a struggle between the two, seduction becomes necessary to get them to buy into a new structure which cannot work as it should, and to which top management is not yet willing to cede the necessary autonomy, by masking that fact. Seduced into committing themselves to the new organization, managers are disillusioned when despite their best efforts the system does not work, and top management do not deliver the rewards, the authority or the information to make it work. Seduced and abandoned, they see behind the mask and are shocked and disappointed. At this point, a common response is to fall back on commitment, but an empty commitment, working harder and longer but without imagination or enthusiasm. Another, perhaps more common response, is to fall back on the old ways of hierarchy, making the struggle between hierarchy and heterarchy even harder for heterarchy to win, as Alistair observes happening. Thus the vertical links on the diagram are as important as the horizontal and need to be considered together, and any organization response to these problems needs to take a similar view, to realize how damaging to the other criteria and the whole effort not delivering on any one of them can be.

The revolution in information technology, global politics and socio-economic technologies has meant that some organizations are, and have to be, different from any observable historically, and that post-modernism is not merely a project (if it ever was) but a condition, or set of conditions, which affects the emergent processes of getting things done whilst at the same time being imminent within them. Stark's studied organizations are on the margins – startups in new industries, organizations emerging in postsocialist countries after the traumatic collapse of communism, or Wall Street traders rebuilding their business after 9/11 – and whilst not being typical, they throw light on what is happening to more mainstream organizations. Operating within changing conditions affects the possibilities for defining the nature of "management" and the identity of the "manager" in a way which has not happened since the idea of "modern management" was formed alongside the emergence of Fordism and Taylorism. Some managers tend, and increasingly struggle, to identify with "modern" management principles (which today may appear "traditional" and which less than a century ago were "radical") whilst others, ready to let go of tradition, are still unsure of what, if any principles they can adhere to in grounding their managerial identities, and whether these might conflict with their organizational identities. In this study, I have not sought to promote or recommend "postmodern" management as though it were a program or set of beliefs or commitments, but to argue that as things appear to be changing in ways which have been called "postmodern" by others, there is a need to map clearly the ground between what managers thought they were and what they appear to be becoming.

Michael Hardt and Antonio Negri (2000) offer an analysis in the light of which our managers' experiences are not surprising. They argue that the traditional, modern and postmodern periods are not so much periods that start and end in a linear progression, but that each is defined by the dominance of particular processes that characterize types of dominant relations, both economic and social. In tradition, or the premodern, agriculture was dominant, selves were not very vertically mobile but were socially defined and environmentally embedded and subjects were disciplined, as Foucault notes, through their bodies. With processes of modernization, agriculture becomes subordinated to industry and a series of transformations follows. Agriculture does not die away, but it is transformed into industrialized agriculture, focused on agricultural products rather than commodities. Village populations migrate into towns for work and become urbanized, the working day dominated by the rhythm and appetites of machinery, which they service. Selves become defined by roles and jobs, and are individualized like cogs in a machine especially under Taylorism and Fordism. Working subjects are increasingly less ruled by physical action or threat and more by rules and supervision, leading eventually to regimes of electronic and peer surveillance. With postmodernization, or informatization, the machine metaphor that dominates working and social relations gives way to that of the computer. This means that the physical concentrations required by modernization are no longer necessary – work (and capital) can move to wherever information may flow such that complex products may be manufactured in parts in several different locations, assembled in other locations and locally customized. Customers may even be able to customize their order as it is being manufactured online. Manufacturing industry is no longer the dominant economic sector – material labour gives way to immaterial labour based on knowledge and affect rather than physical skill and energy. Different technologies do not eradicate manufacturing – like agriculture it is transformed into something less labour intensive, more flexible and more intimate with its customers, a form of service industry (agriculture too undergoes another transformation). And as selves became individualized under modernization, under postmodernization they become multiplex.

For Hardt and Negri the connection between modernity and subjectivity is of critical importance – modernization and postmodernization do not just change what we do; they change who we are and who we think we can and should be. We are no longer human cogs in a machine – we are information nodes, human computers. Another critical point that Hardt and Negri make is that there is no one path to development. Ford's plant in the US in the 1930s is not the same as Ford's plant in Brazil in the 1990s although in economic terms the countries may be similar. This is partly because technology is not exported in obsolete forms, but at its most advanced level, so the Brazilian factory is informatized. Secondly, automobile manufacturing was the highest level of manufacturing industry, which was the dominant economic performer in the 1930s. Today, automobile manufacturing is not the dominant performer in manufacturing, and manufacturing is a second-class citizen to certain types of service industry. So the position has changed dramatically and repetition is supplanted by difference.

The managers I studied, talked with, and shared a little of the lives of, were working in once-dominant sectors of once-proud industries. Their identities had always been a matter of negotiation and contestation, but against this background of relative stability and significance. Their experiences provide us with some direct evidence of the impact of postmodernization processes on not only their work, but on their identities, as Hardt and Negri suggest. These processes are never finished, and continue in motion – they involve changing individual subjectivities, shifting power lines, and challenging gender assumptions. What I have tried to do in this book is to give some form to the confusions and conflicts as well as the grounds for consensus present in how the managers I came to know are themselves coming to new and shifting understandings of who they are. Future research on managerial identities requires more investigation of the *fluidity* of identities and how these formations challenge, mould and transform managerial and organizational discourses. Nevertheless, thanks to their help, we now know a little more about what it means to be a manager in a post-modernizing world.

Appendix 1: Research Methodology

In this appendix I explain the interpretative research approach; the inductive (the data presented in Chapter 2) and deductive methodologies (presented in chapters 5 to 7) used in the different stages of this research; and issues and concerns associated with analyzing, selecting and presenting data: indexicality, intertexuality, reflexivity and validity.

A "Constructivist" approach

The general terms interpretivism and constructivism are often considered as "sensitising concepts" (Blumer 1954 cited in Denzin and Lincoln 1994: 221) however the term constructivist is utilized here to refer to an epistemological and ontological orientation that has influenced the research methodology and research methods utilized for data collection and analysis. At a general level constructivism as exemplified by Gergen (1985) is concerned with "the notion that the world that people create in the process of social exchange is a reality *sui generis*" (Schwandt 1998: 240) and therefore represents "the goal of understanding the complex world of lived experience from the point of view of those who live it" (Schwandt 1998: 221). There is an abiding concern for the emic; to understanding and representing individual middle managers' experiences which involve:

> ...particular actors, in particular places, at particular times, fashion meaning out of events and phenomena through prolonged, complex processes of social interaction involving history, language, and action (Schwandt 1998: 221–2).

Theory and knowledge are therefore concerned with the production and organization of differences and committed to the view that knowledge is created by symbolic and language systems. Realist views of theories and knowledge are rejected, meaning and knowledge are subjectively shared social constructions (Gergen 1985: 267) in specific historical and cultural situations. Emphasis is placed on exploring the discourses that individuals draw on to give meaning to their actions in "concrete" social situations, the interpretative work that "actors" do to produce and organize their lives. Understanding "members" practical everyday procedures (the ethnomethods) for representing their realities "makes" member's social circumstances "self-generating". Interpreting and giving meaning to individual experiences relies on the indexical nature of meaning. As Holstein and Gubrium state:

> Objects and events have equivocal or indeterminate meanings without a visible context. It is only through their situated use in talk and interaction that objects and events become concretely meaningful (cited in Denzin and Lincoln 1994: 142).

To research middle managers' identities therefore it is imperative that these identities are shaped by discourse, discourses that are the product of "context" (Parker 1997). Middle managers' identities are therefore seen as "precarious, contradictory and in process, constantly being reconstituted in discourse each time we think or speak" (Weedon 1987: 33) and it is through these discourses that "organization members create a coherent social reality that frames their sense of who they are" (Mumby and Clair 1997: 181). Through a project of deconstruction, the ambivalence of all text; aims to "subvert the meaning of a text to show how its dominant and negotiated meanings can be opposed" (Denzin 1992: 151 cited in Schwandt 1998: 235); expose the abject lying dormant in text; and "analyse[s] how texts address the problems of presence, lived experience, the real and its representations, and the issues of the subjects, authors and their intentionalities" (Denzin 1992: 151 cited in Schwandt 1998: 235). I was therefore concerned with the fluid production and organization of difference within managerial subjectivities. However interpretative/constructivist approaches are charged with criticisms including solipsism and relativism; the privileging of the actors' voices and the authority of researcher to inscribe the meaning of the text.

Between the subject and the object

Whilst sociological and anthropological methods have developed and moved far from the hypothetico-deductive models which dominated social research for most of the last century, the subject-object distinction remains the last boundary to be dissolved. Some hermeneutically based methodologies were developed specifically to mediate between subjectivity and objectivity, and I will outline three which have influenced the methods employed in this book.

The defining characteristics of *ontological hermeneutics* are linguisticality (lives are lived and constructed in language) and historicity (we live in time and *are* our history). In short, the proper interpretation of any social situation can only occur from *within* that situation, and not from detached observation (Schwandt 1998: 224). However, *objective hermeneutics* seeks to make interpretation a more controllable activity than this, retaining a commitment to the usual criteria of validity, reliability, generalizability and hypobook testing which are characteristic of quantitative research. Data are the product of social interaction, thus authenticity (being true to the data) replaces abstract truth and objectivity refers to those aspects of the subject's world which cannot be changed, rather than any inalienable defining qualities of that world (Denzin 1989a: 54–5).

Analytical induction is another attempt to produce generalizable data and test hypotheses from qualitative data. Here, a hypobook is formulated on the basis of a broad consideration of existing data or evidence, and this is tested against a single case study. The hypobook is modified to explain the case and, as long as no applicable negative cases are discovered, the hypobook is elaborated until it can deal with all cases it encounters, when it can be considered to be *practically* proved (Vidich and Lyman 1998: 73–5; Denzin 1989b: 165–70).

The methodology of this book combines inductive and deductive methods, but is informed by the three perspectives noted. From objective hermeneutics there is a recognition that there are some aspects of the subject's world that are literally out of their control, and are experienced as such. Indeed whilst at times these elements may be ontologically absurd, in that they make no logical sense, they are usually experienced as meaningful in context.

Ontological hermeneutics does not require, as does analytical induction, the precise definition of the research issue or its formulation in a crisp hypobook. Rather, the hypobook itself is recognized as a linguistic phenomenon, a *story*. Indeed, rather than a hypobook, a theoretical framework develops as a narrative, which is then placed into the context of other narratives, the stories obtained in interview data. Objective hermeneutics allows these data to identify the objective and subjective dimensions of each case study as they emerge.

In my case, the initial framework was already given. However, situating this framework, which was itself inductively derived, in history indicated that most of the core conditions which had shaped the modern context had changed, according to literature on changes in management, organizational structures and form and the new nature of middle management. Managerial selves were being formed in this emerging situation, and existing literature was used to deduce how we might expect current conditions to have shifted the original framework. Three cases were then used to select individual narratives to illustrate, or otherwise, the predicted shift. The object of this was to gain some indication of how the emerging historical moment might begin to universalize itself in the lives of the managers in the cases selected (Denzin 1989c: 189). In this deductive hermeneutics, issues of whether and how the shift in the criteria for the formulation of managerial identity occurred, and the obstacles in the way of this historical shift, are as important as the theoretical narrative itself.

Research methodology

A qualitative deductive approach was adopted that focused on the generation of individual middle managers' subjective experiences regarding the dimensions of the Management in Three Movements framework in three organizations (Carlux, Chapter 5; Larts, Chapter 6 and Nylons, Chapter 7) to appreciate the historical, cultural and social context. These data were collected from individual face-to-face, semi-structured interviews with the middle managers themselves. The interviews discussed their day-to-day experiences within the organization and their life outside the work place. The texts generated from these interviews are a product of the research engagement that are actively constructed between the researcher and the researched (Shotter 1995), and are already to be regarded as an account that was partially produced collectively. Although the managers I spoke to formed part of a larger sample of managers in each company, and the organizations presented here formed part of a wider research sample, this has little epistemological significance for this book. What is significant is why I selected the managers I did and what are the consequences of considering this selection valid; why I selected the particular features of these managers' accounting practices and with what consequences for the knowledge so generated; and how the notions of accounting practice, accounts and accountability render this methodology coherent.

Starting with the first question first – why I selected the managers I did and what are the consequences of considering this selection valid – a poststructuralist influenced methodology whilst recognizing the socially constructed nature of accounts goes one step further than more modernist approaches such as reflexive sociology or ethnomethodology. Where these approaches take the "normal" situation as perceived by the members of whatever social group they were researching to be characterized by the taken-for-granted features which members recognize in common, they consider accounts to be *exceptionally* produced, occasioned when the micro-social order is breached in order to explain, justify, dismiss or repair such a breach (Garfinkel 1967). Such accounts are therefore non-routine, though common. However, although such research recognizes that even the sense of normality, of the everyday, that members hold in common is an accomplishment, it accepts that such accomplishment is routine and everyday life is relatively highly stable (hence the need for "breaching experiments" by social investigators such as Garfinkel 1967).

The acceleration of communication and the spread of semiotics, the proliferation of information and the broadening of bandwidths of signification in what has been called the "postmodern" has meant that it is much harder to take anything for granted for very long. Indeed, breaching of common-sense understandings takes place itself as an almost routine matter. Postmodern experience, as Bauman (1995) argues, is fragmented because reality, as we apprehend it, is fragmented – life is effectively in fragments. So as breaching occurs not as a protracted series of intermittent but isolated events, but more as a flow of interruption, a soap opera rather than a drama, so accounts produced and occasioned are done so not as exceptional productions but as a *flow of accountability*. In the case of managers, it has long been recognized, as Gowler and Legge (1996) point out that managers are not only a highly verbal social group whose main activity is communication, and whose work is fragmented because information which is topical and current tends to arrive that way, but that they are members of a self-defining species. Managers tell us who they think they are, and constantly do so. Thus it would be a manager's failure to give an account of himself or herself, prompted or otherwise, that would constitute the breach in their social order, the anomaly of them having nothing to say for themselves. Thus to take the epistemological step of analyzing fragments rather than unified accounts merely recognizes the ontological condition of the managers providing those fragments. The move then is from exceptions which require accounts, to flows of accountability, from constructed and unified accounts to fragments-in-process.

I can now turn to the second question of why I selected the particular features of the managers' accounts that I did and with what consequences. Following Silverman's (1975) interpretation of a concept of Wittgenstein, I recognize that any account can be constructed as weakly persuasive simply by virtue of the fact that it constitutes a selection and combination of certain features of a situation rather than others. Such an account seeks to persuade the reader that it is a "correct" and acceptable version of events, and may become more strongly persuasive to the extent that it builds an argument, employs rhetorical devices, and actively contests and dismisses other accounts. Nevertheless, such accounts may have exploratory qualities. First-order persuasive accounts are those offered by participants in a situation and may be of two types – accounts occasioned in the situation as it unfolds, or those offered by participants at a later date. Some commentators would call these latter second-order accounts. Second-order persuasive accounts for us are those offered by analysts to explain the participants' first order accounts, to rebalance elements of them, to connect them to other analytical frames and if necessary to legislate between them. Their persuasiveness is targeted at a wider, more professional audience with an interest in the explanation itself, rather than the situation itself, and are thus offered for different purposes, at a different level of reflection. This distinction, to the extent that it is theoretical and structural, takes place out of the situation and reflects on the situation, has similarities to the anthropological distinction between the emic and the etic, with the significant addition of the concept of persuasiveness.

As stated previously the approach taken in this book is interpretative, but is furthermore persuasive because of the selection of elements of accounts. As I have recognized that accounts themselves are produced from fragments, I have not deconstructed accounts into fragments but merely selected certain fragments from a larger mosaic. I have done this because these fragments seemed to me to be significant to the participants, they resonated with each other across the accounts of the particular managers chosen, they raised the issue of gender in which I had a theoretical interest, and which seemed to be an issue across the much wider data set which I had obtained. These data are representative of the wider data set in so far as they are taken from it and reproduce elements found elsewhere in the set. I would not, however, wish to claim that they were representative in any quantitative sense, or that mine was the only possible interpretation of either these or the wider data set. Indeed, to continue our earlier metaphor, my interpretation is at best only of one recurring pattern within this wider mosaic, and which I think is discernible within other such mosaics.

Finally, why did I select the particular managers I did and what are the consequences of considering this selection valid? I have noted above that identity as a social construction is not a self-authenticating quality. It is an impression achieved through the adoption of one or several masks, of which gender is one, and these masks may be donned or exchanged for others as interactive situations unfold. For Foucault (1980), social analysis is a matter of revealing masks, only to discover other masks – one reveals not the truth but occasionally truth-effects. Accounts are part of this continuing discursive reproduction-deconstruction of unfolding situations, and the flow of accountability is in this sense a continuing masquerade. I chose managers from one company therefore because the masquerade in which they were participating, though having many difference scenes, was the same one in organizational terms and many of the perspectives of the organization were shared by the participants. Secondly, I chose the managers as representatives which enables me to discuss their comments in some detail whilst giving sufficient variety to cover all the necessary elements. Only a couple of female managers are included not because of their female status but because they illustrate the predominance of males at middle management level and in the case of Larts because she was the only female manager in the company. In Carlux there were no female managers in managerial posts. I was attracted to the managers selected in particular because, even as I conducted the interviews, they appeared to be articulating elements which other interviewees had raised, but had not so well exemplified or expressed, and had a range of differing work experiences, educational attainments and family situations.

This book has presented middle managers' accounts from three organizations (from a larger data set) to focus on individual middle managers' subjective experiences within their organizational context. This approach examined in-depth data within a rigorous theoretical and empirical framework that has been missing from much research on middle management (with the exception of

Watson 1994; Watson and Harris 1999), management (with the exception of Knights and Wilmott 1999; Lennie 1999) and women in management (with the exception Wajcman 1998, Marshall 1995). What follows is an exploration of ontological, epistemological and representational issues in the research.

Constructing texts: authors, accounting and reflexivity

Investigating middle managers' subjectivities by focusing on naturally occurring "talk" recognizes that these texts are the product of both the researcher and research participant's negotiation of their subjectivities; subjectivities that are continually in flux, multiple, competing and gendered. The researcher's active role in the construction of "social texts" as Potter and Wetherell comment:

> ...do not merely reflect or mirror objects, events and categories that pre-exist in the social and natural world. Rather they actively construct a version of those things. They do not just describe things, they do things (Potter and Wetherell 1987: 6).

The researcher is therefore recast as the "practical author" (Shotter 1995) in the research process to reflect "the cultural realities being described" (Birth (1990: 551) cited in Linstead 1994: 12) in the generation and construction of the research "reality". Gubrium and Holstein state "circumstances that provide the context for meaning are themselves self-generating" (cited in Denzin and Lincoln 1994: 143). The authors continue to argue that:

> Interpretive activities are simultaneously in and about the settings to which they orient, and that they describe. Socially accomplished realities are thus reflexive; descriptive accounts of settings give shape to those settings whilst simultaneously being shaped by the settings they constitute (Denzin and Lincoln 1994: 143).

Texts are therefore produced in specific contexts, informing and being informed by their local settings. Appreciating the multiple, fragmentary nature of texts and their interpretations and representations, the author has no absolute authority of the research experience with no claim to factual superiority. Linstead and Grafton-Small justly confirms that:

> ... the author is as much a product of the text as the text is a product of the author (Barthes 1981). The text cannot exist as mere words, symbols or actions, though, until it is read or made to have meaning – therefore it depends upon its re-creation by a "reader" or recipient... The text has an intertexuality, a multiplicity of meaning which is inherent rather than a result of variety of interpretations (1992: 343–4).

The active readings of the author and reader of text in the production of meaning and the self-reflexive processes of the author is central to producing a research narrative that could be termed valid. Furthermore, the text's intertexuality has specific implications for analyzing the research data and achieving a transgressive "postmodern" validation of the data that capitalizes on the multiple, the fragmented, the local. Barthes in an earlier account comments:

...the text is plural. Which is not simply to say that it has several meanings but that it accomplishes the very plural of meaning: an irreducible (and not merely an acceptable) plural. The text is not a co-existence of meanings but a passage, an over-crossing... (1977: 199).

Thus the interpretative procedures have the potential to reveal difference. Data collection and analysis therefore relies heavily on the reflexive properties of all concerned in the active construction of texts, meaning being generated from multiple interpretations and interpretative procedures. Woolgar (1988) raises our attention to the "rich and complex interplay" of the observation; text; context; the researcher and the researched; and the adequacy of representation and thus as "agents of representation" we need to pay particular attention to reflexivity as a "tool for improving observational accuracy" and an "impetus for exploring different ways of asking questions about knowledge practices" (Woolgar 1998: 16-17). Reflexivity therefore stems from the relation between the researcher's practices and the research subjects. Reflexivity is achieved in this research by benign introspection (Woolgar 1988: 22), that is reflection, which in this research consisted of the recording of fieldwork confessions, extensive field notes that included the researchers' "gut feelings" and intuitive apprehension of the situations and experiences of the research process. At the heart of the research method was an attempt to grasp the "inside story" whilst at the same time reflecting an adequate portrayal of the subjects' experiences – the stories expressed. Focusing on the processes of reading the situation, recording the texts and fieldnotes, analyzing of the texts, and then representing these texts in an adequate and reflexive manner that allowed for the meaning of these texts to be interpreted and identified with by individual readers assisted the development of a reflexive process for constructing reality. Benign introspection is based on acknowledging differences between the object of study and representation, whereas constitutive reflexivity (Woolgar 1988: 22) denies difference and affirms similarity. Drawing on Garfinkel, Woolgar concurs that constitutive reflexivity is "a connection between... representation and object of study) is a back and forth process. Members' accounts... are constituent features of the settings they make observable" (Garfinkel 1967: 8 cited in Woolgar 1988: 22). Therefore even recognizing the tensions, ambiguities, contradictions inherent in any of the research texts, individual accounts are seen as reflective of the situations.

Silverman (1975), following Wittgenstein's *Philosophical Investigations* and Heidegger, draws our attention to the interpretative processes of the inquiry that informs us that all research accounts, that is the member's original accounts and the researcher's interpretations of these accounts, are selective and increase and decrease in terms of their persuasiveness. Silverman comments:

There is no way in which any account including my own can avoid relying upon and sustaining a persuasive version of the character of the world (Silverman 1975: 27).

These "persuasive accounts" as Silverman concurs illustrate the processes of reflexivity in shaping and representing member's accounts. Additionally any reading and representation of these accounts are persuasive since the processes of selecting and filtering operate throughout our analysis and writing. Silverman states:

writing and reading are always acts of production – of societies, of selves. And that production is both mine and not mine alone. Mine because in my acts of production I re-member my-self. Not mine because "I" exist in and through a dialogue with a tradition that always already precedes me, and with an emerging social order that will be the readings of my text (1975: 42 cited in Linstead (1993: 58)).

In this extract Silverman therefore re-positions himself as a researcher as a member of the engagement to shape and reshape the construction of the text and therefore meaning generated from the interpretative inquiry. This book therefore analyzes the fragmented accounts generated from the constructs of the extended Gowler and Legge framework. Tyler (1986) reminds us that members don't organize their accounts around the categories we use and therefore as researchers we infer from the accounts that they share with the researcher. Tyler argues that postmodern ethnography is:

> fragmentary because it cannot be otherwise. Life in the field is itself fragmentary, not at all organized around familiar ethnological categories... we make do with a collection of indexical anecdotes or telling particulars with which to *portend* that larger unity beyond explicit textualisation (1986: 161).

Following this line of reasoning I used a manual form of analysis that could mediate between the fragments because it was sensitive to the nuances of the research texts. Demonstrating a reflexive awareness in this book has been vital whilst conducting this poststructuralist inquiry. In the field of organization studies Linstead (1994) and Chia (1996) both explore reflexivity from a postmodernist perspective. Chia's critique of "first-order" reflexivity (Steier 1991 cited in Chia 1996: 44) demonstrates the authors' lack of "accounting" (Chia 1996: 44) and therefore the avoidance of reflexively addressing the socially constructed nature of the research process and text. As researchers therefore we are able "to subtly privilege ourselves with the status "observer" making our claims thereby appear more credible than those of others" (ibid.). Chia therefore proposes that it is "meta-reflexive" theorists that create persuasive accounts that are the product of "some consensus regarding their social experiences and therefore 'irony', 'self-reflection' and 'playful seriousness' replace the rational quest for 'certain' or even 'partially true' knowledge of an external organizational reality" (Chia 1996: 45). More importantly, the theories generated and the research texts "mirror the concerns and preoccupations of the theorists themselves and do not, as such, claim any absolute, grounded connexion with a reality beyond" (Chia 1996: 45–6). Chia's postmodern stance reminds then that the poststructuralist approach adopted in this book centres around "uncertainty", "incompleteness", "plurality", and "fragmentation" (Law 1994: 2 cited in Chia: 1996: 47) and for that reason the "processes of ordering and organising (*in organizational research*) are necessarily precarious, incomplete and fragmented" (Chia 1996: 47). The consequences of this methodological orientation therefore is summarized by Linstead who raises our attention to the issues in achieving reflexivity, namely the:

> dilemma of being sensitive to a range of data: the dangers of being dominated by technique, of treating data as "objective", and of researchers becoming separated from the authorship of their data while failing to perceive such a separation in their accounts (1994: 1336).

Thus the active readings of the author and reader of text in the production of meaning and the self-reflexive processes of the author is central to producing a research narrative that could be termed *valid*. Yet management research in particular is dominated by *imperial* forms of validity which actively construct, enforce and standardize gender-neutral research methodologies and methods which are therefore problematic when trying to take a gendered approach to management and organization. Gherardi and Turner (1988) in their booklet "real men don't collect soft data" reveal the gender construction of research methods and their implications for validity. The feminine is downplayed, even cast away when imposing imperial – masculine – forms of validity. Poststructuralist feminism has the potential to give voice to the individuality, originality, novelty, and possibly difference of the researched and researcher throughout the research experience. Moving towards a postmodern account of validity may go hand-in hand with rewriting the feminine into management and organization.

Accordingly, I suggest with Scheurich (1997) that validity is itself a mask, or more accurately several possible masks. Establishing validity consists in rendering one representation meaningful in terms of another, often quite different interpretation, expressed as a set of knowledge criteria. Difference is inevitably and purposefully regarded as something in need of reformulation or explaining away, or even suppression. Whilst the concept of validity has its uses, the fact that it is merely a tool of social analysis and not the object of social analysis is often lost in social research. Recognizing the nature and function of masks in the social research process is itself a project worthy of full and further investigation but it is necessary to make the point that the poststructuralist approach to analysis that I have taken in employing the concepts of fragments and masks, self-reflexively rebounds onto our own practice as researchers and raises specific epistemological questions about the nature of the knowledge produced in any research programme which go far beyond the loose "anything goes" type of radical relativism of which poststructuralism is often unjustly accused.

Appendix 2: Research Methods

To generate data on middle managers' subjectivities this book has appropriated both an inductive (the exploratory study highlighted in Chapter 2) and deductive (the main part of this book) methodologies to develop theory. Prior knowledge from the inductive exploration informed the development of the Management in Three Movements framework and subsequent research design. The organizations at the time of selection were based on those organizations that had undergone major restructuring and ranged from small to large sized companies. The interviewees (middle managers and other individuals such as team leaders, senior managers and shopfloor personnel) were selected and comprised a range of age, gender, race and occupational, professional and hierarchical groups. The organizations were private sector organizations with diverse geographical locations and including manufacturing, engineering, logistics, and privatized utilities. The three organizations presented in this book are all manufacturing organizations. These organizations were selected by pragmatic (available contacts) and theoretical sampling (middle managers in restructured and restructuring organizations).

When access has been achieved initial orientation visits were conducted to collect background, contexual data on the organization from the contact person in each organization. Within the inductive methodology the research involved a flexible, open-ended, opportunistic process of inquiry that was constantly subject to redefinition based on experience and observation in the companies. A pilot study within Carlux was carried to test and develop the interview schedule. Participant observation of the organization's activities and informal conversations generated broad knowledge of the organization (see the contributors to Linstead et al (1996) for the benefits of researcher's immersion in the field). On reflection more time spent in the field in an extensive longitudinal study was required for the depth of knowledge required for exploring the micro-processes of identity construction. After identifying the interview participants exploratory interviews were conducted with the relevant individuals. The Management in Three Movements framework was developed from this inductive data to enable a deductive study when develop theory from the constructs developed. The processes of interviewing and observation will now be discussed.

Interviews

Approximately 20 individual face-to-face, in-depth semi-structured interviews (Strauss and Corbin 1990; Miles and Huberman 1993) in each company with relevant people (middle managers, senior managers, teamleaders, change initiators and implementers) were conducted in the exploratory study to explore, not only middle managers experiences of their roles in the company, but the broader knowledge of middle managers roles in their organizations from significant other individuals as well. The interviews focused on individual's career history, their experiences of working in their organization, their roles and management practices, their familiarity with the organizational changes occurring and how this influenced their roles. The personal responsibilities and commitments of middle managers were investigated to investigate the possible tensions between public and personal spheres of lives specifically focusing on commitment and time. Company documents such as organizational charts and role descriptions were observed and analyzed at the time of the interviews where appropriate.

In the deductive phase of this research approximately ten middle managers were interviewed in each company. The interviews were tape-recorded and fieldwork notes taken during the sessions and directly afterwards to record and reflect my initial impressions and interpretations. These fieldwork notes provided a wealth of information for analyzing and representing the data. The interviews lasted between one and two hours. Informal discussions complemented the interviewing process and provided richness in the data which proved to be enormously beneficial in unravelling the complexities, contradictions and paradoxes within managers' persuasive accounts particularly in relation to issues regarding power, politics and family life. "Sensitive" issues (see Lee 1993) within the research could be revealed in a safer environment. This process although time consuming was fundamental for uncovering "off the record" accounts and formed a great deal of the data obtained. The interview tapes were fully transcribed and although time consuming it enabled me to spend a great deal of time with the text that enriched my initial interpretations and subsequent representations of each manager and their organizations.

Participant observation

All social research in one way or another is a form of participant observation because we cannot study the social world without being part of it (Atkinson and Hammersley 1994) in the inductive phase of this research. Observation of some middle managers' routines and behaviours were conducted with four managers in each company for approximately two days. My role was as researcher was as observer-as-participant (Layder 1993) that maintained only superficial contacts with the people being studied (Burgess 1984) which allowed for greater exploration of middle managers' "lives". Participant observation has the potential of having the capability of being unbiased by the interview, although the researcher's presence and interpretation of the situation heavily influence this method. The middle managers observed were selected from the managers interviewed who expressed most interest in the research.

Data collection and analysis

The data collection phase was longitudinal and I visited each company during a six to 12 month period. Data analysis occurred through the data collection (Eisenhardt 1989). Within-case analysis was used to produce orienting theory that is, ideas of the type of data emerging about relationships and events within each company and cross-case analysis across the case organizations to develop substantive theory. Within-case analysis involved detailed write-ups (using the transcribed interviews, observation notes and fieldwork notes) for each company and individual studied and cannot be generalized across case studies (Whyte 1970 cited in Eisenhardt ibid.). These write-ups involved descriptions to generate preliminary ideas about the company and the individuals to "help researchers to cope early in the analysis process with the often enormous volume of data..." to allow "unique patterns to merge before investigators push to generalise patterns across cases. In addition, it gives investigators a rich familiarity with each case which, in turn, accelerates cross-case comparison" (Eisenhardt 1989: 540). Using Eisenhardt's framework for case study analysis, cross-case comparison explored the data in divergent ways using the constructs of the Management in Three Movements framework to explore individual middle managers' texts. This method of analysis also aimed at identifying conflicting issues or differences between the observation data and the interview data. Eisenhardt, although adopting a functionalist research approach, expresses the benefit of cross searching as a way to "force investigators to go beyond initial impressions, especially through the use of structured and diverse lenses on the data... investigators will capture the novel findings which may exist in the data" (1989: 541). Methodological rigour was also achieved by presenting my initial analysis of the data to the participants to determine whether these persuasive accounts resonate with and inform the member's own understandings of their subjective experiences.

Data presentation and analysis

The basic objective for the analysis of this book is the process of individual identity construction and although there are different ways that this could be approached, and even though the book at a theoretical level is prepared to challenge the unitary conceptions of the subject, the choice of individual cases of identity construction as a basic unit of analysis offers a number of advantages. The benefits of using the individual subject as a source of information for investigating individuals' identity construction provides the justification for my adoption of individual one to one interviews. These interviews enabled the access to listen to individual, not just for data gathering but for grasping individuals' stories. Also, individual interviews provide an arena for individuals managers, that are often vulnerable talking to outsiders, to open up in a safe environment to produce more in-depth accounts on not only individual's working experiences but the relationship between the personal and public; the tensions and contradictions in their accounts; and the power dynamics at play in their lives.

However organizations play a distinctive part in shaping individual identities particularly, but not limited to, those aspects of those identities that are related to working within the organization. The blurring of public and private boundaries of individual managers' lives is permeable and this was a focus of the analysis that shapes the construction and reconstruction of individual subjectivities. A key aspect of this socially constructed identity is that it is constructed in conditions of asymmetry that works on the basis that people are not all equally positioned in the organization and within the discourses that shape meaning and so it makes a difference whether you are male/female; black/white; old/young or categorized in terms of any other binaries.

References

Acker, J. (1990) Hierarchies, Jobs, Bodies: A Theory of Gendered Organizations, *Gender and Society*, 4(2): 139–58.

Adler, N. and Kwon, S.W. (2002) Social Capital: Prospects for a New Concept, *The Academy of Management Review*, 27(1): 17–40.

Alimo-Metcalfe, B. (1994) Gender Bias in the Selection and Assessment of Women in Management, in Davidson, M. and Burke, R. (eds) *Women in Management: Current Research Issues*. London: Paul Chapman.

Alimo-Metcalfe, B. (1995) An Investigation of Female and Male Constructs of Leadership and Empowerment, *Women in Management Review*, 10(2): 3–8.

Alvesson, M. (2001) Knowledge Work: Ambiguity, Image and Identity, *Human Relations*, 54(7).

Alvesson, M. (2002) *Understanding Organizational Culture*. London: Sage.

Alvesson, M. and Berg, P.O. (1992) *Corporate Culture and Organizational Symbolism*. New York: de Gruyter.

Alvesson, M. and Billing, Y. (1997) *Understanding Gender and Organizations*. London: Sage.

Alvesson, M. and Karreman, D. (2000) Taking the linguistic turn in organizational research, *The Journal of Applied Behavioral Science (JABS)*, 36(2): 136–58.

Alvesson, M. and Willmott, H. (1998) *Understanding Management*. London: Sage.

Alvesson, M. and Willmott, H. (2002) Identity Regulation as Organizational Control Producing the Appropriate Individual, *Journal of Management Studies*, 39(5): 619–44.

Anthony, P. (1994) *Managing Culture*. Buckingham: Open University Press.

Arthur, M.B., Claman, P.C., and DePhillipi, R.J. (1995) Intelligent Enterprise, Intelligent Career, *Academy of Management Executive*, 9(4): 1–15.

Atkinson, J. (1984) Manpower Strategies for Flexible Organizations, *Personnel Management*, August: 28–31.

Atkinson, P. and Hammersley, M. (1994) Ethnography and Participant Observation, in Denzin, N.K. and Lincoln, Y.S., *Handbook of Qualitative Research*. London: Sage.

Bailyn, L. (1993) *Breaking The Mould: Women, Men and Time in the New Corporate World*. New York: The Free Press.

Balogun, J. and Johnson, G. (2004) Organizational Restructuring and Middle Manager Sensemaking, *Academy of Management Journal*, 47(4): 523–49.

Banerjee, S.B. and Linstead, S.A. (2001) Globalization, Multiculturalism and Other Fictions: The New Colonization for the New Millennium, *Organization*, 8(4): 711–50.

Barker, J. (1993) Tightening the Iron Cage, *Administrative Science Quarterly*, 38(3): 408–37.

Barley, S.R. and Kunda, G. (1992) Design and devotion: surges of rational and normative ideologies of control in managerial discourse, *Administrative Science Quarterly*, 37: 363–99.

Barnes, J. (1990) *Around the World in 10.5 Chapters*. London: Picador.

Barthes, R. (1977) *Image-Music-Text*. Translated by S. Heath. London: Fontana Collins.

Barthes, R. (1981) The Theory of the Text, in Young, R. (ed.) *Untying the Text*. London: Routledge.

Bartlett, C. and Ghoshal, S. (1989) *Managing Across Boundaries: the Transnational Corporation*. New York: Random House Business Books.

Baudrillard, J. (1975) *The Mirror of Production*. New York: Telos Press.

Baudrillard, J. (1981) *The Political Economy of the Sign*. New York: Telos Press.

Baudrillard, J. (1990) *Seduction*. New York: St Martin's Press.

Baudrillard, J. (1998) *Consumer Society: Myths and Structures*. London: Sage.

Bauman, Z. (1989) *Modernity and the Holocaust*. Cambridge: Polity Press.

Bauman, Z. (1992) *Intimations of Postmodernity*. London: Routledge.

Bauman, Z. (1993) *Postmodern Ethics*. Oxford: Basil Blackwell.

Bauman, Z. (1995) *Life in Fragments*. Oxford: Blackwell.

Beck, U. and Beck-Gernsheim, E. (1995) *The Normal Chaos of Love*. Cambridge: Polity Press.

Beech, N. and Huxham, C. (2003) Cycles of Identity Formation in Inter-Organizational Collaborations, *International Studies of Management and Organization*, 33(2): 7–21.

Benbow, N. (1996) *Survival of the Fittest: a survey of managers, experience of and attitudes to work in the post-recession economy*. Corby, UK: Institute of Management.

Benhabib, S. (1992) *Situating the Self*. Cambridge: Polity.

Beunza, D. and Stark, D.(2004) How to Recognize Opportunities: Heterarchical Search in a Trading Room in K. Knorr Cetina and A. Preda (eds) *The Sociology of Financial Markets*. Oxford: Oxford University Press.

Billing, Y.D. and Alvesson, M. (1994) *Gender, Managers and Organizations*. Berlin: de Druyter.

Boje, D.M. and Winsor, R.D. (1993) The Resurrection of Taylorism: Total Quality Management's Hidden Agenda, *Journal of Organizational Change Management*, 6(4): 57–70.

Bologh, R. (1990) *Love or Greatness*. London: Unwin Hyman.

Bourdieu, P. (2001) *Masculine Domination*. Trans. Richard Nice. Cambridge: Polity Press.

Brewis, J. and Linstead, S. (2001) *Sex, Work and Sex Work*. London: Routledge.

Britton, R. (1998) Belief and Imagination. London: Routledge & New Library of Psychoanalysis.

Brockner, J., Tyler, T.R. and Cooper-Schneider, R. (1992) The Influence of Prior Commitment to an Institution on Reactions to Perceived Unfairness: The Higher They Are, The Harder They Fall, *Administrative Science Quarterly*, 37: 241–61.

Brown, A. (1997) Narcissism, Identity and Legitimacy, *Academy of Management Review*, 22(3): 643–86.

Brown, A. (2001) Organization Studies and Identity: towards a research agenda, *Human Relations*, 54(1): 113–21.

Brown, A.D. and Starkey, K. (2000) Organizational Identity and Learning: A Psychodynamic Perspective, *Academy of Management Review*, 25(1): 102–20.

Buchanan, I. and Colebrook, C. (2000) *Deleuze and Feminist Theory*. Edinburgh: Edinburgh University Press.

Burgess, R. (1984) *In the Field: An Introduction to Field Research*. London: Routledge.

Burrell, G. (1992) The Pleasure of Organization. In Alvesson, M. and Willmott, H. (eds) *Critical Management Studies*. London: Sage.

Burrell, G. (1997) *Pandemonium*. London: Sage.

Butler, J. (1999) *Gender Trouble: Feminism and the Subversion of Identity*. New York: Routledge.

Calás, M.B. and Smircich, L. (1991) Voicing Seduction to Silence Leadership, *Organization Studies*, 12(4): 567–602.

Calás, M.B. and Smircich, L. (1992a) Re-writing Gender into Organizational Theorizing: Directions from Feminist Perspectives, in M. Reed and M. Hughes (eds) *Rethinking Organization*. London: Sage.

Calás, M.B. and Smircich, L. (1992b) Using the "F" word: feminist theories and the social consequences of organisational research, in Mills, A. and Tancred, P. (eds) *Gendering Organisational Analysis*. London: Sage.

Calás, M.B. and Smircich, L. (1993) Dangerous Liaisons: The "Feminisation-in Management" Meets "Globalisation", *Business Horizons*, March–April: 73–83.

Calás, M.B. and Smircich, L. (1996) From "The Woman's" Point of View: Feminist Approaches to Organization Studies, in S.R. Clegg, C. Hardy and W.R. Nord (eds) *Handbook of Organization Studies*. London: Sage.

Cameron, K.S., Freeman, S.J. and Mishra, A.K. (1991) Best Practices in White-Collar Downsizing: Managing contradictions, *Academy of Management Executive*, 5(3): 57–73.

Carr, A. (1998) Identity, Compliance and Dissent in Organizations: A Psychoanalytic Perspective, *Organization*, 5(1): 81–99.

Casey, C. (1995) *Work, Self and Society: After Industrialism*. London: Routledge.

Casey, C. (1996) Corporate Transformations: Designer Culture, Designer Employees and "Post-occupational" Solidarity, *Organization*, 3(3): 317–39.

Castells, M. (1996) *The Rise of the Network Society*. Oxford: Blackwell.

Castells, M. (1997) *The Power of Identity*. Oxford: Blackwell.

Charlesworth, K. (1997) *A Question of Balance?: a survey of managers' changing professional and personal roles*. Corby: The Institute of Management.

Chia, R. (1996) The Problem of Reflexivity in Organizational Research: Towards a Postmodern Science of Organization, *Organisation*, 3(1): 31–59.

Cixous, H. (1998) *Stigmata: Escaping Texts*. London: Routledge.

Cixous, H. and Clement, C. (1986) *The Newly Born Woman*. Theory and History of Literature, Vol. 24. Minneapolis: University of Minnesota Press.

Clark, P. (1985) Context of the Shift, in Lincoln, Y.S. (ed.) *Organization Theory and Inquiry*, Beverly Hills, CA: Sage.

Clegg, S. (1990) *Modern Organizations: Studies in the Postmodern World*. London: Sage.

Clegg, S. (1994) Power Relations and the Constitution of the Resistant Subject, in Jermier, J.M., Knights, D., and Nord, W.N. (1994) *Resistance and Power in Organizations*. London: Routledge.

Cockburn, C. (1991) *In The Way of Women: Men's Resistance to Sex Equality in Organisations*. Macmillan: Basingstoke.

Cohen, A. (1994) *Self consciousness: an alternative anthropology of identity*. London: Routledge.

Collinson, D. (1992) *Managing the Shopfloor*. Berlin: de Druyter.

Collinson, D. (1994) Strategies of Resistance: Power, Knowledge and Subjectivity in the Workplace, in Jermier, J.M., Knights, D., and Nord, W.N. *Resistance and Power in Organizations*. London: Routledge.

Collinson, D. (2003) Identities and Insecurities: selves at work, *Organization*, 10(3): 527–47.

Collinson, D.L. and Collinson, M. (1997) Delayering Managers: Time-Space Surveillance and its Gendered Effects, *Organization*, 4(3): 375–407.

Collinson, D. and Hearn, J. (1994) Naming Men as Men: Implications for Work, Organization and Management, *Gender, Work and Organization*, 1(1): 2–22.

Collinson, D. and Hearn, J. (1996) *Men as Managers, Managers as Men*. London: Sage.

Collinson, D.L., Knights, D., and Collinson, M. (1990) *Managing to Discriminate*. London: Routledge.

Connell, R.W. (1995) *Masculinities*. Sydney: Allen and Unwin.

Craib, I. (1998) *Experiencing Identity*. London: Sage.

Crook, S., Pakulski, J., and Waters, M. (1992) *Postmodernization: Change in Advanced Society*. London: Sage.

Cunliffe, A. (2001) Managers as Practical Authors: Reconstructing our Understanding of Management Practice, *Journal of Management Studies*, 38(3): 351–71.

Davidow, W.H. and Malone, M.S. (1992) *The Virtual Corporation*. London: Harper Business.

Davidson, M.J. and Cooper, C.L. (1992) *Shattering the Glass Ceiling: The Woman Manager*. London: Paul Chapman.

Davies, K. (1990) *Women and Time: Weaving the Strands of Everyday Life*. Aldershot: Avebury.

De Certeau, M. (1984) *The Practice of Everyday Life*. Berkeley: University of California Press.

Denzin, N.K. (1989a) *Interpretive Biography*. London: Sage.

Denzin, N.K. (1989b) *The Research Act: A Theoretical Introduction to Sociological Methods*. 3rd ed. London: Prentice Hall.

Denzin, N.K. (1989c) *Interpretative Interactionalism*. Newbury Park, CA: Sage.

Denzin, N.K. and Lincoln, Y.S. (1994) *Handbook of Qualitative Research*. London: Sage.

Derrida, J. (1976) *Of Grammatology*, translated by G.C. Spivak, The Introduction. Baltimore: John Hopkins Press.

Derrida, J. (1978) *Writing and Difference*. Chicago: University of Chicago Press.

Derrida, J. (1995) *The Gift of Death*. London: Chicago Press.

Devanna, M.A. and Tichy, N. (1986) *The Transformational Leader*. New York: John Wiley & Sons Inc.

Dickens, L. (1998) What HRM Means for Gender Equality, *Human Resource Management Journal*, 8(1): 23–40.

Dickson, J. (1977) The Plight of the Middle Manager, *Management Today*, December: 66–9.

Doherty, N., Bank, J., and Vinnicombe, S. (1995) Managing Survivors: The Experience of Survivors in BT and the British Financial Sector. Bedford: Cranfield University.

Donaldson, M. (1991) *Time of Our Lives*. Sydney: George Allen & Unwin.

Donaldson, M. (1996) *Taking our Time: Remaking the Temporal Order*. Perth: University of Western Australia Press.

Dopson, S. and Neumann, J.E. (1998) Uncertainty, Contrariness and the Double-Bind: Middle Managers' Reactions to Changing Contracts, *British Journal of Management*, 9: S53–S70.

Dopson, S. and Stewart, R. (1990) What *is* Happening to Middle Management? *British Journal of Management*, 1: 3–16.

Downs, A. (1997) *Beyond The Looking Glass: Overcoming the Seductive Culture of Corporate Narcissism*. New York: Amacom.

du Gay, P. (1991) Enterprise Culture and the Ideology of Excellence, *New Formations*, 13: 45–61.

du Gay, P. (1993) Entrepreneurial Management in the Public Sector, *Work, Employment and Society*, 7(4): 643–8.

du Gay, P. (1996) *Consumption and Identity at Work*. London: Sage.

du Gay, P. (2000) *In Praise of Bureaucracy: Weber, Organization, Ethics*. London: Sage.

Duncomb, J.E. and Marsden, D. (1995) "Workaholics" and "Whinging Women": Theorising Intimacy and Emotion Work – The Last Frontier of Gender Inequality? *The Sociological Review*, 150–67.

Dunford, R. and Heiler, K. (1994) Human Resource Management and Downsizing: Managing the Tensions, paper presented at the 4th *Annual Conference of IHRM*, Gold Coast, July 5–8.

Dutton, J.E. and Dukerich, J.M. (1991) Keeping and Eye on the Mirror: Image and Identity in Organizational Adaptation, *Academy of Management Journal*, 34: 239–63.

Edwards, R. (1979) *Contested Terrain: the Transformation of the Workplace in the Twentieth Century*. New York: Basic Books.

Edwards, R., Collinson, D., and Rocca, D. (1995) Workplace Resistance in Western Europe: A Preliminary Overview and Research Agenda, *European Journal of Industrial Relations*, 1(3): 283–316.

Edwards, C., Robinson, O., Welchman, R., and Woodhall, J. (1999) Lost Opportunities? Organisational Restructuring and Women Managers, *Human Resource Management Journal*, 9(1): 55–64.

Edwards, C., Welchman, R., and Woodhall, J. (1996) Organisational Change and Women Managers' Careers: The Restructuring of Disadvantage? *Employee Relations*, 18(5): 25–45.

Eisenhardt, K.M. (1989) Building Theories from Case Study Research, *Academy of Management Review*, 14: 532–50.

Elliot, A. (1996) *Subject to Ourselves: Social Theory, Psychoanalysis and Postmodernity*. London: Polity Press.

Fairclough, N. (1992) *Discourse and Social Change*. Cambridge: Polity.

Fagenson, E. (1993) *Women in Management: Trends, Issues and Challenges in Managerial Diversity*. Newbury Park: Sage.

Fayol, H. (1949) *General and Industrial Management*. London: Pitman.

Featherstone, M. (1991) *Consumer Culture and Postmodernism*. London: Sage.

Ferguson, K. (1984) *The Feminist Case Against Bureaucracy*. Philadelphia: Temple University Press.

Fineman, S. (1983) Work meanings, non-work, and the taken for granted, *Journal of Management Studies*, 20: 143–57.

Fleming, P. and Sewell, G. (2002) Looking for the Good Soldier Švejk: Alternative Modalities of Resistance in the Contemporary Workplace, *Sociology*, 36(4): 857–74.

Fleming, P. and Spicer, A. (2003) Working at a Cynical Distance: Implications for Power, Subjectivity and Resistance Organization, 10(1): 157–79.

Floyd, S.W. and Wooldridge, B. (1997) Middle Management's Strategic Influence and Organizational Performance, *Journal of Management Studies*, 34(3): 465–85.

Fondas, N. (1997) Feminisation Unveiled: Management Qualities in Contemporary Writings, *Academy of Management Review*, 22(1): 257–82.

Ford, J.D., Ford, L.W., and McNamara, R.T. (2002) Resistance and the Background Conversations of Change, *Journal of Organizational Change Management*, 15(2): 105–21.

Foucault, M. (1972) *The Archaeology of Knowledge*. London: Tavistock.

Foucault, M. (1976) *The Birth of the Clinic*. London: Tavistock.

Foucault, M. (1977) *Madness and Civilisation*. London: Tavistock.

Foucault, M. (1979a) The History of Sexuality Vol. 1. New York: Vintage.

Foucault, M. (1979b) *Discipline and Punish: the birth of the prison*. Harmondsworth: Penguin.

Foucault, M. (1980) *Power/Knowledge*. Brighton: Harvester Wheatsheaf.

Friedman, J. (1992) Narcissism, roots and postmodernity: the construction of selfhood in the global crisis, in Lash, S. and Friedman, J. (1992) *Modernity and Identity*. Oxford: Blackwell.

Frost, P.J., Moore, L.F., Louis, M.R., Lundberg, C.C., and Martin, J. (eds) (1991) *Reframing Organizational Culture*. London: Sage.

Fulop, L. and Linstead, S. (1999) *Management: A Critical Text*. Basingstoke, Hampshire: Macmillan.

Gabbard, G. (1996) *Psychodynamic Psychiatry in Clinical Practice*. Washington: American Psychiatric Press.

Gabriel, Y. (1999) Beyond Happy Families: A Critical Re-evaluation of the Control-Resistance-Identity Triangle, *Human Relations*, 52(2): 179–203.

Gabriel, Y. (2004a) *Myths, Stories, And Organizations: Premodern Narratives For Our Times*. Oxford: Oxford University Press.

Gabriel, Y. (2004b) Narratives, stories and texts, in Grant, D., Hardy, C., Oswick, C., Putnam, L.L. (ed.), *The SAGE Handbook Of Organizational Discourse*. London: Sage.

Gabriel, Y. and D.S. Griffiths (2004) Stories in organizational research, in Cassell, C., Symon, G. (ed.), *Essential Guide To Qualitative Methods In Organizational Research*. London: Sage.

Galpin, S. and Sims, D. (1999) Narratives and Identity in Flexible Working and Teleworking Organizations, in Jackson, P. (1999) *Virtual Working: Social and Organizational Dynamics*. London: Routledge.

Garfinkel, H. (1967) *Studies in Ethnomethodology*. Englewood Cliffs, NJ: Prentice-Hall.

Garsten, C. and Grey, C. (1997) How to Become Oneself: Discourses of Subjectivity in Post-bureaucratic Organizations, *Organization*, 4(2): 211–28.

Gergen, K.J. (1985) The Social Constructionist Movement in Modern Psychology, *American Psychologist*, 40: 266–75.

Gheradi, S. and Turner, B. (1988) Real Men Don't Collect Soft Data. Trento: *Quaderni del Dipartimento di Politica Sociale*, 13.

Giddens, A. (1991) *Modernity and Self-Identity*. Cambridge: Polity Press.

Gioia, D.A., Schultz, M., and Corley, K.G. (2000) Organizational Identity, Image and Adaptive Instability, *Academy of Management Review*, 25(1): 63–91.

Girard, M. and Stark, D. (2003) "Heterarchies of Worth in Manhattan-based New Media Firms", *Theory, Culture and Society*, vol. 20, no. 3, pp. 77–105.

Girard, M. and Stark, D. (2005) Heterarchies of Value: Distributing Intelligence and Organizing Diversity in a New Media Startup, in Collier and A. Ong (eds)

Global Assemblages: Technology, Politics, and Ethics as Anthropological Problems. Oxford: Blackwell.

Goffman, E. (1959) *The Presentation of Self in Everyday Life.* New Jersey: Anchor Books.

Goode, J. and Bagilhole, B. (1998) Gendering the Management of Change in Higher Education: A Case Study, *Gender, Work and Organization,* 5(3): 148–64.

Gowler, D. and Legge, K. (1983) The Meaning of Management and the Management of Meaning: A View from Social Anthropology in M.J. Earl (ed.) *Perspectives on Management.* Oxford: Oxford University Press.

Gowler, D. and Legge, K. (1996) The Meaning of Management and The Management of Meaning, in Linstead, S., Grafton-Small, R., and Jeffcutt, P. (eds) *Understanding Management.* London: Sage.

Grafton-Small, R. (2005) Identity Aesthetics: Asymmetry and the Assault on Order in Pullen, A. and Linstead, S., *Organization and Identity.* London: Routledge.

Grant, D., Hardy, C., Oswick, C., and Putnam, L. (2004) *Handbook of Organizational Discourse.* London: Sage.

Grant, D., Keenoy, T., and Oswick, C. (1998) *Discourse and Organization.* London: Sage.

Grey, C. (1994) Career as a Project of the Self and Labour Process Discipline, *Sociology,* 28(2): 479–97.

Grint, K. (1995) *Management: A Sociological Introduction.* Cambridge: Polity Press.

Grosz, E. (1994) *Volatile Bodies: Towards a Corporeal Feminism.* Bloomington and Indianapolis: Indiana University Press.

Guest, D. and Peccei, R. (1992) Employee Involvement: Redundancy as a Critical Case, Human, *Resource Management Journal,* 2(3): 34–59.

Hales, C. (1993) *Managing Through Organizations.* London: Routledge.

Hamilton, P. (1997) Rhetorical Discourses of Local Pay, *Organization,* 4(2): 229–54.

Hammer, M. and Champy, J. (1993) *Reengineering the Corporation.* New York: HarperCollins.

Hancock, P. (1999) Baudrillard and the Metaphysics of Motivation: A Reappraisal of Corporate Culturalism in the Light of the Work and Ideas of Jean Baudrillard, *Journal of Management Studies,* 36(2): 145–65.

Hancock, P. and Tyler, M. (2001) *Work, Postmodernism and Organization: A Critical Introduction.* London: Sage.

Handy, C. (1992) *The Age of Unreason.* Cambridge, MA: Harvard Business School Press.

Hardt, M. and Negri, A. (2000) *Empire.* MA: Cambridge University Press.

Hardy, C., Lawrence, T. and Grant, D. (2005) Discourse and Collaboration: The Role of Conversations and collective Identity", *Academy of Management Review,* 30(1): 1–20.

Harvey, D. (1990) *The Condition of Postmodernity.* Oxford: Blackwell.

Hassard, J. (1993) Postmodernism and Organizational Analysis: An Overview, in J. Hassard and M. Parker (eds) *Postmodernism and Organisations.* London: Sage.

Hatch, M.J. and Schultz, M. (2004a) Introduction, in Hatch, M. and Schultz, M. (eds) *Organizational Identity: A Reader.* Oxford: Blackwell.

Hatch, M.J. and Schultz, M. (2004b) The Dynamics of Organizational Identity, in Hatch, M. and Schultz, M. (eds) *Organizational Identity: A Reader.* Oxford: Blackwell.

Hearn, J. and Parkin, W.P. (1983) Gender and Organizations: A Selective Review and a Critique of a Neglected Area, *Organization Studies*, 4(3): 219–42.

Hearn, J. and Parkin, W.P. (1995) *"Sex" at "Work": The Power and Paradox of Organizational Sexuality*. Hemel Hempstead: Prentice-Hall.

Hearn, J., Sheppard, D., Tancred-Sheriff, P., and Burrell, G. (1989) *The Sexuality of Organization*. London: Sage.

Heckscher, C. (1995) *White Collar Blues: Management Loyalties in an Age of Corporate Restructuring*. New York: Basic Books.

Henriques, J., Hollway, W., Urwin, C., Venn, C., and Walkerdine, V. (1984) *Changing the Subject: Psychology, Social Regulation and Subjectivity*. London: Methuen.

Hill, S. (1991) How do you Manage the Flexible Firm? The Total Quality Model, *Work, Employment and Society*, 5(3): 397–416.

Hirchorn, L. (1997) *Reworking Authority: Leading and Following in the Post-modern Organization*. London: MIT Press.

Hochschild, A.R. (1997) *The Time Bind: When Work Becomes Home and Home Becomes Work*. New York: Metropolitan Books.

Hodge, R. and Kress, G. (1988) *Social Semiotics*. Cambridge: Polity.

Holmes, J. (2001) *Ideas in Psychoanalysis: Narcissism*. Cambridge: Icon Books.

Höpfl, H. (2000) The Suffering Mother and the Miserable Son: Organizing Women and Organizing Women's Writing, *Gender, Work and Organization*, April, vol. 7, no. 2, pp. 98–105(8).

Höpfl, H. (2002a) Hitchcock's Vertigo and the Tragic Sublime, *Journal of Organizational Change Management*, 15(1): 21–34.

Höpfl, H. (2002b) Playing the Part: Reflections on Aspects of Mere Performance in the Customer-Client Relationship, *Journal of Management Studies*, 39(2): 255–67.

Höpfl, H. and Linstead, S. (1993) Passion and Performance: Suffering and the Carrying of Organisational Roles, in Fineman, S. (ed.) *Emotion in Organisations*. London: Sage.

Inkson, K. (1993) Do Careers Exist? Studies of Managerial Job Change in the 90s, paper presented to the *ANZAM Conference*, Deakin University.

Inkson, K. (1995) Effects of Changing Economic Conditions on Managerial job Changes and Careers, *British Journal of Management*, 6(3): 183–94.

Jackall, R. (1988) *Moral Mazes: The World of Corporate Managers*. Oxford: Oxford University Press.

Jackson, P. (1999) Introduction: From New Designs to New Dynamics, in Jackson, P. (ed.) *Virtual Working: Social and Organizational Dynamics*. London: Routledge.

Jacobson, S.W. and Jacques, R. (1990) Of Knowers, Knowing, and the Known: A Gender Framework for Revisioning Organizational and Management Scholarship, paper presented at *The Academy of Management Annual Meeting*: Women in Management Division (August).

Jaques, E. (2000a) In Praise of Hierarchy, *Harvard Business Review*, January–February: 127–33.

Jaques, E. (2000b) Response to Lissl, *Harvard Business Review*, May–June: 215–16.

Jermier, J.M., Knights, D., and Nord, W.N. (1994) *Resistance and Power in Organizations*. London: Routledge.

Joseph Rowntree Foundation (1999) Job Insecurity and Work Intensification: Flexibility and the Changing Boundaries of Work, *People Management*, September 2nd: 16.

Kanter, R.M. (1977) *Men and Women of the Corporation*. New York: Basic Books.

Kanter, R.M. (1983) *The Change Masters*. New York: Simon & Schuster.

Kanter, R.M. (1989a) *When Giants Learn to Dance: Mastering the Challenge of Strategy, Management and Careers in the 1990s*. New York: Free Press.

Kanter, R.M. (1989b) The New Managerial Work, *Harvard Business Review*, November–December: 85–92.

Keenoy, T., Oswick, C., and Grant, D. (1997) Organizational Discourses: Text and Context, *Organization*, 4(2): 147–58.

Keillor, G. (1994) *The Book of Guys*. London: Faber and Faber.

Kellner, D. (1992) Popular Culture and the Construction of Postmodern Identities, Lash, S. and Friedman, J. (1992) *Modernity and Identity*. Oxford: Blackwell.

Kemske, F. (1996) *Human Resources*. North Haven, CT: Catbird Press.

Kerfoot, D. (1999) The Organization of Intimacy: Managerialism, Masculinity and the Masculine Subject, in Whitehead, S. and Moodley, R. (eds) (1999) *Transforming Managers: Gendering Change in the Public Sector*. London: UCL Press.

Kerfoot, D. and Knights, D. (1993) Masculinity, Management and Manipulation, *Journal of Management Studies*, 30(4): 659–79.

Kerfoot, D. and Knights, D. (1996) The Best is Yet to Come: The Quest for Embodiment in Managerial Work, in Collinson, D. and Hearn, J. (1996) *Men as Managers, Managers as Men*. London: Sage.

Kerfoot, D. and Knights, D. (1998) Managing Masculinity in Contemporary Organizational Life: A "Man"agerial Project, *Organization*, 5(1): 7–26.

Kerfoot, D. and Knights, D. (1999) Man Management: Ironies of Modern Management in an "Old" University, in Whitehead, S. and Moodley, R. (eds) (1999) *Transforming Managers: Gendering Change in the Public Sector*. London: UCL Press.

Kets De Vries, M. (1995) (2nd ed.) *Organizational Paradoxes: Clinical Approaches to Management*. London: Routledge.

Kleege, G. (2000) Wearing the Mask Inside Out, *Social Research*, 67(1): 47–59.

Knights, D. (1990) Subjectivity, Power and the Labour Process, in Knights, D. and Willmott, H. *Labour Process Theory*. London: Macmillan.

Knights, D. (1992) Changing Spaces: The Disruptive Power of Epistemological Location for the Management and Organizational Sciences, *Academy of Management Review*, 17(3): 514–36.

Knights, D. (2001) The "New Economy" and the "New Man": Virtual Transitions or Transitional Virtualities, *Keynote address to Conference of Asia-Pacific Researchers in Organization Studies (APROS)*, Baptist University, Hong Kong, December.

Knights, D. (2002) Writing Organizational Analysis into Foucault, *Organization*, 9(4): 575–93.

Knights, D. and McCabe, D. (2000) Ain't Misbehavin? Opportunities for Resistance Under New Forms of "Quality?" Management, *Sociology*, 34(3): 421–36.

Knights, D. and Vurdubakis, T. (1994) Foucault, Power and All That, in Jermier, J.M., Knights, D., and Nord, W.N. *Resistance and Power in Organizations*. London: Routledge.

Knights, D. and Willmott, H. (1992) Conceptualising Leadership Processes: A Study of Senior Managers in a Financial Services Company, *Journal of Management Studies*, 29(6): 761–82.

Knights, D. and Willmott, H. C. (1985) Power and Identity in Theory and Practice, *Sociological Review*, 33(1): 22–46.

Knights, D. and Willmott, H. (1999) *Management Lives: Power and Identity in Work Organizations*. London: Sage.

Kondo, D.K. (1990) Crafting Selves: Power, Gender and Discourses of Identity in a Japanese Workplace. Chicago: University of Chicago Press.

Kreitzman, L. (1999) *The 24 Hour Society*. London: Profile Books.

Kristeva, P. (1982) *Powers of Horror: An Essay on Abjection*. Chichester: Columbia University Press.

Kumar, K. (1995) *From Post-Industrial to Post-Modern Society: New Theories of the Contemporary World*. Oxford: Blackwell.

Kunda, G. (1992) Engineered Culture: Control and Commitment in a High Tech Corporation. Philadelphia: Temple University Press.

Kundera, M. (1998) *Identity*. London. Faber and Faber Limited.

Lasch, C. (1979) *The Culture of Narcissism: American Life in an Age of Diminishing Expectations*. London: W.W. Norton and Company.

Lash, S. and Friedman, J. (1992) *Modernity and Identity*. Oxford: Blackwell.

Lash, S. and Urry, J. (1993) *Economies of Signs and Space*. London: Sage.

Lawrence, P.R. and Lorsch, J.W. (1986) *Organization and Environment: Managing Differentiation and Integration*. Boston, Mass.: Harvard Business School Press.

Layder, D. (1993) *New Strategies in Social Research*. Cambridge: Polity.

Ledwith, S. and Colgan, F. (1996) *Women in Organisations: challenging gender politics*. Basingstoke: Macmillan.

Lee, R.M. (1993) *Doing Research on Sensitive Topics*. London: Sage.

Lee, N. and Munro, R. (2001) *The Consumption of Mass*. London: Blackwell.

Lennie, I. (1999) *Beyond Management*. London: Sage.

Leonard, P. (1998) Gendering Change? Management, Masculinity and the Dynamics of Incorporation, *Gender and Education*, 10(1): 71–84.

Letiche, H. (2004) "Jean-Francois Lyotard" in S. Linstead (ed.) *Organization Theory and Postmodern Thought*. London: Sage.

Linstead, A. and Brewis, J. (2004) Introduction in Linstead, A. and Brewis, J. (eds) Beyond Boundaries: towards fluidity in theorising and practice. Special Issue of the journal, *Gender, Work and Organization*, 11(4): 335–62.

Linstead, A. and Catlow, C. (2004) Dilemmas Beyond the Glass Ceiling... the performances of senior women managers in the National Health Service in New Public Management: Dilemmas facing Professionals and Managers in the Public Sector, Barry, J., Chandler, J., and Dent, M. (eds) London: Ashbury Press.

Linstead, A. and Thomas, R. (2002) What Do You Want From Me? A Post-structuralist Feminist Reading of Middle Managers' Identities, *Culture and Organization*, 8(1): 1–20.

Linstead, S.A. (1995) After the Autumn Harvest: rhetoric and representation in an Asian Industrial Dispute, *Studies in Cultures, Organizations and Societies*, 1(2): 231–52.

Linstead, S.A. (1993) Deconstruction in the Study of Organizations, in Hassard, J. and Parker, M. (eds) *Postmodernism and Organizations*. London: Sage.

Linstead, S.A. (1994) Objectivity, Reflexivity and Fiction: Humanity, Inhumanity and the Science of the Social, *Human Relations*, 47(11): 1321–46.

Linstead, S.A. (1996) Panel discussion on The Future of Management Work. *Australian and New Zealand Academy of Management*. University of Wollongong, New South Wales.

Linstead, S.A. (2000a) Gender Blindness or Gender Suppression? A comment on Fiona Wilson's Research Note, *Organisation Studies*, 21(1): 297–303.

Linstead, S.A. (2000b) "Writing like a Man" Review of *Managing Like a Man* Judy Wajcman, Penn State University Press, 1998, *Human Relations*, 53(8): 1106–111.

Linstead, S.A. (2001a) Rhetoric and Organizational Control: A Framework for Analysis, in Westwood, R. and Linstead, S. (2001) *The Language of Organization*. London: Sage.

Linstead, S.A. (2001b) Death in Vegas: Seduction, Kitsch and Sacrifice, *Management*. Special Issue on *Deconstructing Las Vegas*, 4(3): 159–74.

Linstead, S. and Chan, A. (1994) The Sting of Organization: Command, Reciprocity and Change Management, *Journal of Organizational Change Management*, 7(5): 4–19.

Linstead, S.A. and Grafton Small, R. (1992) On Reading Organizational Culture, *Organization Studies*, 13(3): 331–55.

Linstead, S., Grafton Small, R., and Jeffcutt, P. (eds) (1996) *Understanding Management*. London: Sage.

Linstead, S. and Höpfl, H. (eds) (2000) *The Aesthetics of Organization*. London: Sage.

Linstead, S., Fulop, L., and Lilley, S. (2003) *Management and Organization: a critical text*. London: Palgrave.

Littler, C., Wiesner, R., and Dunford, R. (2003) The Dynamics of Delayering: changing management structures in three countries, *Journal of Management Studies*, 40(2): 225–56.

Livian, Y.-F. and Burgoyne, J.G. (eds) (1997) *Middle Managers in Europe*. London: Routledge.

Lyotard, J-F. (1984) *The Postmodern Condition*. Manchester: Manchester University Press.

Maile, S. (1995) The Gendered Nature of Managerial Discourse: The case of a Local Authority, *Gender, Work and Organisation*, 2(2): 76–87.

Marshall, J. (1984) *Women Managers: Travellers in a Male World*. Chichester: John Wiley.

Marshall, J. (1995) *Women Managers Moving On: Exploring Career and Life Choices*. London: Routledge.

May, T. (1999) From Banana Time to Just-In-Time: Power and Resistance at Work, *Sociology*, 33(4): 737–83.

McGovern, P., Hope-Hailey, V., and Stiles, P. (1998) The Managerial Career after Downsizing: case studies form the "Leading Edge", *Work, Employment and Society*, 12(3): 457–77.

McKinlay, A. (2002) "Dead Selves": The Birth of the Modern Career, *Organization*, 9(4): 595–614.

McKinlay, A. and Starkey, K. (eds) (1997) *Foucault, Management and Organization Theory*. London: Sage.

McNay, L. (2000) *Gender and Agency: Reconfiguring the Subject in Feminist and Social Theory*. Cambridge: Polity.

Mead, G. (1934) *Mind, Self and Society*. Chicago: University of Chicago Press.

Merton, R. (1957) *Social Theory and Social Structure*. Glencoe, IL: Free Press.

Messner, M. (1992) *Power at Play, Sports and the Problem of Masculinity*. Boston: Bacon Press.

Messner, M.A. (1997) *Politics of Masculinities: Men in Movements*. Alta Mira Press.

Metcalfe, B. and Linstead, A. (2003) Gendering Teamwork: Re-Writing the Feminine, *Gender, Work and Organization*, 10(1): 94–119.

Miles, M.B. and Huberman, A.M. (1993) *Qualitative Data Analysis: A Sourcebook of New Methods*. Newbury Park, CA: Sage.

Mills, A. and Tancred, P. (1992) (eds) *Gendering Organisational Analysis*. Newbury Park, CA: Sage.

Mintzberg, H. (1971) Managerial Work: Analysis and Observation, *Management Science*, October: B97–110.

Mintzberg, H. (1973) *The Nature of Managerial Work*. New York: Harper and Row.

Moodley, R. (1999) Masculine Managerial Masks and the "Other" Subject, in Whitehead, S. and Moodley, R. (eds) (1999) *Transforming Managers: Gendering Change in the Public Sector*. London: UCL Press.

Morgan, G. (1986) *Images of Organization*. London: Sage.

Morgan, G. (1996) The Gender of Bureaucracy, in Collinson, D. and Hearn, J. (1996) (eds) *Men as Managers, Managers as Men: Critical Perspectives on Men, Masculinities and Management*. London: Sage.

Moss, J. (1998) (ed.) *The Later Foucault*. London: Sage.

Mullholland, K. (1998) "Survivors" versus "Movers and Shakers": the reconstitution of management and careers in the privatised utilities, in Thompson, P. and Warhurst, C. (eds) (1998) *Workplaces of the Future*. Basingstoke: Macmillan.

Mumby, D.K. and Clair, R. (1997) Organisational Discourse, in van Dijk T.A. (ed.) *Discourse as Structure and Process* 2. London: Sage.

Neumann, J.E., Holti, R., and Standing, H. (1995) *Change Everything at Once! The Tavistock Institute's Guide to "Teamworking" in Manufacturing*. Didcock: Management Books 2000.

Newell, H. and Dopson, S. (1996) Muddle in the Middle: Organizational Restructuring and Middle Management Careers, *Personnel Review*, 25(4): 4–20.

Newman, J. (1995) Gender and Cultural Change, in Itzin, C. and Newman, J. (eds) *Gender, Culture and Organizational Change*. London: Routledge.

Nicholson, L. (ed.) (1990) *Feminism/Postmodernism*. London: Routledge.

Nietzsche, F. (1997) *Beyond Good and Evil: Prelude to a Philosophy of the Future* tr. H. Zimmern. New York: Dover.

Noer, D.M. (1993) *Healing the Wounds: Overcoming the Trauma of Layoffs and Revitalizing Downsized Organizations*. San Francisco: Jossey Bass.

Nonaka, I. and Takeuchi, H. (1995) *The Knowledge-Creating Company*. New York: Oxford University Press.

Noon, M. and Blyton, P. (2002) (2nd ed.) *The Realities of Work*. Palgrave.

O'Doherty, D. and Willmott, H. (1999) Debating Labour Process Theory: The Issue of Subjectivity and the Relevance of Poststructuralism, paper presented at the 5th *"Critical Perspectives on Accounting Conference: Ethical Dimensions of Accounting Change*. Baruch College, New York, April.

Oakley, A. (1981) Interviewing Women: A Contradiction in Terms? in Roberts, H. (ed.) *Doing Feminist Research*. London: Routledge.

Parker, I. (1989) Discourse and Power, in Shotter, J. and Gergen, K.J. (eds) (1989) *Texts of Identity*. London: Sage.

Parker, M. (1997) Dividing Organizations and Multiplying Identities, in Hetherington, K. and Munro, R. (eds) *Ideas of Difference*. Oxford: Blackwell/The Sociological Review.

Parker, M. (2000) *Organizational Culture and Identity*. London: Sage.

Peters, T. (1987) *Thriving on Chaos*. London: Pan.

Peters, T.J. (1992) *Liberation Management*. NY: Macmillan.

Peters, T. and Waterman, R.H. (1982) *In Search of Excellence*. New York: Harper and Row.

Pfeffer, J. (1981) Management as Symbolic Action: The Creation and Maintenance of Organizational Paradigms, in Cummings, L.L. and Staw, B. (eds) *Research in Organizational Behaviour*, 3(1): 1–52.

Pfeffer, J. (1998) *The Human Equation: Building Profits by Putting People First*. New York: Harvard Business School Press.

Piore, M. and Sabel, C. (1984) *The Second Industrial Divide: Possibilities for Prosperity*. New York: Basic Books.

Potter, J. and Wetherell, M. (1987) *Discourse and Social Psychology: Beyond Attitudes and Behaviour*. London: Sage.

Prasad, A. and Prasad, P. (1998) Everyday Struggles at the Workplace: The Nature and Implications of Routine Resistance in Contemporary Organizations, *Research in the Sociology of Organizations*, 15: 225–57.

Prichard, C. (1996) Managing Universities: Is it Men's Work? in Collinson, D.L. and Hearn, J. (eds) *Men as Managers: Managers as Men*. London: Sage.

Prichard, C. and Deem, R. (1999) Wo-managing Further Education: Gender and the Construction of the Manager in the Corporate Colleges of England, *Gender and Education*, 11(3): 323–42.

Pullen, A. (forthcoming) Gendering the Research Self: Social Practice and Corporeal Multiplicity in the Writing of Organizational Research, *Gender, Work and Organizations*.

Pullen, A. and Linstead, S. (eds) (2005a) *Organization and Identity*. London: Routledge.

Pullen, A. and Linstead, S. (2005b) Un-gendering the Future in Pullen, A. and Linstead, S. (eds) *Organization and Identity*. London: Routledge.

Ray, C.A. (1986) Corporate Culture: the Last Frontier of Control? *Journal of Management Studies*, 23(3): 287–98.

Redman, T., Wilkinson, A., and Snape, E. (1997) Stuck in the Middle? Managers in Building Societies, *Work, Employment and Society*, 11(1): 101–14.

Reed, M. (1997) In Praise of Duality and Dualism: Rethinking Agency and Structure in Organizational Analysis, *Organization Studies*, 18(1): 21–42.

Reskin, B. and Roos, P. (1990) *Job Queues, Gender Queues: Explaining Women's Inroads into Male Occupations*. Philadelphia: Temple University Press.

Ritzer, G. (1999) *Enchanting the Disenchanted World*. Newbury Park, CA: Pine Forge Press.

Ritzer, G. (2004) *The Globalization of Nothing*. Thousand Oaks, CA: Pine Forge Press.

Rosener, J. (1990) Ways Women Lead, *Harvard Business Review*, November–December: 119–25.

Rosenfeld, H. (1965) On the psychopathology or narcissism: A clinical approach, *International Journal of Psycho-Analysis*, 45: 332–7.

Sampson, E.E. (1989) The Deconstruction of the Self, in Shotter, J. and Gergen, K.J. (eds) *Texts of Identity*. London: Sage.

Savage, M. and Witz, A. (1992) *Gender and Bureaucracy*. Oxford: Blackwell.

Sawicki, J. (1991) *Disciplining Foucault: Feminism, Power and the Body*. London: Routledge.

Scarbrough, H. (1998) The Unmaking of Management? Change and Continuity in British Management in the 1990s, *Human Relations*, 51(6): 691–715.

Scarbrough, H. and Burrell, G. (1996) The Axeman Cometh: The Changing Roles and Knowledge of Middle Managers, in S. Clegg and G. Palmer (eds) *The Politics of Management Knowledge*. London: Sage.

Scase, R. and Goffee, R. (1989) *Reluctant Managers*. London: Unwin Hyman.

Schein, E.H. (1997) *Organizational Culture and Leadership*. London: Jossey-Bass.

Scheurich, J.J. (1997) *Research Method in the Postmodern*. London: Falmer Press.

Schwandt, T.A. (1998) Constructivist, Interpretivist Approaches to Human Inquiry, in Denzin, N.K. and Lincoln, Y.S. (eds) *The Landscape of Qualitative Research: Theories and Issues*. Thousand Oaks, CA: Sage.

Schwartz, H. (1990) *Narcissistic Processes and Corporate Decay*. New York: New York University Press.

Scott, J.C. (1985) *Weapons of the Weak: Everyday Forms of Peasant Resistance*. New Haven, CT: Yale University Press.

Scott, J.C. (1990) *Domination and the Arts of Resistance: Hidden Transcripts*. New Haven, CT: Yale University Press.

Scott, J. (1992) *Domination and The Arts of Resistance: Hidden Transcripts*. New Haven: Yale University Press.

Semler, R. (1993) *Maverick: The Success Story Behind the World's Most Unusual Workplace*. London: Warner Books.

Sewell, G. (1998) The Discipline of Teams: The Control of Team-Based Industrial Work through Electronic and Peer Surveillance. *Administrative Science Quarterly*, 43(2): 397–428.

Sewell, G. and Wilkinson, B. (1992) Someone to Watch Over Me: Surveillance, Discipline and Just-in Time Labour Process, *Sociology*, 26(2): 271–89.

Sheppard, D.L. (1989) Organisations, Power and Sexuality: The Image and Self-Image of Women Managers, in Hearn, J., Sheppard, D.L., Tancred-Sheriff, P., and Burrell, G. (eds) *The Sexuality of Organisation*. London: Sage.

Shotter, J. (1995) The Manager as a Practical Author: A Rhetorical-Responsive, Social Constructionist Approach to Social-Organizational Problems, in Hosking, D.M., Dachler, H.P. and Gergen, K.J. (eds) (1995) *Management and Organisation: Relational Alternatives to Individualism*. Aldershot: Avebury.

Shotter, J. and Gergen, K.J. (eds) (1989) *Texts of Identity*. London: Sage.

Sievers, B. (1992) *Work, Death and Life Itself*. Berlin: de Druyter.

Silverman, D. (1975) *Reading Castaneda*. London: Routledge.

Simon, H.A. (1960) *Administrative behaviour: a study of decision-making process in administrative organization*. New York: Free Press.

Simon, W. (1997) *Postmodern Sexualities*. London: Routledge.

Sims, D. (2003) Knowing, loving and the Velveteen Rabbit. Y. Gabriel (ed.) In *Myths, stories and organizations*. Oxford: Oxford University Press.

Sinclair, A. (1992) The Tyranny of a Team Ideology, *Organisation Studies*, 13(4): 611–26.

Sinclair, A. (1994) Trials at the Top: Chief Executives Talk about Men, *Women and Australian Executive Culture*. Melbourne: The Australian Centre at the University of Melbourne.

Sinclair, A. (1998) *Doing Leadership Differently: Gender, power and Sexuality in a Changing Business Culture*. Melbourne: Melbourne University Press.

Smircich, L. and Morgan, G. (1982) Leadership: The Management of Meaning, *Journal of Applied Behavioural Science*, 18(2): 257–73.

Smith, C. and Wilkinson, B. (1983) From schoolboy hunches to departmental lunches, *Sociological Review*.

Sotirin, P. and Gottfried, H. (1999) The Ambivalent Dynamics of Secretarial "Bitching": Control, Resistance, and the Construction of Identity, *Organization*, 6(1).

Stark, D. (1999) "Heterarchy: Distributing Intelligence and Organizing Diversity" in J. Clippinger, (ed.) *The Biology of Business: Decoding the Natural Laws of Enterprise*. San Francisco: Jossey-Bass Publishers.

Stark, D. (2001) "Ambiguous Assets for Uncertain Environments: Heterarchy in Postsocialist Firms", in DiMaggio, P. *The Twenty-First Century Firm: Changing Economic Organization in International Perspective*. Princeton, NJ: Princeton University Press.

Stewart, R. (1976) *The Realities of Management*. Harmondsworth: Penguin.

Stewart, R. (1989) Studies of Managerial Jobs and Behaviour: The Ways Forward, *Journal of Management Studies*, 26(1): 1–9.

Stewart, R. (1993) *The Reality of Organizations: A Guide for Managers*. Basingstoke: Macmillan.

Stone, A.R. (1995) *The War of Desire and Technology at the Close of the Mechanical Age*. London: MIT Press.

Strati, A. (1999) *Organization and Aesthetics*. London: Sage.

Strauss, A. and Corbin, J. (1990) *Basics of Qualitative Research*. Newbury Park, CA: Sage.

Sullivan, O. (1997) Time Waits for No (Wo) man: An Investigation of the Gendered Experience of Domestic Time, *Sociology*, 31(2): 221–39.

Thomas, R. and Dunkerly, D. (1999) Careering Downwards? Middle Managers' Experiences in the Downsizing Organization, *British Journal of Management*, 10(2).

Thomas, R. and Linstead, A. (2002) Losing the Plot?: Middle Managers and Identity, *Organization*, 9(1): 71–93.

Thompson, P. and Ackroyd, S. (1999) Organizational *Misbehaviour*. London: Sage.

Thompson, P. and McHugh, D. (1995) *Work Organizations*. London: Macmillan.

Thompson, P. and Warhurst, C. (eds) (1998) *Workplaces of the Future*. Basingstoke: Macmillan.

Thornhill, A. and Gibbons, A. (1995) The Positive Management of Redundancy Survivors: Issues and Lessons. *British Journal of Management*, 7(3): 5–12.

Thornhill, A. and Saunders, M. (1997) Downsizing, Delayering: But Where's The Commitment? *Personnel Review*, 26(2).

Tienari, J. (1999) The first wave washed up onshore: reform, feminization and gender segregation, *Gender, Work and Organization*, 6(1): 1–19.

Townley, B. (1992) *Reframing Human Resource Management: Power, Ethics and the Subject at Work*. London: Sage.

Tyler, M. (2005) Women in Change Management: Simone De Beauvoir and the Co-optation of Otherness, *Journal of Organizational Change Management*, 18(6).

Tyler, S. (1986) Postmodern ethnography: From Document of the Occult to Occult Document? in J. Clifford and G.E. Marcus (eds) *Writing Culture*. London: University of California Press, pp. 122–40.

Urwick, L. (1952) *Notes on the Theory of Organisation*. New York: American Management Association.

Vidich, A.J. and Lyman, S.M. (1998) Qualitative Methods: Their History in Sociology and Anthropology in N.K. Denzin and Y.S. Lincoln (eds) *The Landscape of Qualitative Research: Theories and Issues*. London: Sage.

Vinnicombe, S. and Colwill, N.L. (1995) *The Essence of Women in Management.* London: Prentice-Hall.

Virilio, P. (1991) *The Lost Dimension.* New York: Semiotext(e).

Wajcman, J. (2004) *Technofeminism.* Oxford: Polity.

Wajcman, J. (1998) *Managing like a Man: Women and Men in Corporate Management.* Oxford: Polity Press.

Walby, S. (1997) *Gender Transformation.* London: Routledge.

Watson, T. (1994) *In Search of Management.* London: Routledge.

Watson, T. (1995a) Discourse and Argument in Organizational Sense Making: A Reflexive Tale, *Organizational Studies*, 16(5): 805–11.

Watson, T. (1995b) Shaping the Story: Rhetoric, Persuasion and Creative Writing in Organizational Ethnography, *Studies in Cultures, Organizations and Societies*, 1(2): 301–11.

Watson, T. and Harris, P. (1999) *The Emergent Manager.* London: Sage.

Watson, T. and Watson, D. (1999) Human Resourcing in Practice: Managing Employment Issues in the University, *Journal of Management Studies*, 36(4): 483–504.

Weedon, C. (1999) *Feminism, Theory and the Politics of Difference.* Oxford: Blackwell.

Weedon, C. (1987) *Feminist Practice and Poststructuralist Theory.* Oxford: Blackwell.

Weick, K.E. (1979) *The Social Psychology of Organizing.* London: McGraw Hill.

Westwood, R. (2001) Appropriating the Other in Discourses of Comparative Management, in Westwood, R. and Linstead, S. (2001) *The Language of Organization.* London: Sage.

Wheatley, M. (1992) *The Future of Management.* Institute of Management, Corby.

Whitehead, S. (1998) Disrupted Selves: Resistance and Identity Work in the Managerial Arena, *Gender and Education*, 10(2): 199–215.

Whitehead, S. (2001) Woman as Manager: A Seductive Ontology, *Gender, Work and Organization*, 8(1): 84–107.

Whitehead, S. and Moodley, R. (eds) (1999) *Transforming Managers: Gendering Change in the Public Sector.* London: UCL Press.

Willmott, H. (1984) Images and Ideals of Managerial Work: A Critical Examination of Conceptual and Empirical Accounts, *Journal of Management Studies*, 2(3): 349–68.

Willmott, H. (1993) Strength is Ignorance; Slavery is Freedom: Managing Culture in Modern Organizations, *Journal of Management Studies*, 30(4): 515–52.

Willmott, H. (1997) Rethinking Management and Managerial Work: Capitalism, Control and Subjectivity, *Human Relations*, 50(11): 1329–59.

Wilson, F. (1995) *Organizational Behaviour.* London: Oxford Press.

Wilson, F. (1996) Organizational Theory: Blind and Deaf to Gender? *Organization Studies*, 17(5): 825–42.

Woodhall, J., Edwards, C., and Welchman, R. (1997) Organisational Restructuring and the Achievement of an Equal Opportunity Culture, *Gender, Work and Organisation*, 4(1): 2–13.

Woolgar, S. (1988) Reflexivity is the Ethnographer of the Text, in *Knowledge and Reflexivity – New frontiers in the Sociology of Knowledge.* London: Sage.

Worrall, L. and Cooper, C. (1998) *The Quality of Working Life.* London: Institute of Management.

Zuboff, S. (1998) *In the Age of the Smart Machine.* Cambridge, MA: Harvard University Press.

Author Index

Subject Index